INVENTING MORMONISM

T0124816

INVENTING MORMONISM

TRADITION

AND THE

HISTORICAL

RECORD

H. MICHAEL MARQUARDT & WESLEY P. WALTERS

Smith Research Associates

∞ *Inventing Mormonism*: *Tradition and the Historical Record*
was printed on acid-free paper and was composed, printed, and
bound in the United States of America.

Clothbound ©1994; paperbound ©1998
by H. Michael Marquardt. All rights reserved.
Distributed by Signature Books, Inc.,
Salt Lake City, Utah.

09   08   07   06   05   6   5   4   3   2

Library of Congress Cataloging-in-Publication Data

Marquardt, H. Michael.
Inventing Mormonism : tradition and the historical record /
H. Michael Marquardt and Wesley P. Walters.
p.   cm.
Includes bibliographical references and index.
ISBN: 1-56085-039-6, cloth
ISBN: 1-56085-108-2, paper
1. Smith, Joseph, 1805-1844. 2. Mormon Church—Presidents—
Biography.   3. Mormon Church—New York—History—19th Century.
4. Palmyra (N.Y.)—History—19th Century.   I. Walters, Wesley P.
II. Title.
BX8695.S6M25   1993
289.3'092—dc20   93-13603
[B]   CIP

CONTENTS

PREFACE

This book is the result of many years of research into the early history of the Joseph Smith family and the origins of the Mormon church. Our primary objective has been to find and present historical records, such as tax lists and censuses, and recollections of people living at the time and place where Mormonism began. We were interested not only in Mormonism specifically but also in the general social and intellectual climate of western New York during the 1820s. By evaluating the body of this documentary material as a whole we hope to bring new insights to the study of Mormon beginnings.

We follow original spelling as far as possible when quoting various sources, although in a few manuscripts we have supplied punctuation and capital letters to facilitate readability. Words in manuscripts that appear above the line are indicated by angled brackets < >. Crossed-out and repeated words are usually deleted. Page numbers for some newspapers are added where in the original there is no actual page number. Source notations and other comments are contained in the notes at the end of each chapter. References to Mormon scripture are usually provided in their standard abbreviations; thus BC refers to Book of Commandments, D&C to Doctrine and Covenants, PGP to Pearl of Great Price, etc.

Among the places where we conducted research are: the historical department of the Church of Jesus Christ of Latter-day Saints (LDS), Salt Lake City, Utah; the library-archives of the Reorganized Church of Jesus Christ of Latter Day Saints (RLDS), Independence, Missouri; J. Willard Marriott Library, University of Utah, Salt Lake City; Harold B. Lee Library, Brigham Young University, Provo, Utah; Library of Congress, Washington, D.C.; Town Clerk's Office, Palmyra, New York; Town Clerk's Office, Manchester, New York;

Town Clerk's Office, Bainbridge, New York; Office of History, Norwich, New York; Ontario County Records Center and Archives, and Ontario County Historical Society, both in Canandaigua, New York; Wayne County Historical Society, Lyons, New York; Amistad Research Center, New Orleans, Louisiana; Presbyterian Historical Society and Historical Society of Pennsylvania, both in Philadelphia, Pennsylvania; Princeton University Library, Princeton, New Jersey; American Antiquarian Society, Worcester, Massachusetts; Utah State Historical Society and LDS Family History Library, both in Salt Lake City, Utah. We express our appreciation to these repositories and their staffs. We also benefitted greatly from the many helpful suggestions of friends and readers.

On 9 November 1990 Wesley P. Walters passed away. Following his death, the final editing was completed with the help of his wife Helen. This book is dedicated to Wes's memory.

H. M. M.

PROLOGUE

Mormonism is rooted in the life and activities of its founder, Joseph Smith, Jr., much as Christianity is rooted in the life of Jesus. The story of Jesus was not written by Jesus himself but professes to be told by associates and eyewitnesses. Gospel writer Luke indicates the important role of witnesses in preserving oral tradition (Luke 1:1-4). Joseph Smith was also surrounded by witnesses and observers—family members, schoolmates, neighbors, friends, critics, local government officials, judges, constables. These accounts and records, sometimes brief and obscure, found in damp basements of courthouses, old archives, and crumbling books also provide evidence of his life and activites.

As early as 1831 John Whitmer, an early Mormon convert, was appointed to write and keep a history of the new church. In the fall of 1832 Joseph Smith and his close friend Frederick G. Williams worked on a brief history of the fledgling faith, but it was never completed and remained unpublished until the 1960s. In 1834-35 Oliver Cowdery, cofounder of the church, published a history in the form of a series of letters. Cowdery's narrative, the first account published in a church periodical, appeared in the *Latter Day Saints' Messenger and Advocate*. These letters were later copied into Joseph Smith's journal and considered part of his own history.

By 1838 both early chroniclers, Whitmer and Cowdery, were no longer in good standing with Smith. In April 1838 Smith and his counselor Sidney Rigdon wrote to Whitmer and asked him to return his record.[1] When Whitmer refused, they wrote their own history: "Friday, April the 27th 1838 This day was chiefly spent writing a history of this Church from the earliest period of its existance [sic] up to this date, By Presidents Joseph Smith, Jr., Sidney Rigdon, [and] myself [George W. Robinson, scribe]."[2]

The initial draft of this history was written during a four-day period by George W. Robinson. In 1839 it was copied by James Mulholland, another of Smith's scribes, into what is known today as the Manuscript History of the Church, Book A-1. The A-1 book was revised before and after its first publication and is now considered to be Smith's official narrative. It incorporates an account of Smith's early religious calling and has served as the basis for virtually all later official and semi-official histories of the church.

The earliest part of this history was published in installments in the Mormon newspaper *Times and Seasons* in Nauvoo, Illinois, between March and May 1842.[3] Later it was reprinted in *The Latter Day Saints' Millennial Star* in England. In 1851 it was included in a pamphlet, *The Pearl of Great Price.* This was presented in revised form at a general conference of the church in Salt Lake City on 10 October 1880 and accepted as scripture. It has since been widely circulated and is regarded by Mormons as an important starting point in any investigation of the history of Mormonism.

We present the following extract from the Manuscript History written in 1839 by Mulholland before it was edited for publication as an essential introduction to our discussion. It is followed by a section of maps and a chronology.

Owing to the many reports which have been put in circulation by evil disposed and designing persons in relation to the rise and progress of the Church of Latter day Saints, all of which have been designed by the authors thereof to militate against its character as a church, and its progress in the world; I have been induced to write this history so as to disabuse the publick mind, and put all enquirers after truth into possession of the facts as they have transpired in relation both to myself and the Church as far as I have such facts in [my] possession.

In this history I will present the various events in relation to this Church in truth and righteousness as they have transpired, or as they at present exist, being now the eighth year since the organization of said Church.

I was born in the year of our Lord One thousand Eight hundred and five, on the twenty third day of December, in the town of Sharon, Windsor County, State of Vermont. My father Joseph Smith Senior left the State of Vermont and moved to Palmyra, Ontario, (now Wayne) County, in the State of New York when I was in my tenth year.

In about four years after my father's arrival at Palmyra, he moved with his family into Manchester in the same County of Ontario. His family consisting of eleven souls, namely, My Father Joseph Smith, My Mother Lucy Smith whose name previous to her marriage was Mack, daughter of Solomon Mack, My brothers Alvin (who is now dead), Hyrum, Myself, Samuel Harrison, William, Don Carloss [Carlos], and my Sisters Soph[r]onia, Cath[e]rine and Lucy.

Sometime in the second year after our removal to Manchester, there was in the place where we lived an unusual excitement on the subject of religion. It commenced with the Methodists, but soon became general among all the sects in that region of country, indeed the whole district of Country seemed affected by it and great multitudes united themselves to the different religious parties, which created no small stir and division among the people, Some crying, "Lo here" and some Lo there. Some were contending for the Methodist faith, Some for the Presbyterian, and some for the Baptist; for notwithstanding the great love which the converts to these different faiths expressed at the time of their conversion, and the great Zeal manifested by the respective Clergy who were active in getting up and promoting this extraordinary scene of religious feeling in order to have everybody converted as they were pleased to call it, let them join what sect they pleased, yet when the Converts began to file off some to one party and some to another, it was seen that the seemingly good feelings of both the Priests and the Converts were more pretended than real, for a scene of great confusion and bad feeling ensued; Priest contending against priest, and convert against convert so that all their good feelings one for another (if they ever had any) were entirely lost in a strife of words and a contest about opinions.

I was at this time in my fifteenth year. My Fathers family was proselyted to the Presbyterian faith and four of them joined that Church, Namely, My Mother Lucy, My Brothers Hyrum, Samuel Harrison, and my Sister Soph[r]onia.

During this time of great excitement my mind was called up to serious reflection and great uneasiness, but though my feelings were deep and often pungent, still I kept myself aloof from all these parties though I attended their several meetings as occasion would permit. But in [the] process of time my mind became somewhat partial to the Methodist sect, and I felt some desire to be united with them, but so great was the confusion and strife amongst the different denominations that it was impossible for a person young as I was and so unacquainted with men and things to come to any certain conclusion who was right and who was wrong.

My mind at different times was greatly excited the cry and tumult were so great and incessant. The Presbyterians were most decided against the Baptists and Methodists, and used all their powers of either reason or sophistry to prove their errors, or at least to make the people think they were in error. On the other hand the Baptists and Methodists in their turn were equally Zealous in endeavoring to establish their own tenets and disprove all others.

In the midst of this war of words, and tumult of opinions, I often said to myself, what is to be done? Who of all these parties are right? Or are they all wrong together? And if any one of them be right which is it? And how shall I know it?

While I was laboring under the extreme difficulties caused by the contests of these parties of religionists, I was one day reading the Epistle of James, First Chapter and fifth verse which reads, "If any of you lack wisdom, let him ask of God, that giveth to all men liberally and upbraideth not, and it shall be given him.["] Never did any passage of scripture come with more power to the heart of man that [than] this did at this time to mine. It seemed to enter with great force into every feeling of my heart. I reflected on it again and again, knowing that if any person needed wisdom from God, I did, for how to act I did not know and unless I could get more wisdom than I then had would never know, for the teachers of religion of the different sects understood the same passage of Scripture so differently as <to> destroy all confidence in settling the question by an appeal to the Bible. At length I came to the conclusion that I must either remain in darkness and confusion or else I must do as James directs, that is, Ask of God. I at last came to the determination to ask of God, concluding that if he gave wisdom to them that lacked wisdom, and would give liberally and not upbraid, I might venture.

So in accordance with this my determination to ask of God, I retired to the woods to make the attempt. It was on the morning of a beautiful clear day early in the spring of Eightteen hundred and twenty. It was the first time in my life that I had <made> such an attempt, for amidst all <my> anxieties I had never as yet made the attempt to pray vocally.

After I had retired into the place where I had previously designed to go, having looked around me and finding myself alone, I kneeled down and began to offer up the desires of my heart to God. I had scarcely done so, when immediately I was <seized> upon by some power which entirely overcame me and <had> such astonishing influence over me as to bind my tongue so that I could not speak. Thick darkness gathered around me and it seemed to me for a time as if I were doomed to sudden destruction. But exerting all my powers to call upon God to deliver me out of the power of this enemy which had seized upon me, and at the very moment when I was ready to sink into despair and abandon myself to destruction, not to an imaginary ruin but to the power of some actual being from the unseen world who had such a marvelous power as I had never before felt in any being. Just at this moment of great alarm I saw a pillar <of> light exactly over my head above the brightness of the sun, which descended gradually untill it fell upon me.

It no sooner appeared than I found myself delivered from the enemy which held me bound. When the light rested upon me I saw two personages (whose brightness and glory defy all description) standing above me in the air. One of <them> spake unto me calling me by name and said (pointing to the other) "This is my beloved Son, Hear him." My object in going to enquire of the Lord was to know which of all the sects was right, that I might know which to join. No sooner therefore did I get possession of myself so as to be able to speak, than I asked the personages who stood above me in the light, which of all the sects was right, (for at this time it had never entered into my heart that all were wrong) and which I should join. I was answered that I must join none of them, for they were all wrong, and the Personage who addressed me said that all their Creeds were an abomination in his sight, that those professors were all corrupt, that "they draw near to me with their lips but their hearts are far from me, They teach for doctrines the commandments of men, having a form of Godliness but they deny the power thereof." He again forbade me to join with any of them and many other things did he say unto me which I cannot write at this time. When I came to myself again I found myself lying on <my> back looking up into Heaven.

Some few days after I had this vision I happened to be in company with one of the Methodist Preachers who was very active in the before mentioned religious excitement and conversing with him on the subject of religion I took occasion to give him an account of the vision which I had had. I was greatly surprised at his behaviour, he treated my communication not only lightly but with great contempt, saying it was all of the Devil, that there was no such thing as visions or revelations in these days, that all such things had ceased with the apostles and that there never would be any more of them.

I soon found however that my telling the story had excited a great deal of prejudice against me among professors of religion and was the cause of great persecution which continued to increase and though I was an obscure boy only between fourteen and fifteen years of age and my circumstances in life such as to make a boy of no consequence in the world, yet men of high standing would take notice sufficiently to excite the public mind against me and create a hot persecution, and this was common <among> all the sects: all united to persecute me. . . . However it was nevertheless a fact, that I had had a vision. . . . I had actual[l]y seen a light and in the midst of that light I saw two personages, and they did in reality speak <un>to me, or one of them did, . . . for I had seen a vision, I knew it, and I knew that God knew it, and I could not deny it, neither dare I do it, at least I knew that by so doing <I> would offend God and come under condemnation.

I had now got my mind satisfied so far as the sectarian world was concerned, that it was not my duty to join any of them, but continue as I was untill further directed, I had found the testimony of James to be true, that a man who lacked wisdom might ask of God, and obtain and not be upbraided. I continued to pursue my common avocations in life untill the twenty first of September, One thousand Eight hundred and twenty three, all the time suffering severe persecution at the hand of all classes of men, both religious and irreligious because I continued to affirm that I <had> seen a vision.

During the space of time which intervened between the time I had the vision and the year Eighteen hundred and twenty three, (having been forbidden to join any of the religious sects of the day, and being of very tender years and persecuted by those who ought to have been my friends, and to have treated me kindly and if they supposed me to be deluded to have endeavoured in a proper and affectionate manner to have reclaimed me) I was left to all kinds of temptations, and mingling <with> all kinds of society I frequently <fell> into many foolish errors and displayed the weakness of youth and the corruption of human nature which I am sorry to say led me

into divers temptations to the gratification of many appetites offen-
sive in the sight of God.

In consequence of these things I often felt condemned for my
weakness and imperfections; when on the evening of the above
mentioned twenty first of september, after I had retired to my bed
for the night I betook myself to prayer and supplication to Almighty
God for forgiveness of all my sins and follies, and also for a manifestation to me that I might know of my state and standing before
him. For I had full confidence in obtaining a divine manifestation
as I had previously had one.

While I was thus in the act of calling upon God, I discovered a
light appearing in the room which continued to increase untill the
room was lighter than at noonday <when> immediately a personage
<appeared> at my bedside standing in the air for his feet did not
touch the floor. He had on a loose robe of most exquisite whiteness.
It was a whiteness beyond any<thing> earthly I had ever seen, nor
do I believe that any earthly thing could be made to appear so
exceedin[g]ly white and brilliant, His hands were naked and his
arms also a little above the wrists. So also were his feet naked as were
his legs a little above the ankles. His head and neck were also bare.
I could discover that he had no other clothing on but this robe, as
it was open so that I could see into his bosom. Not only was his robe
exceedingly white but his whole person was glorious beyond description, and his countenance truly like lightning. The room was
exceedingly light, but not so very bright as immediately around his
person. When I first looked upon him I was afraid, but the fear soon
left me.

He called me by name and said unto me that he was a messenger
sent from the presence of God to me and that his name was Nephi.[4]
That God had a work for me to do, and that my <name> should be
had for good and evil among all nations kindreds and tongues, or
that it should be both good and evil spoken of among all people.

He said there was a book deposited written upon gold plates,
giving an account of the former inhabitants of this continent and
the source from whence they sprang. He also said that the fullness
of the everlasting Gospel was contained in it as delivered by the
Saviour to the ancient inhabitants. Also that there were two stones
in silver bows and these (put into a breast plate) which constituted
what is called the Urim & Thummim deposited with the plates, and

that was what constituted seers in ancient or former times and that God <had> prepared them for the purpose of translating the book.

After telling me these things he commenced quoting the prophecies of the old testament, he first quoted part of the third chapter of Malachi and he quoted also the fourth or last chapter of the same prophecy though with a little variation from the way it reads in our Bibles. Instead of quoting the first verse as reads in our books he quoted it thus, "For behold the day cometh that shall burn as an oven, and all the proud <yea> and all that do wickedly shall burn as stubble, for <they> that cometh shall burn them saith the Lord of hosts, that it shall leave them neither root nor branch."

And again he quoted the fifth verse thus, "Behold I will reveal unto you the Priesthood by the hand of Elijah the prophet before the coming of the great and dreadful day of the Lord." He also quoted the next verse differently. "And he shall plant in the hearts of the children the promises made to the fathers, and the hearts of the children shall turn to their fathers, if it were not so the whole earth would be utterly wasted at his coming." In addition to these he quoted the Eleventh Chapter of Isaiah saying that it was about to be fulfilled. He quoted also the third chapter of Acts, twenty second and twenty third verses precisely as they stand in our new testament. He said that that prophet was Christ, but the day had not yet come when "they who would not hear his voice should be cut off from among the people," but soon would come.

He also quoted the second chapter of Joel from the twenty eight to the last verse. He also said that this was not yet fulfilled but was soon to be. And he further stated the fullness of the gentiles was soon to come in. He quoted many other passages of scripture and offered many explanations which cannot be mentioned here. Again he told me that when I got those plates of which he had spoken (for the time that they should be obtained was not yet fulfilled) I should not show <them> to any person, neither the breastplate with the Urim and Thummim only to those to whom I should be commanded to show them. If I did I should be destroyed.

While he was conversing with me about the plates the vision was opened to my mind that I could see the place where the plates were deposited and that so clearly and distinctly that I knew the place again when I visited it.

After this communication I saw the light in the room begin to gather immediately around the person of him who had been speaking to me, and it continued to do so untill the room was again left dark except just round him, when instantly I saw as it were a conduit open right up into heaven, and he ascended up till he entirely disappeared and the room was left as it had been before this heavenly light had made its appearance.

I lay musing on the singularity of the scene and marvelling greatly at what had been told me by this extraordinary messenger, when in the midst of my meditation I suddenly discovered that my room was again beginning to get lighted, and in an instant as it were, the same heavenly messenger was again by my bedside. He commenced and again related the very same things which he had done at his first visit without the least variation which having done, he informed me of great judgements which were coming upon the earth, with great desolations by famine, sword, and pestilence, and that these grievous judgements would come on the earth in this generation: Having related these things he again ascended as he had done before.

By this time so deep were the impressions made on my mind that sleep had fled from my eyes and I lay overwhelmed in astonishment at what I had both seen and heard:

But what was my surprise when again I beheld the same messenger at my bed side, and heard him rehearse or repeat over again to me the same things as before and added a caution to me, telling me that Satan would try to tempt me (in consequence of the indigent circumstances of my father's family) to get the plates for the purpose of getting rich, This he forbid me, saying that I must have no other object in view in getting the plates but to glorify God, and must not be influenced by any other motive but that of building his kingdom, otherwise I could not get them.

After this third visit he again ascended up into heaven as before and I was again left to ponder on the strangeness of what I had just experienced, when almost immediately after the heavenly messenger had ascended from me the third time, the cock crew, and I found that day was approaching so that our interviews must have occupied the whole of that night. I shortly after arose from my bed, and as usual went to the necessary labors of the day, but in attempting to labor as at other times, I found my strength so exhausted as rendered me entirely unable.

My father who was laboring along <with> me discovered something to be wrong with me and told me to go home. I started with the intention of going to the house, but in attempting to cross the fence out of the field where we were, my strength entirely failed me and I fell helpless on the ground and for a time was quite unconscious of any thing. The first thing that I can recollect was a voice speaking unto me calling me by name. I looked up and beheld the same messenger standing over my head surrounded by light as before. He then again related unto me all that he had related to me the previous night, and commanded me to go to my father and tell him of the vision and commandments which I had received.

I obeyed. I returned back to my father in the field and rehearsed the whole matter to him. He replyed to me, that it was of God, and to go and do as commanded by the messenger. I left the field and went to the place where the messenger had told me the plates were deposited, and owing to the distinctness of the vision which I had had concerning it, I knew the place the instant that I arrived there.

Under a stone of considerable size, lay the plates deposited in a stone box. This stone was thick and rounding in the middle on the upper side, and thinner towards the edges, so that the middle part of it was visible above the ground, but the edge all round was covered with earth. Having removed the earth and obtained a lever which I got fixed under the edge of the stone, and with a little exertion raised it up, I looked in and there indeed did I behold the plates, the Urim and Thummim and the Breastplate as stated by the messenger.

The box in which they lay was formed by laying stones together in some kind of cement, in the bottom of the box were laid two stones crossways of the box, and on these stones lay the plates and the other things with them. I made an attempt to take them out but was forbidden by the messenger and was again informed that the time <for> bringing them forth had not yet arrived, neither would untill four years from that time, but he told me that I should come to that place precisely in one year from that time, and that he would there meet with me, and that I should continue to do so untill the time should come for obtaining the plates.

Accordingly as I had been commanded I went at the end of each year, and at each time I found the same messenger there and received instruction and intelligence from him at each of our interviews respecting what the Lord was going to do, and how and in what manner his kingdom was to be conducted in the last days.[5]

NOTES

1. "Indeed Sir," the two men wrote Whitmer, "we never Supposed you capable of writing a history, but were willing to let it come out under your name notwithstanding it would real[l]y not be yours but ours. We are still willing to honour you if you can be made to know your own interest and give up your notes, so that they can be corrected, and made fit for the press. But if not, we have all the materials for another, which we Shall commence this week to write" (letter, 9 Apr. 1838, "Scriptory Book of Joseph Smith Jr.," kept by George W. Robinson, historical department, Church of Jesus Christ of Latter-day Saints, Salt Lake City, Utah, hereafter LDS archives; compare Scott H. Faulring, ed., *An American Prophet's Record: The Diaries and Journals of Joseph Smith* [Salt Lake City: Signature Books in association with Smith Research Associates, 1987], 171; see also Dean C. Jessee, ed., *The Papers of Joseph Smith* [Salt Lake City: Deseret Book Co., 1992], 2:227).

2. Faulring, 176-77. The entries for writing this history continue, "Monday, the 30th This day was Spent by the First Presidency in writing the history of the Church and in resitation of grammer lessions which resitations is attended to <each> morning previous to writing. Tuesday, 1st May 1838 This day was Also spent in writing Church History by the First Presidency. Wednesday, 2nd This day was also spent in writing history and <receiving> lectures on grammer by President Rigdon" (179-80). The Scriptory Book does not mention participation by Smith's brother Hyrum, the third member of the presidency of the church, in writing the new history.

3. Smith started publishing his history in the 15 March 1842 issue, stating that it was an "extract from my journal" (*Times and Seasons* 3:726).

4. A week after it was recorded that the personage's name was Nephi, Smith spent the afternoon "in answering the questions proposed in the Elders Journal" (Scriptory Book, 39, entry for 8 May 1838). Question number four was, "How, and where did you obtain the book of Mormon?" Smith answered, "Moroni, the person who deposited the plates, from whence the book of Mormon was translated, in a hill in Manchester, Ontario County, New York, being dead, and raised again therefrom, appeared unto me, and told me where they were; and gave me directions how to obtain them. I obtained them, and the Urim and Thummim with them; by the means of which, I translated the plates; and thus came the book of Mormon" (*Elders' Journal* 1 [July 1838]: 42-43). Some writers have concluded that both Moroni and Nephi visited Smith, others feel that the name Nephi was a clerical error in the manuscript, though it was never corrected by Smith. The current

version in the Pearl of Great Price says it was Moroni who appeared in the bedroom.

5. Manuscript History of the Church, Book A-1: 1-7, LDS archives. Crossed out words and words added for the *Times and Seasons* publication are not included. Additions made after the first publication in Nauvoo are also excluded.

MAPS

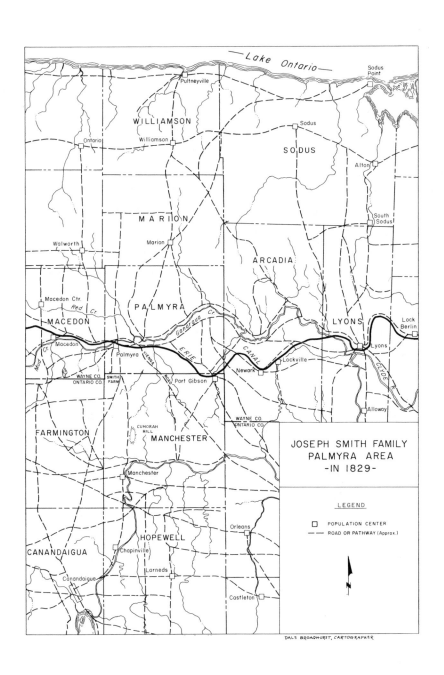

JOSEPH SMITH FAMILY
PALMYRA AREA
-IN 1829-

LEGEND

☐ POPULATION CENTER
— — — ROAD OR PATHWAY (Approx.)

DALE BROADHURST, CARTOGRAPHER

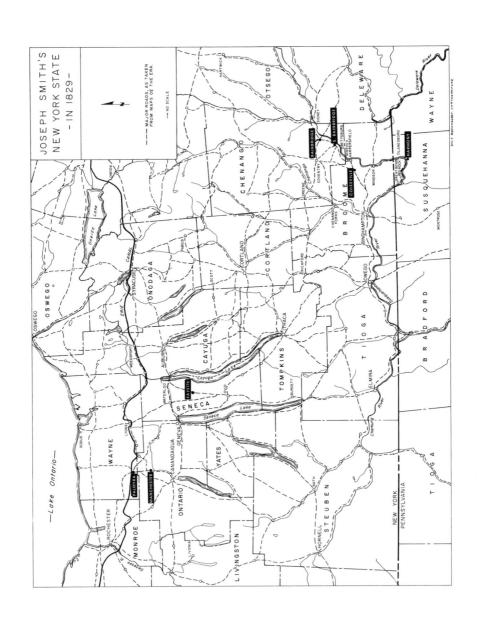

JOSEPH SMITH'S
NEW YORK STATE
- IN 1829 -

----- MAJOR ROADS, AS TAKEN
FROM MAPS OF THE ERA.

→ NO SCALE

THE JOSEPH SMITH, SR., FAMILY

	Birthdate	Birthplace	Death Date
Father: Joseph Smith [Sr.]	12 July 1771	Topsfield, Massachusetts	14 Sept. 1840
Mother: Lucy Mack (m. 24 Jan. 1796)	8 July 1775	Gilsum, New Hampshire	14 May 1856

Children	Birthdate	Birthplace	Death Date
1. male child	about 1797	Tunbridge, Vermont	about 1797
2. Alvin	11 Feb. 1798	Tunbridge, Vermont	19 Nov. 1823
3. Hyrum	9 Feb. 1800	Tunbridge, Vermont	27 June 1844
4. Sophronia	17 May 1803	Tunbridge, Vermont	28 Aug. 1871
5. Joseph (Jr.)	23 Dec. 1805	Sharon, Vermont	27 June 1844
6. Samuel Harrison	13 Mar. 1808	Tunbridge Vermont	30 July 1844
7. Ephraim	13 Mar. 1810	Royalton, Vermont	24 Mar. 1810
8. William	13 Mar. 1811	Royalton, Vermont	13 Nov. 1893
9. Catherine	28 July 1812	Lebanon, New Hampshire	2 Feb. 1900
10. Don Carlos	25 Mar. 1816	Norwich, Vermont	7 Aug. 1841
11. Lucy	18 July 1821	Palmyra, New York	9 Dec. 1882

A CHRONOLOGY OF MORMON ORIGINS

1817

April   Joseph Smith, Sr., is living in the village of
             Palmyra, New York, on Road District 26.

1818

April   Joseph Sr. is residing in Palmyra village.

1819

April   Joseph Sr. is still residing in Palmyra village.

1820

April   Joseph Sr. and family are located at the south
             end of Stafford Road in Palmyra Township;
             Alvin Smith is residing in the village of Palmyra.

1820-21

             Joseph Smith, Jr., later reports he has a personal
             forgiveness of sins; he is an exhorter for the
             Methodist class in Palmyra and attends a local
             debating club.

1820

13 June   The Smith family is living on land owned by
             Samuel Jennings.

22 June   Tax on 300 acres of Lot 1 in Farmington (later
             Manchester) is to be paid by Nicholas Evertson heirs.

14 July   Power of attorney is given to Zachariah Seymour.

Summer   Joseph Sr. and Alvin article for 100 acres of land
              in Farmington, Lot 1, from Zachariah Seymour,
              land agent for Nicholas Evertson's heirs.

1821

April   Joseph Sr., Alvin, and Hyrum Smith are residing
              at the south end of Stafford Road in Palmyra.

7 July   Joseph Sr. is taxed for 100 acres of Lot 1.

18 July   Daughter Lucy Smith is born in Palmyra Township.

1822

              Joseph Jr. is present when Willard Chase finds a
              stone in a well on the Chase property. Joseph
              borrows the stone.

April   Joseph Sr. and Alvin are listed on south end
              of Stafford Road in Palmyra.

29 June   Lot 1 valuation is still $700 for 100 acres for
              Joseph Sr.

2 July   Zachariah Seymour, the land agent from
              whom Joseph Sr. and Alvin articled the 100 acres
              and to whom they made payments, dies.

1823

24 July   A $300 assessment increase on land shows
              improvements on the Smiths' Manchester
              property.

1822-24

              Joseph Jr. tells that by looking in Willard Chase's
              stone he can see hidden treasures, all things in

caves, in and under the earth, and spirits in ancient dress in charge of the treasures.

1823

November
The Smiths' frame house in Manchester commences to be built.

19 November
Alvin Smith dies.

September 1824 to Spring 1825

Revival of religion commences with the Methodists, followed by the Baptists and Presbyterians, in the Palmyra vicinity. Joseph Jr. hears discourses by Reverend Lane of the Methodist church and attends meetings.

1825

Spring
Lucy, Hyrum, Samuel Harrison, and Sophronia Smith join Palmyra's Presbyterian church. Joseph Jr. is inclined toward the Methodist faith.

October-
November
Joseph goes with his father to southern New York and near Harmony (now Oakland), Pennsylvania, to obtain money to pay off their Manchester farm; they hunt for a gold/silver mine with a number of treasure seekers. At home of Isaac Hale, Joseph Jr. meets Hale's daughter Emma. The treasure seeking company stays at Hale's home.

December
The Smiths' farm, on which they are delinquent, is sold to Lemuel Durfee. The Smiths remain as renters.

October 1825 to March 1826

Joseph Jr. works for Josiah Stowell for five months and goes to school. He uses two stones to search for treasure and prays for help in the endeavor.

1826

20 March
During a court examination before Justice Albert Neely, Joseph Jr. states that by looking at a stone he can discover treasures hidden in the bowels of the earth, gold mines, coined money, and lost property.

Fall
Joseph Jr. works for Joseph Knight at Colesville, New York.

1827

18 January
Joseph Jr. and Emma Hale are married at South Bainbridge, New York.

January
Josiah Stowell moves Joseph and Emma to Manchester.

1827
Peter Ingersoll moves Emma's furniture from Harmony, Pennsylvania, to Manchester. Joseph Jr. tells his father-in-law he will give up glass-looking.

10 March
Joseph Jr. receives a receipt for credit of four dollars on Abraham Fish's account.

16 April
Samuel Harrison Smith begins to work for Lemuel Durfee, Sr., in payment for use of the house where the Smiths reside.

June
Joseph Sr. tells Willard Chase that some years previous a spirit had appeared to his son Joseph Jr. and informed him about a book or record of gold.

August	Joseph Jr. works two days mowing for Lemuel Durfee, Sr.
20 September	Joseph Knight and Josiah Stowell visit the Smith home.
22 September	Joseph Jr. visits a nearby hill taking Emma with him in Joseph Knight's wagon. He finds gold plates in a stone box and hides the plates in a fallen tree top. He also finds with the plates a sword, breastplate, and a pair of spectacles (also called Urim and Thummim). Joseph tells Joseph Knight the plates "appear to be Gold" and through the glasses or spectacles "I can see any thing."
September	Joseph Jr. goes to Macedon and works for Mrs. Wells.
September/ October	Joseph Jr. takes the gold plates from the hiding spot in the fallen tree top and runs home with them. He tells Willard Chase that if it had not been for the stone, he would not have obtained the book. A group of treasure seekers begins looking for the plates. Lucy Smith mentions that Joseph hid the plates in a wood box which was smashed by people searching for the record.
October	The Martin Harris family hears about the gold plates from Lucy. Mrs. Harris and her daughter go to the Smith home. Martin talks to members of the Smith family and Joseph Jr. about how the book was found. Joseph says that an angel appeared to him and told him it was God's work and that he located the plates by looking in the stone found on the Chase property. The angel told him he must quit the company of the money-diggers, translate the plates, and publish them to the world. Martin responds, "If the Lord

will show me that it is his work, you can have all the money you want."

November/December Martin Harris gets Joseph Jr. out of debt and gives him $50. Alva Hale comes from Harmony to pick up Joseph and Emma. Alva moves them to Harmony. The plates are placed in a barrel containing beans.

Winter 1827-28

Joseph Jr. tells his wife's neighbors about the gold plates.

1828

February Hyrum Smith and Martin Harris travel to Harmony, Pennsylvania, to see Joseph Jr. Harris takes a set of characters copied from the gold plates to New York City.

12 April Harris becomes a scribe at Harmony. The contents of the book are for the first time dictated by Joseph Jr.

14 June Harris takes the manuscript pages home. At Palmyra he reads from the manuscript in the evenings to his family and some friends.

15 June A male child is born to Joseph and Emma but dies the same day at Harmony. Emma hovers near death.

June/July Joseph Jr. travels to Manchester and learns that the manuscript is lost.

July A revelation concerning the lost pages is given at Harmony (BC 2; LDS D&C 3; RLDS D&C 2). This is Joseph's first recorded revelation.

September Lucy, Hyrum, and Samuel Smith stop attending Palmyra's Presbyterian church.

HARMONY, PENNSYLVANIA

Fall-Winter   Samuel Smith, Emma Hale Smith, and Reuben
                 Hale each serve as scribes to Joseph.

1829

February   Lucy and Joseph Sr. travel to Harmony,
                 Pennsylvania. A revelation is received at Harmony
                 (BC 3; LDS and RLDS D&C 4).

March   Martin Harris travels to Harmony and wants to
                 know if Joseph Jr. "had, in his possession, the
                 record of the Nephites." A revelation is received
                 (BC 4; LDS and RLDS D&C 5). Harris returns
                 to Palmyra. Isaac Hale describes the manner in
                 which the record was dictated: a stone placed
                 in a hat.

5 April   Samuel Smith and Oliver Cowdery arrive at
                 Harmony, Pennsylvania.

7 April   Cowdery acts as a scribe to Joseph Jr. Seven
                 revelations are given during April and May
                 (BC 5-11; LDS D&C 6-12; RLDS D&C 3, 6-11).
                 Dictation continues during the summer of 1829
                 at Harmony, Pennsylvania, and concludes at
                 Fayette, New York, about 1 July 1829.

FAYETTE, NEW YORK

June   John Whitmer becomes a scribe. Joseph Jr.
                 receives revelations for members of the
                 Whitmer family (BC 12-14; LDS D&C 14-16;
                 RLDS D&C 12-14) and "instructions relative to
                 building up the church of Christ" (BC 15;
                 LDS D&C 18; RLDS D&C 16).

14 June   Oliver Cowdery writes to Hyrum Smith.

June   A revelation is received for Oliver Cowdery,
                 David Whitmer, and Martin Harris "previous to

their viewing the plates containing the book of Mormon" (LDS D&C 17; RLDS D&C 15).

PALMYRA, NEW YORK

26 June   The title page of the manuscript Book of Mormon is published in the *Wayne Sentinel.*

ROCHESTER, NEW YORK

Summer   Martin Harris goes to Rochester, New York, to inquire about printing the Book of Mormon. He reports that Joseph found a gold bible and that "By placing the spectacles in a hat and looking into it, Smith interprets the characters into the English language."

PALMYRA, NEW YORK

25 August   Indenture is made between Martin Harris and Egbert Grandin on land and property for enough money ($3,000) to print the Book of Mormon.

August 1829 to March 1830

The Book of Mormon is typeset and printed at Grandin's print shop. John Gilbert sets the type and receives manuscript pages from Hyrum Smith.

HARMONY, PENNSYLVANIA
1829

4-22 October   Joseph Jr. arrives in Harmony and writes to Oliver Cowdery that he has bought a horse from Mr. Stowell and wants someone to come after it.

MANCHESTER, NEW YORK

6 November   Cowdery writes from Manchester that Harris will pick up the horse in two or three weeks.

28 December   Cowdery writes to Joseph Jr. from Manchester: "it may look rather strange to you to find that I have so soon become a printer."

1830

16 January   An agreement between Joseph Sr. and Martin Harris on selling the Book of Mormon is witnessed by Oliver Cowdery.

PALMYRA, NEW YORK

26 March   The *Wayne Sentinel* advertises the Book of Mormon for sale.

MANCHESTER, NEW YORK

[26-31] March   Joseph Jr. arrives in Manchester with Joseph Knight, Sr.; a commandment is given for Harris (BC 16; LDS D&C 19; RLDS D&C 18).

6 April   The Church of Christ is organized; six revelations are received (BC 17-22; LDS D&C 21, 23; RLDS D&C 19, 21). Cowdery is ordained an elder. Joseph Jr. is ordained an elder, also prophet and seer by Cowdery. Joseph Sr., Lucy, Harris, and Sarah Rockwell are baptized in Crooked Brook.

FAYETTE, NEW YORK

11-16 April   A Fayette, New York, branch of the church is established. Cowdery delivers the first public discourse of the church and performs baptisms. A revelation is received regarding individuals who have been baptized in other Christian churches (BC 23; LDS D&C 22; RLDS D&C 20).

18 April   More baptisms are performed by Cowdery.

9 June   The first conference of the church is held; articles and covenants are presented

(BC 24; LDS D&C 20; RLDS D&C 17). Baptisms are performed. Joseph Sr. and Hyrum Smith are ordained priests.

MANCHESTER, NEW YORK

28 June — Joseph Sr. appears in Manchester before Justice Nathan Pierce on behalf of his son Hyrum.

COLESVILLE, NEW YORK

28 June — Baptisms are performed in Colesville, New York, but no confirmations. A Colesville branch is started.

SOUTH BAINBRIDGE, NEW YORK

1 July — Joseph Jr. is brought before Justice Joseph Chamberlain in South Bainbridge, New York.

COLESVILLE, NEW YORK

July — Joseph Jr. is arrested upon warrant and appears before Justice Joel K. Noble in Colesville.

HARMONY, PENNSYLVANIA

July — In Harmony, Pennsylvania, revelations are received, including one for Emma Smith (BC 25-27; LDS D&C 24-26; RLDS D&C 23-25).

4 September — A revelation is recorded concerning sacrament (BC 28; LDS D&C 27; RLDS D&C 26).

September — Joseph Jr. travels from Harmony to Fayette.

FAYETTE, NEW YORK

September — Revelations are given to the church at Fayette and others (BC 29-34; LDS D&C 28-31; RLDS D&C 27-30).

26 September — The second conference of the church commences; total membership is sixty-two.

MANCHESTER, NEW YORK

17 October   In Manchester a missionary covenant to
                  preach to native Americans (Lamanites) is issued.

FAYETTE, NEW YORK

October   In Fayette a revelation to Ezra Thayer and
                  Northrop Sweet is given (BC 35; LDS D&C 33;
                  RLDS D&C 32).

4 November   Orson Pratt arrives in Fayette; Joseph Jr. asks
                  and receives a revelation for him (BC 36;
                  LDS D&C 34; RLDS D&C 33) by gazing at a
                  stone placed in a hat.

December   Revelations are given for Sidney Rigdon and
                  Edward Partridge (BC 37-38; LDS D&C 35-36;
                  RLDS D&C 34-35).

CANANDAIGUA, NEW YORK

December   In Canandaigua, New York, a revelation to
                  Joseph Jr. and Sidney Rigdon instructs them to
                  go to Ohio (BC 39; LDS and RLDS D&C 37).

1831

FAYETTE, NEW YORK

2 January   The third conference of the church takes place
                  in Fayette; revelation is received (BC 40; LDS
                  and RLDS D&C 38).

January   Two revelations concerning James Covell,
                  a Baptist minister, are given (BC 41-42; LDS
                  and RLDS D&C 39-40).

CHAPTER ONE

THE MOVE TO PALMYRA AND MANCHESTER, NEW YORK

When Joseph Smith, Jr., began working on the official history of his life and church, he created a chronological puzzle. When precisely did his family move to Palmyra, New York, and later to the adjoining township of Manchester? In his narrative he places the move two years before an important religious revival which he says preceded his first vision. However, there are problems with this sequence of events.

At the opening of his 1838-39 autobiography Smith reports that his father moved to Palmyra when he was in his tenth year. Joseph Jr. was born on 23 December 1805, which means his "tenth" year was probably 1815. But in three other statements published under his name he says he was "ten years old," meaning the move occurred in 1816.

Next Smith remarks that "in about four years after my father's arrival at Palmyra, he moved with his family into Manchester," the next township south of Palmyra. This dates the family's relocation to Manchester to approximately 1820. Later Smith states, "[I]n the second year after our removal to Manchester, there was in the place where we lived an unusual excitement on the subject of religion." This excitement, he continues, led him to pray in the woods about which church to join. He was answered by the appearance of two heavenly beings, the Father and the Son. According to his account, the religious revival and subsequent vision would have occurred about 1822.

1

However, in the same account Smith specifically dates his vision to "the spring of Eightteen hundred and twenty."[1]

Fortunately, we are not limited to Joseph Smith's history in trying to solve this riddle. From contemporary records we can establish with reasonable certainty the chronology of the Smith family's relocation to Palmyra and later to Manchester (which was called Farmington at the time[2]). Records described in this chapter help determine when the family was dwelling in the village of Palmyra, when they moved to a log cabin on Stafford Road, and finally when they took up residence on a farm in Manchester. Analysis of these dates and events is important since they provide the historical setting for the revival and the visions that Joseph Jr. later related experiencing. In addition, Joseph's mother Lucy Mack Smith dictated in 1844-45 her own history of the Smith family.[3] Undoubtedly her history contains some errors, but it remains an important record of her family's life during the years they lived in Palmyra and Manchester.

Lucy first describes her husband Joseph's preceding the rest of the family in moving from Vermont to Palmyra, New York, sometime after 1815. Leaving Norwich, Vermont, Joseph Sr. was followed for a short distance by his eldest sons Alvin and Hyrum who watched as their father left alone for Palmyra. He would send for his family when he was ready for them.

Lucy then expressed considerable joy at the subsequent reunion with her husband. She described the family's long-range plans after locating to the village of Palmyra:

> We <all> now Sat down and maturely councilled together as to what course it was best to take, how we sho[u]ld proceed to buisness in our then destitute circumstances. It was agreed by each one of us that it was <most> advisable to ap[p]ly all our energies together and endeavor to obtain a Piece of land as this was then a new country and land was bow [low], being in its rude state, but it was almost a time of famine. Wheat was $2.50 per bushel and other things in proportion. How shall we, said My Husband, be able to sustain ourselves and have anything left to buy land? As I had done considerable at painting oil cloth coverings for tables stands &c. I concluded to set up the buisness and if prospered I would try to supply the wants of the family. In this I succeeded so well that it was not

long till we not only had an abundance of good and wholesome provision but I soon began to replenish my household furniture, a fine stock of which I had sacraficed entirely in moving.[4]

Lucy's craft enterprise prospered, and the family later contracted for one hundred acres in the township of Farmington (now Manchester), immediately south of Palmyra township.

Joseph Sr. is first found in Palmyra on the road tax list for April 1817 as a resident on Main Street.[5] New York law established a system for maintaining roads which required that each township be divided into road districts and that all men in each district be required to work on the roads. Each district was under the supervision of a path master or overseer elected at an annual town meeting held on the first Tuesday of April. At the same meeting three commissioners of highways were to be elected. The overseer had sixteen days from the date of his election to list every male living in his district, twenty-one years or older (a free man) or property owner (a freeholder). Each man devoted at least one day a year to keeping the roads in repair in the district in which he lived. This included clearing brush, stones, and fallen trees; repairing bridges; filling holes; and in the winter clearing paths through the snow. A man could hire someone to serve in his place, but failure to fulfill the obligation in person or by proxy resulted in a fine enforceable by law.[6]

Joseph Sr.'s name first appears in Road District 26 for April 1817, consistent with his having arrived in the latter part of 1816. The town's "Record of Roads" shows that District 26 began on Main Street in the center of the village of Palmyra (the so-called "Four Corners" where four churches now stand) near where the road from Canandaigua intersected and ran west until it crossed into what is now Macedon Township. The district included a small portion of present Walworth Road on the north side of Mud Creek and also a road running south toward the adjoining township of Farmington.[7] This 1817 list basically follows the order in which individual properties were situated as one moves west on Main Street, with Joseph Smith, Sr., listed as living at the west end of Main Street. Joseph Sr.'s name occurs again at the same location in District 26 in 1818 and 1819.

In April 1820 Alvin Smith's name appears for the first time on the road tax list among the merchants on Main Street. Alvin had turned twenty-one in February 1819 and his absence from the 1819 road list may indicate he had been hired out. Residing on Main Street may represent the cake and beer shop the Smiths reportedly operated in town.[8] However, Joseph Sr.'s name appears at the end of the list, showing he was now living outside the business district and near the Palmyra-Farmington town line, where the road district ended.

The Smith family's cabin would be mentioned two months later in the "Palmyra Town Book" as "Joseph Smiths dwelling house," located about fifty feet north of the line dividing Palmyra from Farmington. It stood about two miles south of Main Street on property owned by Samuel Jennings, a merchant with whom the Smiths did business. When the road survey crew on 13 June 1820 laid out the extension of Stafford Road to join Main Street to the north, they used the cabin as a reference point. The survey reads: "Minutes of the survey of a public Highway beginning on the south line . . . in the town of Palmyra three rods fourteen links southeas[t] of Joseph Smiths dwelling house."[9]

The Smith cabin location is further supported by Orsamus Turner, who in 1818 began work as a young apprentice printer at the office of the local *Palmyra Register*. He recalled that he first saw the Smith family in the winter of 1819-20 living "in a rude log house, with but a small spot underbrushed around it" near the town line.[10] This cabin on the outskirts of Palmyra should not be confused with a cabin the family would eventually build on land in nearby Farmington/Manchester.

Lucy subsequently reported that the family contracted for 100 acres of "Everson" (Evertson) land held by the estate of Nicholas Evertson, an attorney in New York City who had acquired considerable land holdings in western New York before his death in 1807. It was June 1820 before Evertson's executors conveyed to Caspar W. Eddy, a New York City physician, power of attorney to sell his holdings. Eddy traveled to Canandaigua, New York, the seat of Ontario County, and on 14 July 1820 transferred his power of attorney to his friend Zachariah Seymour.[11] Seymour had long been a land agent in the area and was a close associate of Oliver Phelps, who with his partner Nathaniel Gorham had opened a land office in Canandaigua and had instituted the practice of "articling" for real estate.

Articling was a way for hard-working but cash-poor pioneers to obtain possession of land by buying on an installment plan. Under this arrangement a schedule of payments was outlined in an "Articles of Agreement" which stipulated the following conditions: the deed was held by the seller until the final payment was made; if the buyer defaulted he lost all right to the land as well as to any improvements, and the seller could then resell it.[12]

It was by this method that the Smiths became property owners. The land deed of Squire Stoddard, who in November 1825 acquired the lot adjoining the Smith's Manchester farm, noted that the north line of his property was "the south line of lands heretofore articled to Joseph and Alvin Smith."[13]

The usual pattern of payment involved breaking the price down into three or more installments, each due a year apart on the original date of the contract. Often the first payment was further broken into easily met segments, such as $10 down, $18 within 90 days, and the balance within the year. When the anniversary date of the contract arrived, the entire second payment was then due. Although title was retained by the seller, the property tax was ordinarily paid by the buyer and was expressly stipulated in some contracts. Sometimes specific requirements were added, such as building a cabin at least eighteen feet by eighteen feet within a year or clearing a specified acreage of land within that period. Often the record of payments was kept on the back of these Articles of Agreement.[14]

Joseph Sr. and Alvin would have had to "article" for their land shortly after July 1820. Joseph Sr. is listed in the Farmington (Manchester) 1820 census (which was enrolled between 7 August 1820 and 5 February 1821), suggesting that the articling was completed no later than February 1821. The ages of the male family members were: under 10, 2 (William and Don Carlos); 16-26, 2 (Alvin and Hyrum); and over 45, 1 (Joseph Sr.). Female members were: under 10, 1 (Catherine); 16-26, 1 (Sophronia); and 26-45, 1 (Lucy Mack Smith). Both Joseph Jr. (age fourteen) and his younger brother Samuel Harrison (age twelve) were missing from the census.[15]

The new Smith farm encompassed approximately one hundred

acres, one third of the original Lot No. 1 in that township. According to the assessment roll for 22 June 1820, the entire three hundred acres of Lot 1 were taxed to the heirs of Nicholas Evertson at that time. In the following year's assessment (7 July 1821) only two hundred acres were taxed to the Evertson heirs, while the balance was assessed to Joseph Smith.[16]

After contracting for the farm, Lucy reports, "In one year's time we made nearly all of the first payment. The Agent adivised [advised] us to build a log house on the land and commence clearing it, we did so. It was not long till we had 30 acres ready for cultivation. But the second payment was now coming due and no means as yet of meeting it."[17] As a result Alvin left Palmyra to raise "the second payment and the remmainder of the first," and returned with "the necessary amount of money for all except the last payment." If the Smiths contracted for the land soon after Seymour received his power of attorney to sell it, around 1 August 1820, then the rest of the first payment and all of the second payment would have been paid to Seymour by 1 August 1821. Lucy adds that they were unable to make the third and last payment (which would have been 1 August 1822) because the land agent died. Seymour did indeed die on 2 July 1822, corroborating this part of her story and establishing the fact that the Smiths contracted for the land sometime after mid-July 1820.[18]

Lucy mentions that "in one year's time" after they contracted for the property, the land agent told them they should build a cabin on their land, which "we did." However, it cannot be precisely determined from her account when this log house was built. That this refers to their Farmington farm and not the Palmyra property is clear from several key facts. First, the Smiths were living in the Palmyra cabin when the road supervisors mentioned it in June 1820 before the Smiths could have contracted for the Farmington land. In addition, William Smith, Joseph Jr.'s younger brother, declared concerning the Farmington/Manchester property, "The improvements made on this farm was first commenced by building a log house at no small expense, and at a later date a frame house at a cost of several hundred dollars."[19] William would hardly call a cabin built on Samuel Jennings's land in Palmyra an improvement on their own farm across the line in Manchester.

From the Palmyra road tax list it is clear that at least Joseph Sr. and Alvin were still living in Palmyra as late as April 1822. It is probable that the Smiths did not move to the Manchester farm until after the summer of 1822. It could not be earlier than July 1821 because Smith family genealogy mentions the birth of a daughter named Lucy, the youngest child of the family. The genealogy specifically states that Lucy was "born in Palmyra."[20]

That some members of the Smith family did not move until after April 1822 is witnessed by the Palmyra road tax list. In 1821 the name of Hyrum Smith, who had turned twenty-one in February, appeared with Alvin and Joseph Sr. on the Palmyra road tax list. In the April 1822 road tax list, the elder Smith and Alvin again appear, so that as of April 1822 the father and oldest son had not yet moved to their Manchester farm, since they were taxed as Palmyra residents. Hyrum's name is missing from the 1822 list. This could indicate that other members of the family had been working on their one hundred acres and had built a cabin sometime in 1821. It is also possible that Hyrum and perhaps other Smith children had moved there to relieve the crowded conditions in their Palmyra cabin. But it could also indicate that Hyrum had hired out to work on a farm in a neighboring town.

When the one hundred acres first went on the assessment roll in July 1821, taxed to Joseph Sr., the parcel was valued at $700, $7 an acre. This was approximately what uncleared land in the area was selling for at the time. The remaining two hundred acres of Lot No. 1 were taxed to the Evertson heirs at a value of $1,400.[21] The same value appeared in the 29 June 1822 assessment.[22] However, by 24 July 1823 the value of the Smith property had jumped to $1,000. This is an increase of over 40 percent, yet the average property value for the whole township rose only 4 percent that year. This indicates that for the first time a cabin had been built and sufficient land had been cleared so that under New York law the assessed value had to be raised.[23]

Lucy's narrative corroborates the assessment roll evidence for an 1822 move to the Manchester property. She introduces events leading up to her son Alvin's death in late 1823 by saying: "In the spring after we moved onto the farm we commenced making Mapel [maple] sugar of which we averaged 1000 lbs per year. We then began to make preparations for building a house, as the Land Agent of whom we purchased our farm was dead and we could not make the last payment."[24]

Next Lucy remarks that the third harvest had "arrived since we opened our new farm." Wheat harvest in New York fell during the latter part of July. By contracting for the property sometime after mid-July 1820, the harvest for that year was over. The first harvest for the Smiths would have been in the summer of 1821. Accordingly the third harvest would be the summer of 1823. At this point Lucy relates the story of the angel's visit informing her son Joseph Jr. of the gold plates. She reports that he attempted that September to obtain the plates but was denied permission. Finally she reports that in November the family succeeded in raising their frame house and had the necessary materials on hand for its completion. However, Alvin's sudden sickness on 15 November and his death four days later on 19 November 1823 left the house incomplete. Lucy remembered that on his death-bed Alvin told Hyrum, "I now want you to go on and finish the House."[25]

Once it is clear that the frame house was not raised until November 1823, then the increase of $300 in the assessed valuation, four months earlier in July 1823, must refer to some other improvements, including completion of the log cabin on their farm. This conclusion is further confirmed when Lucy introduces events of 1823 with the words, "In the spring after we moved onto the farm." This clearly fixes the date of their move to the farm as occurring in 1822.

Some indirect evidence supporting an 1822 date for the Smiths' move to their Manchester property comes from the dating of the Palmyra revival. Joseph Jr.'s 1838-39 account reports that the revival occurred the second year after the family's move to the farm, although it mistakenly places it in 1820.[26] Lucy's account specifically locates the revival after Alvin's death in 1823. Contemporary evidence shows that the revival occurred during the last months of 1824 and early months of 1825. Thus if the revival, which broke out in 1824, occurred two years after the Smiths moved to their Manchester farm, as Joseph's history says, then their move would have indeed occurred in 1822.

NOTES

1. Willard Bean was one of the first Mormon writers to point out the discrepancies. He reasoned: "If the family lived four years in Palmyra, and the religious agitation took place two years later, it would place the date of the vision in the Sacred Grove in the spring of 1822." He adds, "[I]t will readily be seen that our historians have two too many years jammed into the period between the arrival of the Smiths in 1816 and the date of the vision in the spring of 1820" (*A.B.C. History of Palmyra and the Beginning of "Mormonism"* [Palmyra, NY: Palmyra Courier Co., 1938], 35).

Mormon writers have provided various explanations for these problems. In the 1840s Willard Richards's insertion into Smith's manuscript history the words "or thereabouts" in regard to the arrival in Palmyra—"in my tenth year. <*or thereabouts*>"—and with respect to Smith's vision—when he was "between fourteen and fifteen years of age <*or thereabouts*>"—may be the earliest attempt to resolve this problem (Dean C. Jessee, ed. *The Papers of Joseph Smith* [Salt Lake City: Deseret Book Co., 1989], 1:269, 274, emphasis added). In 1968 historian Marvin S. Hill reduced the Smith family's stay in Palmyra to two years. He explained, "Joseph Smith Jr. erroneously said four years were passed in Palmyra" ("The Role of Christian Primitivism in the Origin and Development of the Mormon Kingdom, 1830-1844," Ph.D. diss., University of Chicago, 1968, 39 and n2). Most Mormon writers follow the 1818 date for the move to Manchester. See Leonard J. Arrington and Davis Bitton, *The Mormon Experience: A History of the Latter-day Saints* (New York: Alfred A. Knopf, 1979), 5; and Richard L. Bushman, *Joseph Smith and the Beginnings of Mormonism* (Urbana: University of Illinois Press, 1984), 47-48.

2. In March 1821 Farmington was divided in half. The west half retained the name Farmington, the east half, south of Palmyra, became Burt for just over a year and then Manchester on 16 April 1822.

3. Lucy Mack Smith, Preliminary Manuscript (MS), "History of Lucy Smith," 40. This manuscript was dictated to Martha Jane Coray and the original is in archives, historical department, Church of Jesus Christ of Latter-day Saints, Salt Lake City, Utah (hereafter LDS archives). The page numbering used in our book corresponds to a typed transcript in LDS archives and to page numbers in the photocopy of the manuscript. Where the manuscript has lacunae, the first publication of Lucy's history, *Biographical Sketches of Joseph Smith the Prophet, and His Progenitors for Many Generations* (Liverpool: Published for Orson Pratt by S. W. Richards, 1853), is used. Orson Pratt used a manuscript that had been revised by Martha and Howard Coray from the earlier preliminary manuscript. Extracts were inserted in this

revision from the "History of Joseph Smith" published in the *Times and Seasons* (Nauvoo, Illinois).

In the notes that follow, the Preliminary Manuscript is cited where available, the second citation will be to the first publication of it, shortened to *Biographical Sketches*, and the third citation to the current edition titled, *History of Joseph Smith By His Mother, Lucy Mack Smith* (Salt Lake City: Book-craft, 1958), shortened to *History of Joseph Smith*.

4. Lucy Mack Smith, Preliminary MS, 42-43; *Biographical Sketches* (1853), 70; *History of Joseph Smith* (1958), 63-64.

5. Palmyra Highway Tax Record, Palmyra, New York, Copies of Old Village Records, 1793-1867, microfilm #812869, LDS Family History Library, Salt Lake City, Utah; microfilm 900, reel #60 at Harold B. Lee Library, Brigham Young University, Provo, Utah. A copy is also in the King's Daughters Library, Palmyra, New York. The record is labeled at the beginning, "A Copy of the Several Lists of the Mens Names Liable to Work on the Highways in the Town of Palmyra in the Year 1804." The original record cannot be located at the present time, and a typescript made by Doris Nesbitt is the only copy. Richard Palmer of the Palmyra Historical Society suggested that the original book may have been destroyed when in about 1976 someone took the wrong boxes to the town dump.

The post office serving the Smith family was in Palmyra. Joseph Smith, Sr., is included in a list of unclaimed letters at the Palmyra Post Office on 31 December 1818. See *Palmyra Register* 2 (13 Jan. 1819): 4.

6. New York Legislature, *Laws of the State of New York*, 2 vols. (Albany: H.C. Southwick, 1813), 2:125, 128-29, 271-75, 309. The office of Overseer of Highways was not to be taken lightly. The overseer could be fined ten dollars for each time he failed to notify those required to work on the roads and for each delinquency in performing any other task assigned him. Two weeks prior to the town meeting the following year he was required to certify what work had been done, by whom, and to report anyone who had not fulfilled his obligation.

7. Palmyra, New York, "Record of Roads of the Town of Palmyra, 1793-1901," 94-95, 104; microfilm copy in the State Library, Albany, New York, Film 74-29-1.

8. Pomeroy Tucker, *The Origin, Rise, and Progress of Mormonism* (New York: D. Appleton & Co., 1867), 12.

9. "Palmyra Town Book" (Old Town Record [1793-1870]), 221. Also recorded in "Record of Roads," (1793-1901), 120, Town Clerk's Office, Palmyra, New York. The "Record of Roads" book reads "dwelling home," while the "Town Book" reads "dwelling house." Both are recopied from a

now missing original road record book, but the latter reading was transcribed earlier.

A 1982 excavation confirmed a dwelling site at this location. See Dale L. Berge, "Archaeological Investigations at the Joseph Smith, Sr., Log Dwelling, Palmyra, New York, Interim Report" (Salt Lake City: Historical Department, Church of Jesus Christ of Latter-day Saints, 1982), 15; and Dale L. Berge, "Archaeological Work at the Smith Log House," *Ensign* 15 (Aug. 1985): 24.

The assertion that "the Smiths inadvertently built their cabin on the Palmyra side" (Donald L. Enders, "A Snug Log House," *Ensign* 15 [Aug. 1985]: 16) instead of on the Manchester property is unlikely. The Palmyra merchant who owned the property on which the home stood, and who knew Smith and extended him credit, would hardly have allowed Smith to mistakenly build on his land. (See Samuel Jennings, Estate Papers, 5 June 1822, now housed in Ontario County Records Center and Archives, Canandaigua, New York, 10, line 23, and 12, line 10, for Joseph Smith Sr.'s debts of $11.50 and $1 respectively at the time of Jenning's death on 1 September 1821.)

Pomeroy Tucker wrote that the land the Smith family lived on was included in the farm of Seth T. Chapman who owned the Manchester property at the time Tucker wrote his book (*Origin, Rise, and Progress of Mormonism*, 13).

10. O[rsamus]. Turner, *History of the Pioneer Settlement of Phelps and Gorham's Purchase* (Rochester, NY: William Alling, 1851), 212-13, 400. This log house was actually in the township of Palmyra.

11. For the probate of Nicholas Evertson's estate, see County of New York, Manhattan Borough, Surrogate's Court, Wills, 47:7-11. On the power of attorney, see Miscellaneous Records, C:342-44, 347-48, Ontario County Records Center and Archives, Canandaigua, New York.

12. Colonel Zachariah Seymour, a Revolutionary War veteran, served under Colonel Oliver Phelps. Seymour acted as land agent in Canandaigua, New York, for school lands owned by Connecticut as well as for private individuals (see Ontario County, Deeds, 17:485; and *Ontario Repository*, 4 Apr. 1820, 1). On Oliver Phelps's "articling" innovation, see John W. Barber and Henry Howe, *Historical Collections of the State of New York* (New York: S. Tuttle, 1842), 406-407, reprinting an extract from the *Rochester Directory* of 1827. Seymour served as co-executor of Phelps's estate. A number of Seymour's papers are in the Phelps's papers both at the State Library in Albany and the Ontario County Historical Society in Canandaigua.

13. Deed recorded in Deed Liber 44:220, Ontario County Records Center and Archives, Canandaigua, New York.

14. An example of a printed Articles of Agreement form used by Sey-

mour, located in the Ontario County Historical Society holdings, is for property in Burt (Manchester), dated 31 May 1821. Examples of printed forms requiring the payment of the assessment tax, building a cabin, clearing acreage, and the reversion clause can be found in the State Library, Albany, New York, among the Phelps papers.

15. See *Ontario Repository*, 8 Aug. 1820, 3; "Census of 1820," *History and Growth of the United States Census* (Washington, D.C., 1900), 134, 137); U.S. 1820 Census Records, Farmington, Ontario County, New York, microfilm #193717, p. 318, Family #524, LDS Family History Library. The *Palmyra Register*, 16 Aug. 1820, asked residents to help prepare the census information themselves.

16. Farmington, New York, Assessment Roll, 7 July 1821, 25, 32, Ontario County Records Center and Archives, Canandaigua, New York.

17. Lucy Mack Smith, Preliminary MS, 43. The statement in her book, completed by the Corays, reads, "In a year, we . . . erected a log house" (*Biographical Sketches* [1853], 70; *History of Joseph Smith* [1958], 64). Whether this is Lucy's clarification or the Corays' understanding of her original draft is impossible to determine. In her manuscript Lucy stated: "So that in 2 years from the time we entered Palmyra, strangers destitute of friends, home or employment. We were able to settle ourselves upon our own land [in] a snug comfortable though humble habitation built and neatly furnished by our industry" (Preliminary MS, 44; *Biographical Sketches* [1853], 71; *History of Joseph Smith* [1958], 65). The two-year time period after arriving in Palmyra mentioned by Lucy appears to be an inaccuracy on her part.

18. Lucy Mack Smith, Preliminary MS, 43, 45-46. On Seymour's death, see the Walter Hubbell Papers, Princeton University Libraries, Princeton, New Jersey: letter from Henry Penfield to James Kent, 8 Aug. 1826, 1; and his eulogy in the *Ontario Repository*, 16 July 1822, a reprint of the previous week's *Ontario Messenger*.

19. "Notes Written on 'Chamber's Life of Joseph Smith.' by William Smith," about 1875, typescript, 17, LDS archives. See Richard L. Anderson, "Joseph Smith's New York Reputation Reappraised," *Brigham Young University Studies* 10 (Spring 1970): 314. Russell R. Rich in the same issue (257) maintained that the Smiths built their cabin on the Manchester property.

20. "Genealogy," Manuscript History, A-1: 10 [separate section], reads, "Lucy Smith, born in Palmyra, Ontario Co. N.Y. July 18, 1821." See Jessee, *Papers of Joseph Smith*, 1:19. Lucy received a patriarchal blessing from her father on 9 December 1834 at the age of thirteen. Her birth date and place were given as 18 July 1821 at Palmyra, Ontario County, New York, in Patriarchal Blessing Book 1:8 and recopied in 2:14, LDS archives. See Milton V. Backman, Jr., *A*

Profile of Latter-day Saints of Kirtland, Ohio and Members of Zion's Camp 1830-1839 (Provo, UT, 1982), 112. Lucy is incorrectly listed as "(wife of Joseph Sr.)." *William Smith on Mormonism* (Lamoni, IA: Herald Steam Book & Job Office, 1883), 5, gives 1821 as the date for the move to Manchester.

21. For examples of land prices, ranging from $3 to $10 an acre, see the Phelps papers in Albany, New York; cf. Fawn M. Brodie, *No Man Knows My History* (New York: A. Knopf, 1945), 10.

22. Manchester, New York, Assessment Roll, 29 June 1822, 16, Ontario County Records Center and Archives, Canandaigua, New York.

23. Manchester, New York, Assessment Roll, 24 July 1823, 17. The 4 percent increase was arrived at by comparing the dollar value per acre of property from 1820 to 1823 and averaging the increase shown in 1823. On increase in evaluation, see *Laws of the State of New York*, 2:510.

24. Lucy Mack Smith, Preliminary MS, 45-46; *Biographical Sketches* (1853), 72; *History of Joseph Smith* (1958), 66. William Smith wrote that the family moved into the township of Manchester and "Here my father purchased one hundred acres of new land heavely [sic] timber[e]d and in the clearing up of this land which was mostly done in the form of fire" ("Notes Written on 'Chamber's Life of Joseph Smith,'" 20).

25. Lucy says that the frame house was still being built when Alvin died but has the year as 1822, which is incorrect (Preliminary MS, 45-46, 51-52; see *Biographical Sketches* [1853], 87; *History of Joseph Smith* [1958], 85). She gives Alvin's death variously as 1822 and 1824, but his tombstone shows he died on 19 November 1823 at the age of twenty-five years. Early sources for the death of Alvin are the following:

1. Gravestone in the General John Swift Memorial Cemetery, Palmyra, New York, inscribed: "In memory of/ Alvin. Son of Joseph/ & Lucy Smith. who/ died Nov. 19. 1823./ in the 25. year of/ his age." (See photograph in Alma P. Burton, *Mormon Trail from Vermont to Utah* [Salt Lake City: Deseret Book Co., 1966], 35.)

2. Day Book of Dr. Gain C. Robinson, 20 Nov. 1823, the day after Alvin's death: "Joseph Smith visit attend 300 [$3.00]," possibly indicating his charge for assisting in the autopsy of Alvin Smith (Gain Robinson Day Book [21 July 1823 to 2 June 1826], King's Daughters Library, Palmyra, New York; microfilm #833096 at LDS Family History Library).

3. *Wayne Sentinel* 2 (29 Sept. 1824): 3, prints an advertisement placed by Joseph Sr. dated "Sept. 25th, 1824," stating he had exhumed Alvin's body to refute rumors that it had been removed for dissection.

26. Manuscript History, Book A-1:1; JS-H 1:5, PGP; Jessee, *Papers of Joseph Smith*, 1:269.

CHAPTER TWO

THE PALMYRA REVIVAL

When Joseph Smith, Jr., described his first vision in his 1838-39 account, he dated it to the spring of 1820 and affirmed that this vision was the result of a religious revival, "an unusual excitement on the subject of religion" which took place "in the place where we lived." But he also dated it "sometime in the second year after our removal to Manchester." As shown in the previous chapter, the Smith family did not move onto their Manchester farm until 1822. The second year after this move would have been 1824, not 1820. An examination of newspaper accounts, religious periodicals, church records, and personal narratives shows that there were no significant gains in church memberships or any other signs of revival in Palmyra in 1820. There was a stirring and momentous revival there with all the features that Joseph Smith's history mentions during the fall and winter of 1824-25.

Smith stated that the revival that stirred him also led his mother, sister, and two brothers to join the Presbyterian church, while he was drawn to the Methodists.[1] In the preliminary draft of his mother's history, Lucy adds details which suggest an 1824 date for the revival as well. She begins by linking the revival to the death of her son Alvin. After relating the family's sorrow after his death, when "we could not be comforted because he was not," she adds a short statement, subsequently crossed out: "About this time their [there] was a great revival in religion and the whole neighborhood was very much aroused to the subject, and we among the rest flocked to the meeting house to see if their [there] was a word of comfort for us that might

15

releive [relieve] our over charged feelings."[2] Her "over-charged feelings" were the result of her oldest son Alvin dying suddenly the previous year (1823).

A year after this event she was still seeking consolation for her wounded soul and hoped to find it at the town meeting house where the revival was in full progress and frequent meetings held. Her manuscript continues:

> There was <at this time> a man then laboring in that place to effect a union of all the churches, that all denominations might be agreed to worship God with one mind, and one heart. This I thought looked right, and tried to persuade my Husband to join with them as I wished to do so myself and it was the inclination of them all [her children] except Joseph. He refused from the first to attend the meeting with us. He would say, Mother, I do not wish to prevent you from going to meeting or joining any church you like or any of the Family who desire the like, only do not ask me to <do so> for I do not wish to go. But I will take my Bible and go out into the woods and learn more in two hours than you could if you were to go to meeting two years. My husband also declined attending the meetings after the first but did not object to myself and such of the children as chose <going or becoming> church members.

Lucy notes that Joseph warned her about those involved, and her description of his warning suggests that the church she was intending to join was indeed the local Presbyterian church:

> Now you look at deacon <Jessup>. . . . suppose that (one of his poor neighbors) owed him the value of one cow. This man has eight small children; suppose the poor man should be taken sick & die leaving his wife with one cow but destitute of every means of support for herself and family. Now I tell you that deacon Jess<u>p, <religious> as he is, would not hesitate to take the last cow from the widow and orphans rather than loose the debt.[3]

Henry Jessup was a long-time Presbyterian, one of the original trustees of the Western Presbyterian Church of Palmyra at its incorporation on 18 March 1817.[4]

According to Joseph, his older brother Hyrum joined the Presbyterian church along with his mother as a result of the revival. Willard

Chase, a neighbor, mentioned that in 1825 Hyrum asked to borrow his seer stone. Though reluctant to let the stone go, Chase said he honored Hyrum's request because Hyrum "had made a profession of religion" and Chase felt he could now be trusted to return it.[5]

In his 1838-39 account Joseph Smith remembered that great multitudes joined the Baptist, Methodist, and Presbyterian churches during the revival. Church membership rolls are carefully kept, and in most cases can still be traced.

Membership rolls of "the first Baptized Church in Palmyra," which had a frame meetinghouse west of the village of Palmyra in Macedon township, reveal that during the entire year of 1820 only eight people were received on profession of faith and baptized. However during the period between October 1824 and April 1825, even though the church was without a pastor at the time, 94 individuals were baptized and added to the membership roll.

For Baptists the awakening began on 20 October 1824, when church minutes show that "Michael Egleston, Erastus Spear, Lorenzo Spear, Abagail Spear, Belena Byxbe, Minerva Titus, Sophia Rogers, and Harriot Rogers told their Christian experience to the Church and were fellowshipped by the Church and on Thursday following were Baptized by Elder Bradley and Received into the Church." The minutes of 20 November mentioned eight more individuals baptized; the 24 November minutes name an additional twelve. In December nineteen more were added by conversion. In the first four months of 1825 there were forty-five additional baptisms. For the one year period from October 1824 to the end of September 1825 there were a total of 94 persons baptized, an increase of 87 members. Membership increased from 132 to 219 (65 percent).[6]

The same pattern characterizes Methodist membership records, which give the total membership of the dozen or so preaching points serviced by a circuit-riding preacher. The increase of 208 reported in the summer of 1825 for the previous year demonstrates that this had proved to be a banner year for the Ontario circuit on which Palmyra was located. In contrast, the circuit had constantly lost members during the period between 1819 and 1821—twenty-six in 1819, six in 1820, and forty-nine in 1821.[7]

Presbyterian membership rolls paint an identical picture. Although the first volume of the local church's minutes is missing, records of the Geneva Presbytery to which the church belonged and reported are still extant, and these clearly reflect the revival in the congregation in Palmyra. The minutes show that by 21 September 1825 when figures were in for a revival over the winter of 1824-25 "99 have been admitted on examination." As early as February 1825 the Presbytery was called on, in glowing terms, to

> bless the Lord for the displays of sovereign grace which have been made <within our boundaries> during the past year. In the congregation of Palmyra, the Lord has appeared in his glory to build up Zion. More than a hundred have been hopefully brought into the kingdom of the Redeemer. The distinguishing doctrines of grace have proved eminently the sword of the Spirit, by which the rebellion of man's heart has been slain. The fruits of holiness in this revival even now are conspicuous. The exertions for the promotion of divine knowledge are greater than formerly. Sabbath Schools, Bible classes, Missionary & Tract Societies are receiving unusual attention, & their salutary influence is apparent.[8]

Presbytery records for 1820 suggest some anticipation of a revival in the church of Phelps (located at Oaks Corners some fourteen miles from Palmyra) and at Canandaigua (some thirteen miles away), neither of which materialized, but nothing for the Palmyra church. Newly discovered evidence in the "Presbyterial Reports to the Synod of Geneva" confirms the scarcity of converts in the conference year of 1820. The presbytery reported to synod only fourteen additions to the Western Presbyterian Church of Palmyra for the period between February 1820 and March 1821. If four Smiths joined that year, this left only ten others to join all year.[9]

This pattern of growth is confirmed by Reverend James Hotchkin, who in 1845 began writing the official history of the rise of the Presbyterian denomination in western New York. The Synod of New York backed this effort and requested all the churches to open their records to him. Hotchkin was especially interested in revivals. His account for the Palmyra church shows revivals in 1817 and in 1824 but nothing in the intervening years.[10]

The revival over the winter of 1816-17, which affected mainly the

Presbyterian church of Palmyra, received coverage in at least a dozen periodicals, including among others the *Christian Herald and Seaman's Magazine*, the *Religious Remembrancer*, the *American Baptist Magazine*, and the *Boston Recorder*.[11]

The 1824-25 revival likewise received enthusiastic write-ups in an equal number of publications.[12] But there is total silence in these same periodicals about any revival in Palmyra between 1819 and 1821.[13]

The 1824-25 date can also be confirmed by checking the names of reported participants. William Smith, Joseph's brother, was interviewed in June 1841 by James Murdock, who read back his notes for correction. William recalled that "About the year 1823, there was a revival of religion in that region, and Joseph was one of several hopeful converts."[14] In his own book, *William Smith on Mormonism*, published in 1883, William wrote, "In 1822 and 1823, the people in our neighborhood were very much stirred up with regard to religious matters by the preaching of a Mr. Lane, an Elder of the Methodist Church, and celebrated throughout the country as a 'great revival preacher.'"[15] In addition to Lane, William recalled the involvement of Benjamin Stockton:

> Rev. Stockton was the president of the meeting and suggested that it was their meeting and under their care and they had a church there and they [the Smiths] ought to join the Presbyterians, but as father did not like Rev. Stockton very well, our folks hesitated and the next evening a Rev. Mr. Lane of the Methodists preached a sermon on "what church shall I join?" And the burden of his discourse was to ask God, using as a text, "If any man lack wisdom let him ask of God who giveth to all men liberally."[16]

William's description of the revival fits the pattern of the period. Once a revival had broken out, regular and frequent meetings would be scheduled at the town meetinghouse to advance it. Since Presbyterians were dominant in Palmyra, one could well expect Reverend Benjamin Stockton, their pastor, to preside and to expect the converts to join the church located in the village itself. The Baptist building was about a mile west of the center of the village, and Methodists were a mile east on Vienna Road, so Joseph Smith's expression of the revivals in his "region of country" was a good way to describe the situation.

It is important to note that any extended series of revival meetings at which Stockton presided must fall in 1824 or later because he did not become pastor of the Palmyra Presbyterian church until 18 February 1824.[17] Reverend James Hotchkin in cataloging the revivals in the churches of Geneva Presbytery wrote of the Palmyra church that a "copious shower of grace passed over this region in 1824 under the labors of Mr. Stockton, and a large number were gathered into the church, some of whom are now pillars in Christ's house."[18]

Stockton was pastor of the Skaneateles church in central New York from 4 March 1818 until 30 June 1822.[19] He visited Palmyra for a speech to the Youth Missionary Society in October 1822, and the newspaper described him then as "Rev. Stockton of Skaneateles."[20] He appeared again in the Palmyra paper when he performed a wedding on 26 November 1823, just a week after Alvin's death.[21] According to William Smith, Stockton was present the previous week and preached Alvin's funeral sermon. In this sermon Stockton implied that Alvin "had gone to hell, for Alvin was not a church member, but he was a good boy and my [William's] father did not like it."[22] William noted that when the revival meetings closed and Stockton insisted that the converts join the Presbyterian church, "our folks hesitated" because of his insinuation about Alvin.

"Rev. Mr. Lane," the other person mentioned by William Smith as participating in the revival, is George Lane, a talented Methodist preacher.[23] Lane is also mentioned by Oliver Cowdery, who worked with Joseph Smith beginning in 1829. In the Mormon periodical, *Latter Day Saints' Messenger and Advocate*, Cowdery commenced a "full history of the rise of the church of Latter Day Saints," published during 1834-35. For details of this account he said he relied on information furnished by Joseph Smith.[24] Cowdery begins with Smith as a young man of seventeen who is stirred by a revival in 1823 through the preaching of Lane:

One Mr. Lane, a presiding Elder of the Methodist church, visited Palmyra, and vicinity. Elder Lane was a tallented man possessing a good share of literary endowments, and apparent humility. There was a great awakening, or excitement raised on the subject of religion, and much enquiry for the word of life. Large additions were made to the Methodist, Presbyterian, and Baptist churches. — Mr. Lane's manner of communication was peculiarly calculated to awaken the intellect of the hearer, and arouse the sinner to look about him for safety — much good instruction was always drawn from his discourses on the scriptures, and in common with others, our brother's mind became awakened. For a length of time the reformation seemed to move in a harmonious manner, but, as the *excitement* ceased . . . a general struggle was made by the leading characters of the different sects, for proselytes. . . . In this general strife for followers, his mother, one sister, and two of his natural brothers, were persuaded to unite with the Presbyterians. . . . After strong solicitations to unite with one of those different societies, and seeing the apparent proselyting disposition manifested with equal warmth for each, his mind was led to more seriously contemplate the importance of a move of this kind.[25]

That Cowdery has not overdrawn the effectiveness of Lane's preaching is evident from the comments of a fellow minister in the Methodist Genesee Conference, George Peck:

As a preacher he [Rev. George Lane] was thoroughly orthodox, systematic, and earnest. His sermons exhibited a thorough acquaintance with the Scriptures and with the human heart. In the palmy days of his itinerancy he was often overwhelmingly eloquent. Sometimes under his powerful appeals vast congregations were moved like the trees of the forest before a mighty wind. Many a stout-hearted sinner was broken down, and cried aloud for mercy under his all but irresistible appeals. His language was unstudied, but chaste, correct, simple, and forcible.[26]

In 1823 Lane was living in the area of Wilkes-Barre, Pennsylvania, and was not appointed presiding elder of the Ontario District in which Palmyra was located until July 1824.[27] He presided only until January 1825 when illness in his family forced him temporarily to leave the ministry.[28]

As presiding elder Lane was responsible to ride from circuit to circuit in the Ontario District and hold the quarterly business meetings for each circuit. Each preaching point or congregation on the circuit sent delegates to the quarterly meeting, and at its conclusion the presiding elder would travel on to the next circuit of the district to preside at its quarterly meeting.

According to Lane's report, published in the *Methodist Magazine* (Apr. 1825), the Lord's work in Palmyra and vicinity "commenced in the spring, and progressed moderately until the time of the quarterly meeting, which was held on the 25th and 26th of September" 1824.[29] A note in the local Palmyra newspaper of 15 September showed the progress of the work over the spring and summer, shortly before Lane came on the scene at the September conference: "A reformation is going on in this town to a great extent. The love of God has been shed abroad in the hearts of many, and the outpouring of the Spirit seems to have taken a strong hold. About twenty-five have recently obtained a hope in the Lord, and joined the Methodist Church, and many more are desirous of becoming members."[30]

This verifies Joseph Smith's description of the revival as having "commenced with the Methodists." By September the revival had not yet touched the Baptist church, for at the annual meeting of the Ontario Baptist Association held on 22 September, the church reported only two baptisms for the entire previous year.[31] Similarly the local Presbyterian church remained untouched, for the report of the Presbytery for 8 September stated, "there has been no remarkable revival of religion within our bounds."[32]

Lane's personal report dated 25 January 1825 presents a detailed account of the revival's progress. He describes events occurring in the vicinity of Palmyra, focusing on how youth were especially affected:

> From Catharine [circuit] I went to Ontario circuit, where the Lord had already begun a gracious work in Palmyra. . . . About this time [25 and 26 September 1824] it appeared to break out afresh. Monday evening, after the quarterly meeting, there were four converted, and on the following evening, at a prayer meeting at Dr. Chase's, there were seven. Among these was a young woman by the name of Lucy Stoddard.

Nineteen-year-old Lucy Stoddard was a cousin of Calvin Stoddard, who would later marry Smith's sister Sophronia and who would a few months after this also be touched by the revival.[33]

From this point Lane's account is largely taken up with Lucy Stoddard's conversion experience. Her calm and joyful acceptance of illness and death, just a few weeks after her conversion the last week of September 1824, helped fan the flames of revival among the young people of the village:

> The great deep of her heart was broken up; she saw clearly that she was a child of wrath, and in danger of hell. With this view of her sad condition, she fell prostrate at the feet of her offended sovereign, and in the bitterest anguish cried for mercy. In this situation, however, she was not suffered long to continue before she obtained a most satisfactory evidence of her acceptance with God through the merits of Jesus Christ. Her soul was unspeakably happy, and with great emphasis she exhorted others to come and share with her the inestimable blessing.

A week after her conversion she married Hiram Wilcox. Lane continues:

> The same week she was married she was attacked by a bilious remittent fever, which terminated in a typhus fever. . . . at length, her disorder took such a turn as to convince her and others, that her stay in this world would be but short. The patience with which she endured her afflictions, which were sometimes very severe, was remarkable; not a murmur was heard to escape her lips. . . . From Saturday night to the time of her dissolution, which took place on Monday following, she seemed wholly swallowed up in God.

Lane describes her dying moments and the dramatic impression left on her friends. He reports that

> when life appeared almost extinct, she raised her trembling hands, and clapped them three times, crying, "Hallelujah! hallelujah! hallelujah! glory to God in the highest!" From this time she lay in perfect composure until twelve o'clock on Monday, November 1st, when she breathed her last without a struggle or a groan, after an illness of three weeks and two days, and just five weeks from the time of her conversion. The effect produced by this death was the happiest. While it confounded the infidel, it greatly strengthened believers, especially young converts.[34]

Stoddard was not the only one whose death challenged friends to prepare for heaven. In Manchester township, which joined Palmyra on the south, a deadly epidemic broke out and spread through Phelps township to the east. This "sweeping mortality," as it was called by Benjamin Farley, a Christian-Connection preacher, was regarded by him as an act of God to prepare people's hearts to seek salvation. Writing from Phelps, he reported in a letter to the *Gospel Luminary* dated 28 January 1825:

> It has been a great time of lament[a]tion and mourning; children removed from parents, and parents from children. The scene has been truly alarming. . . . I was called upon almost every day to attend on funeral solemnities, and often two in a day; until I was attacked myself with the same fatal disorder, which brought me near to the grave.

Such widespread death inevitably made people think of the need to prepare for eternity. Farley continued:

> Since those d[a]ys of death and mourning, the Lord has graciously visited this place in mercy. Many have been brought to sing the new song, while scores are enquiring what they must do to be saved. The work is not confined to one neighborhood, but is becoming general. In Palmyra it is judged that more than one hundred have recently experienced salvation; and in the vicinity of Sulphur Springs [now Clifton Springs, Manchester township] about the same number. The work in the above mentioned places is among the methodists and presbyterians. Congregations are uncommonly large and attentive. . . . the harvest truly is great.[35]

The actual numbers of converts in Palmyra may have been larger than Farley's January 1825 letter estimated, for two months previously the *Western Recorder* had already reported "one hundred or more" converts for Palmyra: "A revival of religion has lately commenced in the town of Palmyra, N.Y. It is stated by one of the subjects of this glorious work, that one hundred or more persons, it is thought, have lately been brought out of darkness into marvelous light. — Persons of all ages and classes are the subjects of this work of grace."[36]

By mid-December the number was said to have swelled to near

two hundred. Reverend Reuben Winchell in a letter dated "Dec 20th, 1824" written from Avon, New York, reported that while he was recently preaching at West Bloomfield he heard that the number of converts was about two hundred. He wrote: "In Palmyra, a town about 30 miles North East of this, God has triumphed gloriously. About 200, as I am informed, are sharers in this great and precious work."[37]

Even these figures may be too conservative, for Lane placed the number of Methodist converts alone at "upward of one hundred and fifty" by mid-December:

> December 11th and 12th our quarterly meeting for Ontario circuit was held in Ontario. . . . Here I found that the work which had for some time been going on in Palmyra, had broken out from the village like a mighty flame, and was spreading in every direction. When I left the place, December 22[n]d, there had, in the village and its vicinity, upward of one hundred and fifty joined the [Methodist] society, besides a number that had joined other churches, and many that had joined no church.[38]

By the time Lane left the area the third week in December, many people needed only an invitation in order to be baptized. On Christmas day a Baptist preacher wrote to a friend that "As I came on my journey this way, I tarried a few days, and baptized eight."[39]

Meanwhile revivals were spreading as well in the neighboring towns. By February revivals were reported in Williamson and Ontario to the north, in Manchester, Sulphur Springs, and Vienna to the southeast, in Lyons to the east, and in Macedon to the west. Even towns at a greater distance from Palmyra began to experience revival fires, with Mendon to the west and Geneva to the southeast sharing in the divine outpouring.

A steady stream of reports of the spreading revival continued to flow from the papers and periodicals in early 1825. On 13 January Methodist preacher J. B. Alverson wrote from Canandaigua about Methodist gains:

> In Geneva the work has increased considerably. . . . On Ontario circuit . . . the prospects are very promising. Two hundred have been added since conference [i.e. July 1824]. On Lyons [circuit] the Lord

continues to visit the people in great mercy. At Clyde the prospect is great . . . Sixty-one have experienced religion since this revival commenced, and forty-one have joined the society.[40]

By February townships bordering on Lake Ontario were described as touched by revival fires. According to West Bloomfield's *Gospel Luminary* for February 1825, "We learn that a powerful reformation has been spreading for several months past, in the towns of *Palmyra*, *Williamson* and *Ontario*. The work we are informed still continues in those places."[41]

West Bloomfield itself was tasting the reformation blessing. "It has been a gr[ad]ual scene of reform[a]tion with us ever since April last" (1824), wrote David Millard in a communication dated 25 February 1825. Though not as powerful as the revival had been, still he found that "Our meetings are yet crowded and solemn, and some appear to be seeking the one thing nee[d]ful. On the 11th, inst. I baptized *twenty* happy converts. . . . On the 19th I baptized *five* more. Several others are expected to go forward in this ordinance soon." Millard, who had been preaching at West Bloomfield since 1817, closed his report by noting: "Such a season of extensive and powerful revivals, was probably never known in this western country, since its first settlement."[42]

By March the work was subsiding in the village of Palmyra, but it continued to spread in adjacent towns. Gorham, considerably south of Vienna, was followed by the area of Clyde, farther east beyond Lyons, where during the first part of May about 150 were reported converted. By this time "no recent cases of conviction" were reported from Palmyra itself, but the work was advancing in the Sulphur Springs area and still continuing at Geneva, twenty-five miles distant.[43] This generalized 1824-25 revival activity fits completely Joseph Smith's statement that the revival occurred not only in the place where he lived but "became general among all the sects in that region of country" and that "the whole district of country seemed affected by it."

As converts began filling churches, leaders took stock of their numbers. By January Methodists estimated that on their Ontario circuit two hundred had joined their society. A Baptist pastor in

Bristol, New York, reported to a friend under the date of 9 March 1825 that in the immediate area of Palmyra, "Multitudes have abandoned their false hopes and false schemes. . . . About three hundred have united with the Baptist, Presbyterian, and Methodist churches; and to each in about equal numbers."[44]

The Palmyra newspaper for 2 March 1825 reprinted a report from the *Religious Advocate* of Rochester:

> More than two hundred souls have become the hopeful subjects of divine grace in Palmyra, Macedon, Manchester, Phelps, Lyons, and Ontario, since the late revival commenced. — This is a powerful work; it is among old and young, but mostly among young people. Many are ready to exclaim, "what hath God wrought!" "It is the Lord's doing, and it is marvellous in our eyes." The cry is yet from various parts, "come over and help us." There are large and attentive congregations in every part, who hear as for their lives. Such intelligence must be pleasing to every child of God, who rightly estimate the value of immortal souls, and wishes well to the cause of Zion.

Since the *Religious Advocate* was a Presbyterian-related periodical, the figures undoubtedly reflect Presbyterian gains. A note in the same issue of the Palmyra paper adds this balancing information: "It may be added, that in Palmyra and Macedon, including Methodist, Presbyterian and Baptist Churches, more than 400 have already testified that the Lord is good. The work is still progressing. In the neighboring towns, the number is great and fast increasing."[45]

By September 1825 the results of the revival for Palmyra had become a matter of record. The Presbyterian church reported 99 admitted on examination; Baptists had received 94 by profession of faith and baptism; the Methodist circuit showed an increase of 208. Cowdery's claim of "large additions" and Smith's statement that "great multitudes united themselves to the different religious parties" were scarcely overstatements. Thus the revival matching the detailed descriptions of both Cowdery and Smith took place during the fall of 1824 through the spring of 1825 both "in Palmyra" (Cowdery) and "the neighborhood" where Smith lived (Smith), as well as in the surrounding "vicinity," "region," and "whole district of country."

Despite such evidence supporting the 1824-25 date, two main lines of argument have been advanced to confirm Smith's 1820 revival date. The first maintains that Smith was merely alluding to revivals which were common in western New York state at this period. Proponents of this theory point out that he was in Missouri when he wrote his 1838-39 account. Thus when he spoke of a revival "in the place where we lived," he was designating the whole of western New York. In support of this apologists point to a number of revivals or substantial membership increases occurring during 1820 in towns close enough for Smith to reach on foot. They point to David Marks who, as a teenager, attended revivals up to thirty miles from his home. Since Smith was a robust lad, he could have done the same. In 1969 *Brigham Young University Studies* published a map showing nine revival sites which Smith could have visited in 1820, with distances from the Smith homestead shown in five-mile increments.[46] However, the map is flawed, with four villages placed significantly closer than they appear on accurate maps of the area and other sites listed where there was no religious excitement at all.[47]

However, this argument overlooks—and negates—Cowdery's and Smith's own assertion of a revival "in Palmyra" and "vicinity," as well as the names of pastors responsible for the development. Smith in an 1843 interview with a reporter for the *New York Spectator* stated that it was "among the different religious denominations in the neighborhood where I lived."[48] Lucy says that she and her children in company with their whole neighborhood "flocked to the meeting house." This description does not suggest a ten-to-fifteen-mile walk.

The definitive indication that the revival was local comes in Smith's remarks about the "great confusion and bad feelings" ensuing at the end of the meetings. Even the most ardent defenders of an 1820 date recognize that this strife over converts was local, resulting in Smith's family being proselyted to the local Presbyterian church.

The second line of argument seeks to establish one specific revival, characterized by several of the features his account describes, close enough to his home he could have attended. According to this argument, an awakening took place at the village of Vienna, some eleven miles from Palmyra, between the summer of 1819 and the summer of 1820. The features seen as echoing Smith's account include: the presence of George Lane at Vienna, a camp meeting in the area, and a substantial membership increase.[49] However, there is no evidence that such a revival ever occurred.

Lane was at Vienna in July 1819 attending the annual meeting of the Methodist Genesee Conference, at which he was appointed to serve in Pennsylvania.[50] There is no record that he preached or that a camp meeting was held in connection with this conference. In 1826, when a camp meeting was actually held, the conference minutes contain reference to the ministers who were put in charge of the arrangements for the meeting. No indication of any such arrangements appears in the 1819 minutes.

The idea of a revival at Vienna comes from a misreading and subsequent joining of two unrelated sources. The first statement comes from journalist Orsamus Turner, who from 1818 to 1822 was apprenticed in the office of the Palmyra newspaper. In his reminiscences published thirty years later, Turner remembered attending the local debating society with Smith. He also recalled that "after catching a spark of Methodism in the camp meeting, away down in the woods, on the Vienna road, he [Smith] was a very passable exhorter in evening meetings."[51]

The reference to "camp meeting" alludes to a camp grounds site used by Methodists at that time. This camp was about a mile outside the village of Palmyra, "away down in the woods" on the road running southeast to Vienna. At this site in 1822, Methodists built their first house of worship. Much later, in 1826, about a mile southeast of this chapel a camp meeting was held by the conference which drew a crowd of 10,000 people. It was undoubtedly this camp meeting site which also received mention in the Palmyra paper during the last week of June 1820, not for a crowd of 10,000, but for a man who died from consuming too much alcohol purchased at "the grog-shops" on the edge of the campgrounds.[52] Camp meetings were often held by Methodists but did not often spark a significant revival. When revivals did occur, they were customarily reported in the *Methodist Magazine*.

However, Turner's comment has been misread as referring to a camp meeting at the village of Vienna itself which touched off a whirlwind revival. This conclusion requires uniting Turner's comment with an unrelated and misdated event first mentioned in 1886. In that year M. P. Blakeslee, pastor of the Methodist church in Phelps village (until 1855 called Vienna), attempted to write "Notes for a History of Methodism in Phelps."[53] He had been in touch with Serepta March Baker, the widow of a Methodist preacher, and with Harry Sarsnett, a black man, both of whom had been converted in the same revival. Blakeslee described this revival some sixty years after the event:

> For 1820, Loring Grant and John Baggerly were the preachers. . . .
> In some way the name of Elisha House, an ordained local preacher of ability, became associated with the circuit. Our venerable colored citizen, Mr. Harry Sarsnett, remembers a camp-meeting held by him on the Granger camp-ground, situated on the rise of land south of the railroad, on the farm of V. W. Gates. The year was one flaming spiritual advance. Mrs. Baker says the revival was a religious cyclone which swept over the whole region round about and the kingdom of darkness was terribly shaken. The membership of the circuit arose [sic] from three hundred and seventy-six to six hundred and fifty [correct figures are 374 to 654].[54]

A careful reading of Blakeslee's narrative reveals three important points. First, Blakeslee is not referring to the campground on the Vienna road, since the Vienna road from Palmyra enters the village of Vienna at its northwest side, north of the railroad. The Granger campground was located south of the railroad and southeast of Vienna towards Oaks Corners.[55]

Second, when Blakeslee speaks of the year 1820 he does not mean the calendar year 1820 but the conference year 1820, which began at the annual meeting in either July or August and ran to the following summer's meeting. This is evident from his statement that "For 1820, Loring Grant and John Baggerly were the preachers." The published Minutes shows that these two preachers were not assigned to the Lyons circuit until 20 July 1820 and served until July 1821, too late for a spring 1820 revival. Thus the time Lane was at Vienna and supposedly conducting a camp meeting during July 1819 was an entire year earlier than the revival period picked by Blakeslee, which came in the year following July 1820. It is also significant that the preachers Blakeslee names were not identified with the revival by the man who was converted.

Third, it seems evident that Blakeslee places this flaming revival in 1820 because he noted from the conference's published minutes that in that year the Lyons circuit, which included Vienna, increased its membership by 274. The conference minutes show that as of July 1819 membership on the circuit stood at 673, dropped by 299 to 374 by July 1820, only to rise again by some 280 members to 654 by July 1821. These fluctuations most likely resulted from a typographical error in the printed text for 1820.

This possibility seems especially likely when these apparent gains are compared with the experience of Abner Chase who was appointed presiding elder over the Lyons circuit at the July 1820 conference and served for the next four years. He reports only discouragement until 1823. Chase began his supervision of the Ontario District (of which both Palmyra township and Lyons circuit were a part) on 20 July 1820. This was the very period for which Blakeslee, on the basis of the published membership figures, suggested that a revival swept through the area around Vienna, converting almost three hundred new members. Yet Chase, who was making quarterly visits to the Lyons circuit, knows nothing of such a revival between July 1820 and July 1821. On 1 July 1824 he summarizes his four-year supervision over this district:

> The Lord has been pleased to visit this District (Ontario) in mercy the present year [July 1823-July 1824]. . . . Four years since, Unitarianism or Arianism, seemed to threaten the entire overthrow of the work of God in some Circuits on this District, and on some others, divisions and wild and ranting fanatics, caused the spirits of the faithful in a degree to sink. But the Lord has turned again the captivity of Zion, and made us to rejoice. Though for two or three years [July 1820-July 1823] we saw no great awakenings, yet we saw that truth and rational scriptural piety were evidently gaining ground.
>
> The present year [July 1823-July 1824] we have had some glorious revivals. . . .

Chase cites an awakening on Catherine circuit during "the last year"

(July 1823-July 1824), with more than one hundred added and a meeting house built, but adds that "the greatest and best news" comes from the Lyons circuit. He then reports:

> From the annual Conference [July 1823] where we received our appointment to this [Lyons] circuit, we came directly to our work, in the name of the Lord, hoping and praying for a revival. . . .
>
> We soon perceived the serious attention of the listening multitudes to the word preached, accompanied with tears and cries for salvation in Jesus' name. Nor were they turned empty away. In our prayer-meetings scores of these deeply penitent mourners, witnessed the power of Christ to save.

After reporting that entire families were touched, he continues: "How many have been converted cannot now be easily ascertained; about two hundred and eighty have joined the different societies, on the circuit the present year [July 1823-July 1824]. The work has been gradually progressing for eight or ten months. . . . Indeed we have been all year harvesting, and are yet in the midst thereof." Finally Presiding Elder Chase concludes his 1 July 1824 report by contrasting the fruitlessness of the previous years with the bounty of the present: "This account may appear small when compared with some from larger fields and abler pens, but to us it appears great, who have been so long combatting the enemy, without winning much spoil."[56] Thus Chase's report makes it clear that Blakeslee, writing sixty-two years later, places the revival on the Lyons circuit three years too early. Rather the revival began in the fall of 1823 and was continuing in the summer of 1824.[57]

Contemporary evidence thus requires an 1824-25 date for the revival Smith describes in his 1838-39 official history. Certainly memory at times conflates events, and perhaps Smith in retrospect blended in his mind events from 1820 with a revival occurring four years later. But the problems caused by the dating discrepancy are fundamental ones. That date for the revival provides the circumstances and motivation leading to the first vision and allows the four annual visits to the hill Cumorah, beginning in September 1823 and leading to Smith's obtaining the plates in September 1827. A revival in the spring of 1825 would place the first visit to the hill Cumorah in September 1825 and allow only one visit before Smith finally received the plates.

One historian maintains that the story may have been altered by Smith himself. Marvin S. Hill concluded that the 1838-39 account was "streamlined for publication," making the story "more logical and compelling."[58] Hill concludes this because Smith in 1832 had handwritten an earlier account of his religious experiences into a ledger book.[59] This earlier version varies at several significant points from the later 1838-39 account. It presents Smith's motivation for seeking God in prayer due to his reading the Bible from "age of twelve to fifteen." From this Bible reading he had already concluded that "there was no society or denomination that [was] built upon the gospel of Jesus Christ as recorded in the new testament." In contrast, the 1838-39 account states that prior to his prayer, "it had never entered into my heart that all were wrong."[60]

The absence of a motivating 1824-25 revival from the 1832 account relieves apologists of a serious chronological conflict. Hill, who recognized that the 1838-39 narrative describes the 1824 revival, notes that "an 1824 revival creates problems for the 1838 account" but not for the 1832 account.[61] Hill's point is that we should give priority to the 1832 account as closer to Smith's experience. It is to this earlier account, as well as other evidence, that we now turn in considering Smith's early educational and religious experiences.

NOTES

1. See Manuscript History, Book A-1: 1-2, archives, historical department, Church of Jesus Christ of Latter-day Saints, Salt Lake City, Utah (hereafter LDS archives); JS-H 1:5, 7-8, PGP; Dean C. Jessee, ed., *The Papers of Joseph Smith* (Salt Lake City: Deseret Book Co., 1989), 1:269-70.

2. Lucy Mack Smith, Preliminary Manuscript (MS), "History of Lucy Smith," 55, LDS archives (page numbering corresponds with a typed transcript in LDS archives and with the page numbers in the photocopy of the manuscript).

3. Ibid., 55-56; Lucy Mack Smith, *Biographical Sketches of Joseph Smith the Prophet, and His Progenitors for Many Generations* (Liverpool: Published for Orson Pratt by S.W. Richards, 1853), 90-91, hereafter as *Biographical Sketches*; Lucy Mack Smith, *History of Joseph Smith By His Mother, Lucy Mack Smith* (Salt

Lake City: Bookcraft, 1958), 90-91, hereafter as *History of Joseph Smith*. In the 1853 edition Joseph Smith's *Times and Seasons* account was inserted into Lucy's history (74-78), making it contain two accounts of the same revival but with different dates.

4. Incorporation papers of the Western Presbyterian Church of Palmyra, 18 Mar. 1817, in Miscellaneous Records, Book C:209, Ontario County Clerk's Office, Canandaigua, New York. Henry Jessup was referred to as Deacon Jessup; see *Western Farmer* 1 (12 Dec. 1821): 4.

5. Chase's affidavit in E.D. Howe, *Mormonism Unvailed* (Painesville [OH]: Printed and Published by the Author, 1834), 241.

6. For 1820, see Minutes of the Palmyra Baptist church under the dates of 18 Mar., 17 June, and 19 Aug. 1820. For 1824-25, see the Minutes of the Palmyra Baptist church, 16 Oct., 20, 24 Nov., 4, 5, 18 Dec. 1824; 1, 15, 29 Jan., 19 Feb., 5, 19 Mar., and 3 Apr. 1825. See *Minutes of the Ontario Baptist Association* (Rochester: Printed by Everard Peck, 1825), 5, for published membership figures for the conference year 1824-25.

The records of "The First Baptized [sic] Church in Palmyra" are now in the American Baptist Historical Society in Rochester, New York. In 1835, when part of the congregation organized the Baptist church within the village of Palmyra itself, the original records remained with the part of the church that would eventually become the Macedon Baptist church in the next township to the west.

7. *Minutes of the Annual Conferences of the Methodist Episcopal Church* (1773-1828), published in 1840, report: 446 (1824), 471 (1825), 330 (1819), 345 (1820), and 366 (1821). The records of the Palmyra Methodist church were burned in a fire at Rochester, New York, in 1933.

8. Geneva Presbytery "Records," 21 Sept. 1825, Book D:40; Geneva Synod "Records," 6 Oct. 1825, 431, both in the Presbyterian Historical Society, Philadelphia, Pennsylvania. In the Presbytery's Report to Synod, the Palmyra church reported for the year between 10 September 1824 and 23 September 1825 additions of 103 members and a membership jump from seventy-nine to 178 (130 percent) with forty adult baptisms. See "Presbyterial Reports to the Synod of Geneva," Presbyterian Historical Society.

For the quote, see Geneva Presbytery "Records," 2 Feb. 1825, Book D:27-28.

Evidence of the increase of "Sabbath Schools, Bible Classes, Missionary & Tract Societies" also can be seen in the following three excerpts appearing in the local *Wayne Sentinel* for 15 December 1824:

Messrs. Editors — Please to allow the subscriber . . . the privilege of expressing his gratitude to God, for what He is doing for the people of Palmyra, and likewise his thanks to a number of friends in that village, for assisting him in printing Tracts, and in setting up Sabbath Schools.

The collection taken up on the Sabbath evening, amounting to $7[.]72, by the recommendation of the Rev. Mr. STOCKTON, will afford the subscriber some assistance, and it being divided and partly appropriated to a Juvenile Library, for a Sunday School in Palmyra, it will probably be the means of commencing a Library there for the benefit of the rising generation. . . .

By a Sabbath School Society is meant an institution for collecting the children and youth, of all denominations, whenever most convenient, for the purpose of giving them instructions from the word of God without any attempt to build up any peculiar sect or party. Such parts of the Holy Scriptures ought to be committed to memory as are of the most practical nature, and such as may be considered most useful in pointing out the duty of man to his Maker, and to his fellow creatures; such, for instance, as the Lord's Prayer, the Ten Commandments, Christ's Sermon on the Mount, the xii. of Romans, iii. of Colossians, and iv. of Ephesians. . . .

A MEETING will be held in the Presbyterian house of worship, in this village, on *Thursday evening, the 16th inst.* at half-past 6 o'clock, for the purpose of organizing a RELIGIOUS TRACT SOCIETY. All who feel disposed to encourage the circulation of Scripture truth in the form of small and familiar publications, are invited to attend.

9. Geneva Presbytery "Records," 2 Feb. 1820, Book C:37, and "Presbyterial Reports to the Synod of Geneva." The membership for Palmyra shows an increase over the previous year's report from sixty-one to seventy-one members. This figure includes those who transferred in by letter of recommendation from another congregation as well as those joining upon profession of faith, off-set by those transferring out and those who either died or were dropped from membership.

10. James H. Hotchkin, *A History of the Purchase and Settlement of Western New York, and the Rise, Progress, and Present State of the Presbyterian Church in that Section* (New York: Published by M. W. Dodd, 1848), 378.

11. See accounts in *The Christian Herald and Seaman's Magazine* (28 Sept. 1816; 10 May, 7 June 1817): 2:16; 3:103f, 164; *Religious Remembrancer* (5 Oct., 2 Nov. 1816; 17 May 1817), 4th Series, 24, 39, 151f; *American Baptist Magazine* (July 1817) 1:153; and *Boston Recorder* (17 Sept. 1816; 13 May, 21 Oct. 1817):

1:151; 2:88, 180. See also Joshua Bradley, *Accounts of the Religious Revivals ... from 1815 to 1818* (1819), 223.

12. Accounts of the revival in Palmyra during 1824-25 are reported in *New-York Religious Chronicle* 2 (20 Nov. 1824): 154; 3 (9 Apr. 1825): 58; *Western New York Baptist Magazine* 4 (Feb. 1825): 284; *Western Recorder* 1 (9 Nov. 1824): 90; 2 (29 Mar. 1825): 50; *Boston Recorder* 10 (29 Apr. 1825), 70; 10 (20 May 1825): 82; *The Christian Herald* 8 (Portsmouth, Mar. 1825): 7 (this last publication is the organ of the Christian-Connection church and should not be confused with *The Christian Herald* of Presbyterian affiliation); *Christian Watchman* 5 (20 Nov. 1824): 199; *Baptist Register* (Utica), 3 Dec. 1824; 11 Mar. 1825, 7; *American Baptist*, Feb. 1825; *Zion's Herald* 3 (9 Feb., 11 May 1825), a Methodist weekly in Boston; *American Baptist Magazine* 5 (Apr. 1825): 124-25; and the *New York Observer*, 7 May 1825.

13. The following periodicals were examined without finding a single reference to a Palmyra revival: Baptist: *American Baptist Magazine* (Jan. 1819-Nov. 1821); *Latter-day Luminary* (Feb. 1818-Nov. 1821); *Western New York Baptist Magazine* (Feb. 1819-Nov. 1821). Presbyterian: *Religious Remembrancer* (Jan. 1818-18 Aug. 1821); *The Christian Herald and Seaman's Magazine* (2 Jan. 1819-6 Jan. 1821); *Evangelical Recorder* (5 June 1819-8 Sept. 1821). Methodist: *The Methodist Magazine* (Jan. 1818-Dec. 1821). Congregational: *Religious Intelligencer* (Jan. 1819-May 1821). Christian-Connection: *The Christian Herald* (May 1818-25 May 1821). Other: *Boston Recorder* (Jan. 1818-Dec. 1821); *Palmyra Register* (13 Jan. 1819-27 Dec. 1820). The *Palmyra Register* has revivals reported in the state of New York but not in Palmyra (7 June, 16 Aug., 13 Sept., 4 Oct. 1820). Even when it describes a Methodist camp meeting in the vicinity of the village, it reports only that a man got drunk at the grog shops on the edge of the campground and died the next morning (3 [28 June; 5 July 1820]: 2).

14. Letter of Rev. James Murdock, dated New Haven, 19 June 1841, to the *Congregational Observer*, Hartford and New-Haven, Connecticut, 2 (3 July 1841): 1. Interview of William Smith aboard an Ohio River boat on 18 April 1841. Original of *The Congregational Observer* is located in the Connecticut State Historical Society, Hartford. This interview was republished in the *Peoria Register and North-Western Gazette* 5 (3 Sept. 1841).

15. William Smith, *William Smith on Mormonism* (Lamoni, IA: Herald Steam Book and Job Office, 1883), 6.

16. Interview of William Smith by E. C. Briggs as reported by J. W. Petersen to *Zion's Ensign* 5 (13 Jan. 1894): 6, Independence, Missouri; see also, with minor inaccuracies, *Deseret Evening News* 27 (20 Jan. 1894): 11; *Latter-day Saints' Millennial Star* 56 (26 Feb. 1894): 133-34; *Church News*, 16

Mar. 1968, 11. William stated that "Hyrum, Samuel, Katharine [Sophronia] and mother were members of the Presbyterian church" (*Zion's Ensign* 5:6), which he described as the "Church, of whome the Rev. Mr. Stoc[k]ton was the Presiding Paster" (William Smith, "Notes Written on 'Chamber's Life of Joseph Smith' by William Smith," typescript, 18, LDS archives).

The fact that the names of Smith's mother and brothers appear later as members of the Palmyra Presbyterian church who were dropped for nonattendance is further evidence that the revival Smith had in view affected the local Presbyterian church. See Western Presbyterian Church of Palmyra, "Session Records," 2:11-12. Volume 1, which would have shown the exact date the Smiths joined, has been missing since at least 1932.

17. For his installation, see *Wayne Sentinel* 1 (18 Feb. 1824): 3; (25 Feb. 1824): 2. Also Geneva Presbytery "Records" C:252-54, 274; and Hotchkin *History*, 377. Stockton asked for permission to resign on 5 September 1827 (Geneva Presbytery "Records" D:83) which was agreed to by the local congregation on 18 September (D:85).

18. Hotchkin, *History*, 378.

19. For his installation date, see *Evangelical Recorder* 1 (7 Mar. 1819): 111; or *Religious Intelligencer* 2 (2 May 1818): 800. On the terminal date, see Hotchkin, *History*, 341. Stockton remained a member of Cayuga Presbytery, which included Skaneateles, through 1823 (see Geneva Synod "Records," 1:211, 238, 258, 374) until he transferred to Geneva Presbytery on 3 February 1824 (see Geneva Presbytery "Records" C:252). The Presbytery and Synod records are in the Presbyterian Historical Society, Philadelphia.

20. *Palmyra Herald* 2 (6 Nov. 1822): 3.

21. *Wayne Sentinel* 1 (31 Dec. 1823; 7, 14, 21, 28 Jan. 1824).

22. *Zion's Ensign* 5 (13 Jan. 1894): 6; *Deseret Evening News* 27 (20 Jan. 1894): 11; and *Latter-day Saints' Millennial Star* 56 (26 Feb. 1894): 133.

23. For sketches of Lane's life, see *Minutes of the Annual Conference of the Methodist Episcopal Church* 8 (1860): 40-41; William Sprague, *Annals of the American Methodist Pulpit* 7 (1861): 810-11; Hendrick B. Wright, *Historical Sketches of Plymouth, Luzerne Co., Penna.* (Philadelphia: T.B. Peterson & Brothers, 1873), 309, 346ff; Oscar Jewell Harvey, *The Harvey Book* (1899), 128-34; George Peck, *The Life and Times of Rev. George Peck, D.D.* (New York: Nelson & Phillips, 1874), 96-97, 104, 108-9; George Peck, *Early Methodism Within the Bounds of the Old Genesee Conference from 1788 to 1828* (New York: Carlton & Porter, 1860), 492-95, and scattered references 166-67, 235-38, 309, 346, 428, 431, 441-42, 447-49, 509. Lane's portrait appears in *The Methodist Magazine* 9 (Apr. 1826), and later in H. Wright, *Historical Sketches*, facing 346.

24. *Latter Day Saints' Messenger and Advocate* 1 (Oct. 1834): 13, Kirtland, Ohio. Cowdery states:

> That our narrative may be correct, and particularly the introduction, it is proper to inform our patrons, that our brother J. SMITH jr. has offered to assist us. Indeed, there are many items connected with the fore part of this subject that render his labor indispensible [sic]. With his labor and with authentic documents now in our possession, we hope to render this a pleasing and agreeable narrative, well worth the examination and perusal of the Saints.

Cowdery's eight installments which appeared in the *Messenger and Advocate* were recopied about October-November 1835 and are located in Manuscript History, Book A-1: 46-103 [a separate section], LDS archives. See Jessee, *Papers of Joseph Smith*, 1:26-96. Besides being republished in the *Times and Seasons* (Nauvoo, IL), the letters also appeared in *The Gospel Reflector* (Philadelphia), were published as a pamphlet in Liverpool, England (1844), and were included in *The Prophet* (New York) in 1844.

25. *Messenger and Advocate* 1 (Dec. 1834): 42-43, emphasis in original. When Cowdery first published this account, he gave Smith's age as the "15th year of his life." He corrected this in his next letter, and said that in his previous letter the time of the religious excitement should have been in Smith's seventeenth year: "You will recollect that I mentioned the time of a religious excitement, in Palmyra and vicinity to have been in the 15th year of our brother J. Smith Jr.'s, age—that was an error in the type—it should have been in the 17th.—You will please remember this correction, as it will be necessary for the full understanding of what will follow in time. This would bring the date down to the year 1823" (1 [Feb. 1835]: 78). Cowdery's correction of the date to the year 1823 still presents a problem since Lane was not the presiding elder of the local Methodist circuit until he was appointed a year later in 1824. Smith's 1823 excitement, as Cowdery reported it, was placed prior to the reported first appearance (September 1823) of the angel who guarded the golden plates of the Book of Mormon.

26. George Peck, *Early Methodism*, 494. George Lane was born on 13 April 1784 and died on 6 May 1859.

27. For official confirmation of Lane's assigned field of labor, see *Minutes of the Annual Conferences* (1773-1828), 1:337, 352, 373, 392, 418, 446. In 1823 Lane was serving in the Susquehanna District in central Pennsylvania. In July 1819 Lane went with Reverend George Peck to the annual eight-day business meeting of the Genesee Annual Conference. This was held at Vienna (now Phelps), a village some fifteen miles from the Smith home. The "Journal" of

the conference does not indicate that any preaching services were held, and there is no indication of any revival touched off at Vienna or Palmyra.

28. *Minutes of the Annual Conferences* (1825), 470.

29. Letter of George Lane, dated 25 Jan. 1825, in *Methodist Magazine* 8 (Apr. 1825): 159.

30. *Wayne Sentinel* 1 (15 Sept. 1824): 3.

31. *Minutes of the Ontario Baptist Association* (Convened at Gorham, 22-23 Sept. 1824), 4.

32. Geneva Presbytery "Records," 8 Sept. 1824, D:16.

33. Calvin W. Stoddard, twenty-three years old at the time, was baptized by Elder Malby of the Palmyra Baptist church on Sunday, 3 April 1825, along with his sister Bathsheba. His parents (Silas and Bathsheba), who were in their sixties, had been baptized the month before (Minutes of the Palmyra Baptist Church, 5 Mar. and 3 Apr. 1825). Calvin Stoddard worked for Lemuel Durfee, Sr., as is recorded in Durfee's account books. In 1824 his wage was set at $8.50 per month and later increased to $10 a month for a period of eight months (Lemuel Durfee Account Book, 1813-29, Ontario County Historical Society, Canandaigua, New York). Stoddard married Sophronia Smith, who was then a member of the Palmyra Presbyterian church, on 30 December 1827. There were difficulties with Stoddard regarding open communion, and on 16 August 1828 a committee sent from the church to visit Stoddard reported that he said "that many of them were Devils." He was excluded from the Palmyra Baptist church (Palmyra Baptist Church Minutes, 19 July, 16 Aug. 1828). He later joined the Mormon church.

34. *Methodist Magazine* 8 (Apr. 1825): 159-60.

35. *Gospel Luminary* 1 (Mar. 1825): 65-66.

36. *Western Recorder* 1 (9 Nov. 1824): 90.

37. *American Baptist Magazine* 5 (Feb. 1825): 61-62.

38. *Methodist Magazine* 8 (Apr. 1825): 160.

39. *The Latter Day Luminary* 6 (Feb. 1825): 61.

40. *Methodist Magazine* 8 (Apr. 1825), 161.

41. *Gospel Luminary* 1 (Feb. 1825): 42, emphasis in original.

42. Ibid., 1 (Mar. 1825): 65, emphasis in original.

43. *Western Recorder* 2 (10 May 1825): 74.

44. *American Baptist Magazine* 5 (Apr. 1825): 125, Solomon Goodale writing from Bristol, New York, 9 Mar. 1825.

45. *Wayne Sentinel* 2 (2 Mar. 1825): 3, 4. Unfortunately these reports have been mistakenly misdated to 1820 and used in several Mormon publications to establish an 1820 revival. However, the *Religious Advocate* did not begin publication at Rochester until about 1825, and its account quoted above

refers to the 1824-25 revival. For examples of this account being used to support an 1820 revival date, see Willard Bean, *A.B.C. History of Palmyra and the Beginning of "Mormonism"* (Palmyra, NY: Palmyra Courier Co., 1938), 22; Preston Nibley, *Joseph Smith the Prophet* (Salt Lake City: Deseret News Press, 1946), 21-22; and Gordon B. Hinckley, *Truth Restored: A Short History of the Church of Jesus Christ of Latter-day Saints* (Salt Lake City: Deseret Book Co., 1979), 1-2.

46. Milton V. Backman, Jr., "Awakenings in the Burned-over District: New Light on the Historical Setting of the First Vision," *Brigham Young University Studies* 9 (Spring 1969): 301-20; map, 312-13.

47. Manchester, shown at about four miles distant from Palmyra, is actually five; Canandaigua, shown at ten miles, is actually twelve; Junius, shown as fifteen, is more than half a mile farther, and West Bloomfield, shown as fifteen miles, is nearly eighteen miles.

The two sites which should be eliminated are Victor and Phelps. Phelps and Oaks Corners met as one congregation and had only "prospects" of a revival. Victor should be omitted because the revival there occurred in 1830, not 1820. The *History of Ontario Co. New York* (1876) mistakenly reports a revival in Victor "in the winter of 1820-21, conducted by Reverends Philo Woodworth, Daniel Anderson, and Thomas Carlton." It was not until the summer of 1830 that these three were assigned to the Victor charge. Carlton did not even join the Methodist Church until 1825 and was only twelve years old in 1820. See [W. H. McIntosh] *History of Ontario Co. New York* (Philadelphia: Everts, Ensign, & Everts, 1876), 203. For assignment of Woodworth, Anderson, and Carlton to Victor, see *Minutes of the Annual Conferences* 2:73; for Carlton joining the Methodist church in 1825, see Matthew Simpson, ed., *Cyclopedia of Methodism* (Philadelphia: Everts & Stewart, 1878), 167.

48. *New York Spectator*, 23 Sept. 1843.

49. Milton V. Backman, Jr., *Joseph Smith's First Vision: The First Vision in its Historical Context* (Salt Lake City: Bookcraft, 1971), 53-89, and 2d ed. (1980), 195-210.

50. "Journal of the Genesee Conference, 1810-1828," 1:76-84, transcribed copy of original journal, Wyoming seminary, Kingston, Pennsylvania.

51. O[rsamus]. Turner, *History of The Pioneer Settlement of Phelps and Gorham's Purchase* (Rochester, NY: William Alling, 1851), 214, 400. There was a letter waiting for Turner in the Palmyra Post Office, see listing of 30 June 1821 in *Western Farmer* 1 (4 July 1821): 3.

52. *Palmyra Register* 3 (28 June, 5 July 1820): 2.

53. M. P. Blakeslee, "Notes for a History of Methodism in Phelps, 1886," typescript located in the Phelps Historical Society.

54. Ibid., 7-8.

55. Mabel E. Oaks, town historian for the Township of Phelps, explained to Wesley P. Walters on 22 December 1969: "As to Turner's reference to the 'woods away down on the Vienna Road,' I fully believe now I was in error in interpreting it to mean our Town of Phelps village of Vienna . . . am afraid it was a bit of subconscious wishful thinking, tho I sincerely believed it at the time. I believe now Turner was referring to Palmyra camp grounds."

56. Abner Chase, *Methodist Magazine*, 7 (Nov. 1824): 435-36.

57. For discussions concerning Smith's first vision and the revival, and responses, see Wesley P. Walters, "New Light on Mormon Origins from the Palmyra (N.Y.) Revival," *Bulletin of the Evangelical Theological Society* 10 (Fall 1967): 227-44; revised and enlarged in *Dialogue: A Journal of Mormon Thought* 4 (Spring 1969): 60-81; reply by Richard L. Bushman, "The First Vision Story Revived," ibid.: 82-93; Wesley P. Walters, "A Reply to Dr. Bushman," ibid.: 94-100. For a detailed discussion of Backman's attempt in *Joseph Smith's First Vision* to place an 1819-20 revival at Vienna, see Wesley P. Walters, "Joseph Smith's First Vision Story Revisited," *Journal of Pastoral Practice* 4 (1980): 92-109.

58. Marvin S. Hill, "The First Vision Controversy: A Critique and Reconciliation," *Dialogue: A Journal of Mormon Thought* 15 (Summer 1982): 39.

59. Jessee, *Papers of Joseph Smith*, 1:3-10.

60. Earlier in this account Smith said that he often wondered about the churches of his day, whether they were "all wrong together," which contradicted his later statement that such an idea "never entered into my heart" (Manuscript History A-1:3; JS-H 1:18, PGP; Jessee, *Papers of Joseph Smith*, 1:273).

61. Hill, "The First Vision Controversy," 40. Hill later commented, "When Smith dictated a more polished version in 1838, it was altered in many details and more elaborate" (*Quest for Refuge: The Mormon Flight from American Pluralism* [Salt Lake City: Signature Books, 1989], 9).

CHAPTER THREE

SECULAR AND RELIGIOUS
BACKGROUND

Joseph Smith Jr.'s formal education was limited and sporadic. He received some of his earliest instruction from his parents. His mother, Lucy, explained that her children had been "deprived of school," but that after her family moved from the hills of Vermont to Lebanon, New Hampshire, in 1811, those children "who were old enough attended a school near by."[1]

After the family moved to western New York, Joseph Jr. apparently attended school in the Palmyra area. According to his own account, schooling was irregular because of economic pressures on the family: "as it required the exertions of all that were able to render any assistance for the support of the Family therefore we were deprived of the bennifit of an education. Suffice it to say I was mearly instructid in reading, writing and the ground <rules> of Arithmatic which const[it]uted my whole literary acquirements."[2]

Isaac Butts attended school with Smith in the Palmyra area,[3] as did Christopher M. Stafford, who remembered Joseph as "a dull scholar."[4] William Stafford's son, John Stafford, recalled, "Joe was quite illiterate. After they began to have school at their house, he improved greatly. . . . they had school in their house, and studied the Bible."[5] Young Joseph most likely received some training from his father who at one time had been a school teacher.

Joseph Jr.'s lack of formal schooling sometimes yielded the erroneous impression that he was illiterate. In the latter part of 1825 while

43

Smith was working in northern Pennsylvania, Isaac Hale, his future father-in-law, remarked that he was "not very well educated."[6] Perhaps in response to such impressions, Smith, though almost twenty years old, enrolled in school in the Bainbridge, New York, area while working for Josiah Stowell during the winter of 1825-26. While being examined before Justice Albert Neely on 20 March 1826, Smith testified that he had been "going to school."[7]

Other accounts confirm this. Stowell's son Josiah remembered Joseph as "about 20 years old or there about. I also went to schoal [school] with him one winter."[8] Asa B. Searles reported that he was a fellow student with Joseph in Bainbridge when his brother, Lemuel Searles, was a teacher there.[9] Local tradition holds that "Smith, while here, attended school in District No. 9."[10]

With opportunities for formal education limited, the Smith family, like others on the frontier, relied on other avenues of instruction and information. One source of wide ranging information was the newspaper, which the Smiths received weekly in Palmyra. Orsamus Turner, who served a five-year printer's apprenticeship in Palmyra between 1818 and 1822, recalled that young Joseph came to the village to pick up his father's newspaper: "He used to come into the village of Palmyra with little jags of wood, from his backwoods home; sometimes patronizing a village grocery too freely; sometimes find an odd job to do about the store of Seymour Scovell; and once a week he would stroll into the office of the old Palmyra Register, for his father's paper."[11]

After they moved to their Manchester farm, the Smith family received the *Wayne Sentinel*, a successor to the *Register* and the *Herald*. A notice giving the subscription cost and the published amount of Joseph Sr.'s delinquent bill suggest that the Smiths received the paper for more than two years. The *Sentinel* cost $2.00 per year if picked up at the office. The 11 August 1826 issue listed "Joseph Smith" among delinquent subscribers with the amount due $5.60.[12]

Certainly the Smith family made use of this newspaper. In September 1824 Joseph Sr. placed an advertisement in the *Sentinel* which ran for six weeks. The advertisement concerned a rumor that his oldest son Alvin's remains had been disturbed:

To the Public. Whereas reports have been industriously put in circulation, that my son *Alvin* had been removed from the place of his interment and dissected, which reports, every person possessed of human sensibility must know, are peculiarly calculated to harrow up the mind of a parent and deeply wound the feelings of relations—therefore, for the purpose of ascertaining the truth of such reports, I, with some of my neighbors, this morning repaired to the grave, and removing the earth, found the body which had not been disturbed.

This method is taken for the purpose of satisfying the minds of those who may have heard the report, and of informing those who have put it in circulation, that it is earnestly requested they would desist therefrom; and that it is believed by some, that they have been stimulated more by a desire to injure the reputation of certain persons than a philanthropy for the peace and welfare of myself and friends. JOSEPH SMITH.[13]

The newspaper ran stories on the Hebrew origin of American Indians, a topic subsequently discussed by Joseph Jr. Mordecai M. Noah had embraced this popular theory, and on 11 October 1825 the *Sentinel* reprinted an address by him detailing his opinion: "Those who are conversant with the public and private economy of the Indians, are strongly of [the] opinion that they are the lineal descendants of the Israelites, and my own researches go far to confirm me in the same belief." He then lists a number of reasons for his belief:

The Indians worship one Supreme Being as the fountain of life, and the author of all creation. Like the Israelites of old, they are divided into tribes. . . . their language and dialect are evidently of Hebrew origin. They compute time after the manner of the Israelites. . . . They have their prophets, High Priests, and their sanctum sanctorum. . . . They have their towns and cities of refuge. . . .

After concluding his list of evidences, he reflects:

If the tribes could be brought together, could be made sensible of their origin, could be civilized, and restored to their long lost brethren, what joy to our people, what glory to our God, how clearly have the prophecies been fulfilled, how certain our dispersion, how miraculous our preservation, how providential our deliverance.[14]

The newspaper also followed contemporary religious events, which clearly affected young Joseph and his family. The Smiths could have read of the visions and revelations of Asa Wild, a religious seeker like Joseph's uncle Jason Mack.[15] The paper published in 1823 Asa's claim that God told him that in seven years "there would scarce a sinner be found on earth" and "that every denomination of professing christians had become extremely corrupt; many of which never had any true faith at all."[16]

Wild's claim that existing churches were in error would have found sympathetic ears in the Smith family. Even by the time of young Joseph's birth in 1805, both of his parents had come to rely on personal interpretation of the Bible as the primary guides to religious life. A crucial context for the background and education of young Joseph thus becomes the broader religious questing and experiences of his extended family.

The family of Joseph Sr. originally had ties to the Congregational church. According to records of the Topsfield, Massachusetts, church, his father, Asael, had been baptized as an infant on 11 March 1744. Nearly twenty-eight years later on 8 March 1772, Asael had three of his children baptized: Jesse (about four years old), Priscilla (about two years old), and Joseph (infant).[17] After Asael's family had moved to Tunbridge, Vermont, his son Joseph, at the age of twenty-four, was married to Lucy Mack on 24 January 1796 by Seth Austin, a justice of the peace in Tunbridge.[18]

A year later Joseph, along with his father and his brother Jesse, professed belief in the doctrine that all people will be saved. They were among the dozen men who on 6 December 1797 stated that they had "formed our selves into a Society and wish to be known by the Name or forme of Universalists." As a result they also informed the town clerk that they did not want "to be Charged with any tax toward the Support of any teacher of any Diferant Denomination."[19] Years later Joseph Sr.'s son William remembered that his father's "faith in the universal restoration doctrin[e], however, often brought him in contact with the advocates of the doctrin[e] of endless misrey [misery]." Because of his "belief in the ultimate and final redem[p]tion of all mankind," William claimed it "brought down upon my father the aprobiem [opprobrium] or slur of Old Jo Smith."[20]

Although following a different path, Lucy Mack Smith also came to be of independent religious leanings, emphasizing the Bible and personal experience rather than organized religion. While in Tunbridge she attended Methodist meetings. She wrote that she persuaded her husband to attend with her a few times: "But as soon as his Father and brother Jesse heard that we were attending Methodist meeting they were much displeased and his father came to the door one day and throw Tom Pain[e]'s age of reason into the house and angrily bade him read that untill he believed it."[21] Thomas Paine's *Age of Reason*, which expounded deism, was widely regarded as an atheistic tract. It taught that true religious knowledge is not revealed or taught by any church but attained by reason and that God, after creating the world according to rational laws, withdrew and no longer interacts with nature or humankind.

Lucy was concerned about her husband's spiritual condition and prayed about him. That night she had a dream in which she saw two trees. She understood that one of the trees was her husband's brother Jesse and the other tree was her husband, who would hear and receive the gospel with his whole heart.[22] This belief in visions and dreams formed a significant part of the Smith family's religious life.

In 1802 the Smith family—by then Joseph, Lucy, and their two young sons, Alvin and Hyrum—moved from Tunbridge to Randolph, Vermont. At Randolph Lucy became seriously ill. She promised God that she would serve him if she recovered from her illness. "<I> covenanted with God if he would let me live I would endeavor to get that religion that would enable me to serve him right whether it was in the Bible or where ever it might be found even if it was to be obtained from heaven by prayer and Faith."[23] She prayed to God and heard a voice then say, "Seek and ye shall find, knock and it shall be opened unto you. Let your heart be comforted, ye believe in God, believe also in me."[24]

Lucy later remembered hearing a Presbyterian give a discourse and afterward she "returned saying in my heart there is not on Earth the religion which I seek, I must again turn to my bible. Taking Jesus and his deciples [disciples] for an ensample I will try to obtain from God that which man cannot give nor take away."[25] She followed this course for a number of years, later recovered her health, and "found a minister who was willing to baptize me and leave me free from membership in any church."[26]

Thus by the time of young Joseph's birth his father had embraced the doctrine that all people will be saved, while his mother avoided joining any church, regarding all churches as devoid of "the religion which I seek." Eventually the Smith family moved from Randolph to Sharon, Vermont, where they rented land from Solomon Mack, Lucy's father, and farmed, and "in the winter he [Joseph Sr.] taught school."[27] Here their son Joseph was born two days before Christmas on 23 December 1805.

Religion remained an important focus of the Smith family during young Joseph's childhood. In 1811, when he was five years old, his grandfather, Solomon Mack, published *A Narraitve [sic] of the Life of Solomon Mack*, an account of his life's experiences and religious conversion.[28] After its publication Mack rode on horseback through the surrounding countryside, selling copies of his self-published book. In his narrative, Mack informs readers that until the winter of 1810-11 he gave very little thought to God. In spite of crippling illnesses, he wrote, "I never once thought on the God of my salvation or looked up to him for blessing or protection." He had never read the Bible and "could only recollect some taught parts such as I had heard and laid up for the purpose of ridiculing religious institutions and characters." But at the age of seventy-six, while incapacitated because of illness, he came under conviction of his sins when he "saw a light about a foot from my face as bright as fire. . . . I thought by this that I had but a few moments to live. . . . I prayed that the Lord would have mercy on my soul and deliver me from this horrible pit of sin." The same appearance of light occurred some nights later, and on another occasion he thought he heard the Lord call him by name. Each time he thought he had but a moment to live.

Finally seeking a sign of his acceptance and pardon by God, he asked to have one night entirely free from pain. He wrote, "And blessed be the Lord, I was entirely free from pain that night." He continued: "And the Lord so shined light into my soul that everything appeared new and beautiful. Oh how I loved my neighbors. How I loved my enemies—I could pray for them. Everything appeared delightful." He found this especially so with regard to the Lord: "The love of Christ is beautiful. There is more satisfaction to be taken in the enjoyment of Christ one day, than in half a century serving our master, the devil."[29]

Young Joseph's grandfather was not the only one to tell of seeing lights and encountering God in dreams. At about the same time, his father, according to his mother's later recollections, was having similar experiences: "my husband's mind became much excited upon the subject of religion; yet he would not subscribe to any particular system of faith, but contended for the ancient order, as established by our Lord and Saviour Jesus Christ, and his Apostles."[30] In April 1811, a month after William was born, Joseph Sr. had what Lucy termed his first vision. In this vision he saw a field and the attendant spirit said, "this field is the world which lies ina[n]imate & dumb as to the things pertaining to the true religion or the order of Heavenly things; all is darkness." As the result of this vision, he, like his wife Lucy, came to the opinion that all churches were in darkness. Lucy wrote that her husband "seemed more confirmed than ever, in the opinion that there was no order or class of religionists that knew any more concerning the Kingdom of God, than those of the world, or such as made no profession of religion whatever."[31]

Joseph Sr. had other visions intermittently during young Joseph's childhood. In May 1818 his father had his sixth vision. In this vision he saw himself on judgment day traveling toward "the meeting house" upon which crowds of people were converging. He was told he had arrived too late and the door was shut. "I soon felt that I was perishing and began to pray but my flesh continued to wither on my bones." An angel appeared and asked him if he had done everything necessary to be admitted. The messenger reminded him, "Justice must have its demands and then mercy <has its> claims." Upon hearing this, it entered his mind "to ask God in the name of Jesus and I cried out in the agony of my soul, Oh, Lord, I beseech Thee in the name of Jesus Christ to forgive my sins." "I then felt strengthened and My flesh began to be restored. The angel then said, you must plead the merits of Jesus for he is an advocate with [the] Father and a mediator between God and man. I now was made quite whole, and the door was opened and upon entering I awoke."[32]

Perhaps as the result of such visions Joseph Sr. seems to have consistently avoided organized religion. After he attended one meeting during the 1824-25 revival, Lucy remembered her husband refused to attend further meetings.

William recalled that his father had morning and evening prayers: "I well remember father used to carry his spectacles in his vest pocked [pocket] . . . and when us boys saw him feel for his specks, we knew that was a signal to get ready for prayer."[33] He explained:

> My father's religious customs often become earksome [irksome] or tiresome to me, while in my younger days as I made no profession of Christ[i]anity. Still I was called upon to listen to pray[e]rs boath [both] night and morning. My father's favourit evening humn runs thus:
>
> The day is past and gone
> The evening shades appear
> O may we all remember well
> The night of death draws near.
>
> Again and again was this hymn sung while upon the bending knees. My parents, father and mother, pour[e]d out their souls to God the doner of all blessings, to keep and g[u]ard their children and keep them from sin and from all evil works.[34]

In 1834 Joseph Sr. told of his efforts to provide a religious education for his children, emphasizing the comfort he found in his visionary experiences:

> I have not always set that example before my family that I ought. I have not been diligent in teaching them the commandments of the Lord, but have rather manifested a light and trifling mind. But in all this I have never denied the Lord. Notwithstanding all this my folly, which has been a cause of grief to my family, the Lord has often visited me in visions and in dreams and has brought me, with my family, through many afflictions, and I this day thank his holy name.[35]

The Smith family was not unique in this emphasis on visionary experience as the basis of enlightenment. Feelings of guilt and needing forgiveness were evidence of the working of the Holy Spirit of God in the life of the individual and a prominent part of the revivalistic religious experience. The assurance of forgiveness often came in the form of a vision.

This visionary forgiveness came to youthful seekers as well as more mature ones. In 1816 Elias Smith (no relation) published his account of a very similar experience. For some time as a youth in his early teens he felt a deep sense of being lost:

> My mind was greatly distressed by considering myself a sinner, justly condemned to die. . . . Every wrong ever committed, whether in thought, word, or deed, appeared before me, and things which before appeared small, now rose like mountains between me and my Creator. It appeared to me that I was a criminal brought to the bar, and proved guilty, and deserving death, without one plea in his own behalf.

With such thoughts pressing on his mind, this youth slipped while carrying a piece of timber. He was pinned on the ground next to a log:

> While in this situation, a light appeared to shine from heaven, not only into my head, but into my heart. This was something very strange to me, and what I had never experienced before. My mind seemed to rise in that light to the throne of God and the Lamb. . . . The Lamb once slain appeared to my understanding, and while viewing him, I felt such love to him as I never felt to any thing earthly. My mind was calm and at peace with God through the Lamb of God, that taketh away the sin of the world. The view of the Lamb on mount Sion gave me joy unspeakable and full of glory.[36]

A few years later, Billy Hibbard published his spiritual vision. Writing about it in 1825, he described an event that took place about 1782 when he was nearly twelve years old. He saw himself as a helpless, hopeless sinner:

> I found to my unspeakable grief and dismay, that I was altogether unholy in my nature; my sins had corrupted every part, so that there was nothing in me that was good; I was a complete sink of sin and iniquity; I looked to see if there was no way to escape, if God could not be just and have mercy on me: but no . . . all my hopes of obtaining mercy and getting to Heaven at last, are gone, and gone forever!

He continued in this depressing state of guilt for some days, hoping to find pardon for his sins. Then on a Sunday while reading about the sufferings of Christ, he "had an impression to go in secret and pray":

> when I came to the place of prayer, had kneeled down, and closed my eyes, with my hands uplifted toward the heavens, I saw Jesus Christ at the right hand of God looking down upon me, and God the Father looking upon him. The look of Jesus on me removed the burden of my sins, while he spoke these words, "Be faithful until death and this shall be thy place of rest."

After thus seeing both the Father and the Son in vision the burden of his guilt suddenly was lifted:

> I never had seen Jesus Christ before, nor heard his voice, nor ever had a sense of his intercession at the right hand of God for me till now; and now I could see the justice of God in shewing mercy to me for the sake of his Son Jesus Christ; and not only to me, but to all that would come to him forsaking their sins, and believing that his death and suffering were the only satisfactory sacrifice for sin.

Finally he described the ecstasy of the visionary experience:

> the love of God in Christ and of Christ in God, so completely overcame me, that I was all in tears, crying, Glory! Glory! Glory! Beholding the glory of God by faith, was a rapturous sight. . . . I opened my eyes therefore, while still on my knees; and behold all nature was praising God. The sun and firmament, the trees, birds, and beasts, all appeared stamped with the glory of God. I leaped from my kneeling posture, clapped my hands, and cried, Glory! Glory! Glory! Heaven and earth is full of thy glory.[37]

Another youth, Eleazer Sherman, described a similar deliverance from the guilt of sin. On 10 January 1815 at the age of nineteen, he concluded that "misery and despair must be my lot forever":

> I sunk down in tears, and sorrow overwhelmed my sinking soul. While in this distress, I heard as it were a soft and pleasant voice saying to me, Behold the Lamb of God, that taketh away the sin of the world: And then was presented to my mental view the dear

Saviour, from his birth to his death. He seemed one of the most innocent looking persons ever beheld by mortal eyes.

After appearing on his throne of mercy, the Savior seemed to ask the young man to surrender his life to him. "As soon as I had given up all," he wrote, "I found peace, and the glory of God filled my soul."[38]

The seventh and last vision of Joseph Smith, Sr., occurred, according to his wife, in 1819 or 1820 while he was living in Palmyra.[39] It was about this time that young Joseph would say that he experienced his first vision. The earliest account of that vision survives from 1832 in Joseph Jr.'s own hand.

He begins his narration by pointing out that his parents "spared no pains to instructing me in <the> christian religion." He then describes his youthful religious questing:

At about the age of twelve years my mind become seriously imprest with regard to the all important concerns for the wellfare of my immortal Soul, which led me to searching the scriptures, believeing as I was taught, that they contained the word of God. Thus applying myself to them and my intimate acquaintance with those of differant denominations led me to marvel exce[e]dingly, for I discovered that <they did not> adorn their profession by a holy walk and Godly conversation agreeable to what I found contained in that sacred depository, this was a grief to my Soul. Thus from the age of twelve years to fifteen I pondered many things in my heart . . . my mind become exce[e]dingly distressed for I become convicted of my sins and by searching the scriptures I found that <mankind> did not come unto the Lord but that they had apostatised from the true and liveing faith and there was no society or denomination that built upon the gospel of Jesus Christ as recorded in the new testament.

However, he continued, "I learned in the scriptures that God was the same yesterday, to day and forever." By observing the wonders of nature, Joseph confirmed for himself "well hath the wise man said <it is a> fool <that> saith in his heart there is no God." Thus by considering both the Bible and creation he concluded: "All, all these bear testimony and bespeak an omnipotant and omnipreasant power, a being who makith Laws and decreeeth and bindeth all things in their bounds, who filleth Eternity, who was and is and will be from all

Eternity to Eternity." Thus convinced that the God of the Bible existed, but no denomination any longer taught the New Testament gospel, he continued praying:

> I cried unto the Lord for mercy for there was none else to whom I could go and obtain mercy and the Lord heard my cry in the wilderness and while in <the> attitude of calling upon the Lord <in the 16th year of my age> a piller of light above the brightness of the sun at noon day come down from above and rested upon me and I was filled with the spirit of god and the <Lord> opened the heavens upon me and I saw the Lord and he spake unto me saying, Joseph <my son> thy sins are forgiven thee. . . . behold I am the Lord of glory, I was crucifyed for the world.[40]

Several observations can be drawn from this earliest written narration of Smith's teenage religious experience. First, like his mother, he finds the Bible his only reliable guide and his interpretation of it the only correct one. Second, like his parents, he realizes that no church any longer has the truth; everyone else has apostatized. Third, unlike others, much of his conviction is of the sins of other professing Christians. Finally, like his parents and many others, he feels conviction of his sins and finds forgiveness through a direct vision of the Savior granting him pardon.

Orasmus Turner, the young apprentice working at the Palmyra *Register* newspaper office, noted young Joseph's presence at a Methodist camp meeting and found him "a very passable exhorter."[41] In the Methodist style of worship, a sermon was preached in which points were drawn from a given text or passage from the Bible. After the message, an exhortation was usually given by another speaker who would reemphasize the points made in the preacher's exposition and plead with the people to take seriously the message they had just heard. The Methodist structure provided for the licensing of official exhorters by the District Conference.[42] However, in more informal situations, such as camp meetings and evening services (where the liturgical format used at the morning worship was dispensed with), even those as young as twelve or thirteen could rise and give exhortations.[43] Since Turner completed his apprenticeship and left

Palmyra in the summer of 1822, his words provide a valuable insight into Joseph's religious activities before his seventeenth birthday.

Joseph did not become a licensed exhorter because such persons had to be members in full standing with the denomination. However, Pomeroy Tucker, another early resident of Palmyra, remarked concerning Joseph, "at one time he joined the probationary class of the Methodist church in Palmyra, and made some active demonstrations of engagedness, . . . [but] he soon withdrew from the class."[44] Formal church membership would have required Joseph's meeting with the class leader "at least six months on trial."[45]

Joseph attended a debating club in Palmyra Village, and Turner recalled the following:

> Joseph had a little ambition; and some very laudable aspirations; the mother's intellect occasionally shone out in him feebly, especially when he used to help us solve some portentous questions of moral or political ethics, in our juvenile debating club, which we moved down to the old red school house on Durfee street, to get rid of the annoyance of critics that used to drop in upon us in the village . . . [46]

Joseph wrote about his "intimate acquaintance with those of differant denominations" during his youth and his partiality toward the Methodists. But by the time he was approaching nineteen, during the 1824-25 revival meetings, he felt little need for organized religion. He later wrote in his 1838-39 account: "During this time of great excitement my mind was called up to serious reflection and great uneasiness; but though my feelings were deep and often poignant, still I kept myself aloof from all these parties, though I attended their several meetings as occasion would permit."[47] His mother recalled, "Joseph never said many words upon any subject but always seemed to reflect more deeply than common persons of his age upon everything of a religious nature."[48]

According to his later colleague Oliver Cowdery, Joseph was impressed by the revival preaching of Reverend George Lane. As mentioned in the previous chapter, Lane was the Methodist presiding elder of the Ontario District from July 1824 until January 1825. Cowdery wrote, "much good instruction was always drawn from his

[Lane's] discourses on the scriptures, and in common with others, our brother's [Joseph Smith's] mind became awakened."[49] Joseph would have been eighteen years old when he heard Lane preaching.

After the family discussed "the subject of the diversity of churches," Lucy Smith recalled, Joseph saw an angel who revealed the gold plates: "After we ceased conversation, he went to bed <and was pondering in his mind which of the churches were the true one> but he had not laid there long till <he saw> a bright <light> enter the room where he lay. He looked up and saw an angel of the Lord <standing> by him. The angel spoke, I perceive that you are enquiring in your mind which is the true church. There is not a true church on Earth. No, not one, <and> has not been since Peter took the Keys <of the Melchesidec priesthood after the order of God> into the Kingdom of Heaven. The churches that are now upon the Earth are all man made churches."[50]

Lucy later remembered "listening in breathless anxiety to the <religious> teachings" of her son Joseph, "for Joseph was less inclined to the study of books than any child we had but much more given to reflection and deep study."[51] These teachings would have been the theological expositions resulting from Joseph's deep study expressed within the Smith family.

Joseph Smith's childhood vision, as his 1832 narrative describes, of Christ's appearing and granting him forgiveness for his sins was similar to those of other young people of his day. The later 1838-39 version of his first vision introduces a revival before his vision and creates a chronologically implausible picture.

From what we can learn about the religious background of the Smith family, Joseph Jr.'s parents taught religious values to their children. Though his father did not attend church, he did sing and pray with his family. Joseph Jr.'s religious instruction included hearing ministers' sermons, revival homilies, private family worship, and personal Bible study. Joseph was not uninformed, ignorant, or illiterate.

While the Smith family held Christian beliefs, they also believed in treasures supernaturally buried in the earth which could be obtained only through magical rituals. It is to the well-documented period of what Joseph Jr. called glass looking that we turn our attention in the next chapter.

NOTES

1. Lucy Mack Smith, Preliminary Manuscript (MS), "History of Lucy Smith," 33, archives, historical department, Church of Jesus Christ of Latter-day Saints, Salt Lake City, Utah (hereafter LDS archives), page numbering corresponds with a typed transcript in LDS archives and with the page numbers in the photocopy of the manuscript; Lucy Mack Smith, *Biographical Sketches of Joseph Smith the Prophet, and His Progenitors for Many Generations* (Liverpool: Published for Orson Pratt by S. W. Richards, 1853), 60, hereafter *Biographical Sketches*; Lucy Mack Smith, *History of Joseph Smith By His Mother, Lucy Mack Smith* (Salt Lake City: Bookcraft, 1958), 51, hereafter *History of Joseph Smith*. Joseph would have been about six years old at the time. Later he evidently owned a copy of *First Lines in Arithmetic* (Hartford, CT, 1818), photocopy in the Wilford C. Wood Collection, Wilford C. Wood Museum, Bountiful, Utah.

2. Joseph Smith, "A History of the life of Joseph Smith Jr.," (1832) MS, 1, LDS archives; cf. Dean C. Jessee, ed., *The Papers of Joseph Smith: Autobiographical and Historical Writings* (Salt Lake City: Deseret Book Co., 1989), 1:5. Orson Pratt wrote in 1840: "He could read without much difficulty, and write with a very imperfect hand; and had a very limited understanding of the ground rules of arithmetic" (*Interesting Account of Several Remarkable Visions* [Edinburgh: Printed by Ballantyne and Hughes, 1840], 3).

3. Statement of Isaac Butt, in *Naked Truths About Mormonism* 1 (Jan. 1888): 2, original publication in the Yale University Library.

4. Statement of C. M. Stafford, ibid., 1 (Apr. 1888): 1. For a listing of books in the Manchester Rental Library, see Robert Paul, "Joseph Smith and the Manchester (New York) Library," *Brigham Young University Studies* 22 (Summer 1982): 333-56.

5. *Saints' Herald* 28 (1 June 1881): 167. This material comes from the notes of the interviewer, William Kelley. His notes about John Stafford are "Joe was quite illit- [illiterate] until after they began to have school at their house - they had school at their house. and studied their Bible" (William H. Kelley Papers, Library-Archives, Reorganized Church of Jesus Christ of Latter Day Saints, Independence, Missouri, hereafter RLDS archives).

6. *The Susquehanna Register, and Northern Pennsylvanian* 9 (1 May 1834): 1; also E. D. Howe, *Mormonism Unvailed* (Painesville [OH]: Author, 1834), 263.

7. Charles Marshall, "The Original Prophet. By a Visitor to Salt Lake City," *Fraser's Magazine* 7 (Feb. 1873): 229.

8. Josiah Stowell, Jr., to J. S. Fullmer, 17 Feb. 1843, in LDS archives, and printed in *LDS Church News*, 12 May 1985, 10.

9. *History of Lee County* [Illinois] (Chicago: H. H. Hill and Company, Publishers, 1881), 397. Searles "had many a wrestle [with Joseph]; but young Smith was a large, strong fellow and could handle any of the boys."

10. James H. Smith, *History of Chenango and Madison Counties, New York* (Syracuse, NY: D. Mason & Co., 1880), 154.

11. O[rsamus]. Turner, *History of the Pioneer Settlement of Phelps and Gorham's Purchase* (Rochester, NY: Published by William Alling, 1851), 213-14.

12. *Wayne Sentinel* 1 (Oct. 1823): 1, and 3 (11 Aug. 1826): 3.

13. Ibid., 2 (29 Sept. 1824): 3, emphasis in original. The ad is dated 25 Sept. 1824. This notice also appeared in the issues of 6, 13, 20, 27 Oct., and 3 Nov. 1824.

14. Ibid., 3 (11 Oct. 1825): 1.

15. Lucy Mack Smith, Preliminary MS, 5; *Biographical Sketches* (1853), 21; *History of Joseph Smith* (1958), 9.

16. *Wayne Sentinel* 1 (22 Oct. 1823): 4.

17. George Francis Dow, in section titled: "Baptismal Records of the Church in Topsfield," *The Historical Collections of the Topsfield Historical Society* 1 (Topsfield, MA: Published by the Society, 1895, 2d ed.): 15, 37-38. See also Richard L. Anderson, *Joseph Smith's New England Heritage: Influences of Grandfathers Solomon Mack and Asael Smith* (Salt Lake City: Deseret Book Co., 1971), 189n120, 191n129.

18. Tunbridge Town Records, Book A:129, located in the Tunbridge Town Clerk's Office, Tunbridge, Vermont. Lucy mentions that Austin married them, but this was not included in the 1853 printing of her book (Preliminary MS, 20).

19. Tunbridge Town Records, Book A: 188. See also Larry C. Porter, "A Study of the Origins of the Church of Jesus Christ of Latter-day Saints in the States of New York and Pennsylvania, 1816-1831," Ph.D. diss., Aug. 1971, Brigham Young University, 13.

20. William Smith, "Notes Written on 'Chambers Life of Joseph Smith.' by William Smith," typescript, 18, LDS archives.

21. Lucy Mack Smith, Preliminary MS, 27. The *Age of Reason* incident is not in the 1853 printing. See *Biographical Sketches* (1853), 54; *History of Joseph Smith* (1958), 43.

22. Lucy Mack Smith, *Biographical Sketches* (1853), 55-56; *History of Joseph Smith* (1958), 45.

23. Lucy Mack Smith, Preliminary MS, 22; *Biographical Sketches* (1853), 47; *History of Joseph Smith* (1958), 34. For additional information on the religious background of Joseph and Lucy Smith, see Dan Vogel, *Religious Seekers and the Advent of Mormonism* (Salt Lake City: Signature Books, 1988), 25-28.

24. Lucy Mack Smith, Preliminary MS, 22; *Biographical Sketches* (1853), 47; *History of Joseph Smith* (1958), 34. These words are from Matt. 7:7, Luke 11:9, and John 14:1.

25. Lucy Mack Smith, Preliminary MS, 23; *Biographical Sketches* (1853), 48; *History of Joseph Smith* (1958), 36.

26. Lucy Mack Smith, Preliminary MS, 23-24; *Biographical Sketches* (1853), 48; *History of Joseph Smith* (1958), 36.

27. Lucy Mack Smith, Preliminary MS, 32; *Biographical Sketches* (1853), 56; *History of Joseph Smith* (1958), 46. William Smith wrote about his father, "his occupation in early life was that of a school teacher he was a man well letter[e]d in the common branches of our english studies" ("Notes Written on 'Chambers Life of Joseph Smith,'" 20).

28. Solomon Mack, *A Narraitve of the Life of Solomon Mack, Containing An Account of the Many Severe Accidents he met with during a long series of years, together with the Extraordinary Manner in which he was converted to the Christian Faith* (Windsor [VT]: Printed at the Expense of the Author [1811]). For the text and dating of this work, see Anderson, *Joseph Smith's New England Heritage*, 33-61, 161-62n3.

29. Solomon Mack, *Life*, 11, 20, 22-24.

30. Lucy Mack Smith, *Biographical Sketches* (1853), 56-57; *History of Joseph Smith* (1958), 46.

31. Lucy Mack Smith, Preliminary MS, 28; *Biographical Sketches* (1853), 57-58; *History of Joseph Smith* (1958), 47-48.

32. Lucy Mack Smith, Preliminary MS, 30-31; *Biographical Sketches* (1853), 72; *History of Joseph Smith* (1958), 66.

33. *Zion's Ensign* 5 (13 Jan. 1894): 6; *Deseret Evening News* 27 (20 Jan. 1894); and *Latter-day Saints' Millennial Star* 56 (26 Feb. 1894): 133.

34. William Smith, "Notes Written on 'Chambers Life of Joseph Smith,'" 18. The hymn, written by John Leland, a Baptist minister, was published in the first LDS hymnal. See *A Collection of Sacred Hymns* (Kirtland, OH: F.G. Williams & Co., 1835 [1836]), 62-63.

35. Remarks made by Joseph Smith, Sr., on 9 December 1834 and recorded in his Patriarchal Blessing Book, Book 1 (LDS archives), as quoted

in Richard L. Anderson, *Investigating the Book of Mormon Witnesses* (Salt Lake City: Deseret Book Co., 1981), 141. See also Mark L. McConkie, *The Father of the Prophet: Stories and Insights from the Life of Joseph Smith, Sr.* (Salt Lake City: Bookcraft, 1993), 75-76.

36. Elias Smith, *The Life, Conversion, Preaching, Travels, and Sufferings of Elias Smith* (Portsmouth, NH: Printed by Beck & Foster, 1816), 1:56, 59.

37. B. Hibbard, *Memoirs of the Life and Travels of B. Hibbard* (New York: Printed for and Published by the Author, 1825), 22-24.

38. Eleazer Sherman, *The Narrative of Eleazer Sherman* (Providence: H. H. Brown, 1830), 1:20-21.

39. Lucy Mack Smith, Preliminary MS, 31; *Biographical Sketches* (1853), 74; *History of Joseph Smith* (1958), 68.

40. "A History of the life of Joseph Smith Jr.," 1-2, LDS archives, and Jessee, *Papers of Joseph Smith*, 1:5-6. In June 1830 there was a brief reference to Joseph's experience of forgiveness recorded in the Book of Commandments: "For, after that it truly was manifested unto this first elder [Joseph Smith], that he had received a remission of his sins, he was entangled again in the vanities of the world" (BC 24:6). Joseph saw this experience as his call to start into the ministry. In his 1832 recollection he wrote that he was in his sixteenth year of age (1821) when he received forgiveness. In 1838-39 he recorded both the season and the year, "It was on the morning of a beautiful, clear day, early in the spring of Eightteen hundred and twenty" (Manuscript History, Book A-1:3; JS-H 1:14, PGP; *Papers of Joseph Smith*, 1:272). For various accounts by Joseph Smith and others of this vision, see Milton V. Backman, Jr., *Joseph Smith's First Vision: The First Vision in its Historical Context* (Salt Lake City: Bookcraft, 1971; 2d ed., 1980), and Richard P. Howard, "Joseph Smith's First Vision: An Analysis of Six Contemporary Accounts," *Restoration Studies I* (Independence, MO: Herald Publishing House, 1980), 95-117.

41. Turner, *History of Phelps and Gorham's Purchase*, 214. See also Calvin N. Smith, "Joseph Smith as a Public Speaker," *Improvement Era* 69 (Apr. 1966): 277. The Methodist work in Palmyra was still only a "class meeting" on the circuit at this time. It was not until 3 July 1821 that the Methodist Society of Palmyra was incorporated as a church "by the name of the first Methodist Episcopal Church of Palmyra" (see Miscellaneous Records, Book C: 385-86, in the County Clerk's Office, Ontario County, Canandaigua, New York). Four days later, on 7 July 1821, Durfee Chase deeded to the Methodist Church his property on Vienna Road (see Deeds of Ontario County, Book G:345, Ontario County Records Center and Archives, Canandaigua, New York). It was not until 1822 that they were able to begin construction of a meeting house (see Palmyra *Herald* 2 [19 June 1822]: 2).

42. *The Doctrines and Discipline of the Methodist Episcopal Church* (New York: J. Emory and B. Waugh, 1828), 28, 43, 45, 64, 74, 80. For background on the Methodist Class, see David Lowes Watson, *The Early Methodist Class Meeting: Its Origins and Significance* (Nashville, TN: Discipleship Resources, 1987). Members of the class were to "bear one another's burdens" (94) and "there was no prerequisite for Methodist membership other than a desire for salvation, the societies were open to all, regardless of their spiritual state" (108).

43. *Doctrine and Discipline of the Methodist Episcopal Church*, 71.

44. Pomeroy Tucker, *The Origin, Rise and Progress of Mormonism* (New York: D. Appleton & Co., 1867), 18.

45. *Doctrines and Discipline of the Methodist Episcopal Church*, 80.

46. Turner, *History of Phelps and Gorham's Purchase*, 214. Also published in *Littell's Living Age* 30 (30 Aug. 1851): 429, reprinted from the *Rochester American*. This statement by Turner is cited in John Henry Evans, *Joseph Smith, An American Prophet*, (New York: Macmillan, 1933), 32. The *Western Farmer* 1 (23 Jan. 1822): 3, Palmyra, New York, contained the following: "NOTICE. The young people of the village of Palmyra and its vicinity are requested to attend a Debating school at the school house near Mr. Billings' on Friday next." Notice dated 19 Jan. 1822.

47. Manuscript History, Book A-1: 2; JS-H 1:8, PGP; Jessee, *Papers of Joseph Smith*, 1:270.

48. Lucy Mack Smith, Preliminary MS, 46, not in *Biographical Sketches* or *History of Joseph Smith*.

49. *Messenger and Advocate* 1 (Dec. 1834): 42. In 1879 Joseph and Hiel Lewis, cousins to Joseph's first wife, Emma Hale, stated that Joseph joined the Methodist Episcopal church or class in Harmony, Pennsylvania, in the summer of 1828. There was disagreement about how long Joseph's name remained on class rolls. See the articles in the *Amboy [Illinois] Journal* vol. 24 for the following issues: 23, 30 Apr., 21 May, 4, 11 June, 2, 9, 30 July, and 6 Aug. 1879. See also *Saints' Herald* 26 (15 June 1879): 190-91, and (15 Dec. 1879): 376. It is possible that Joseph attended class with his wife Emma because of the death of their first son on 15 June 1828. That Joseph was a member of the class was not questioned, only the length of time his name remained on the class record. Like so many of the early Methodist records, the early class books of the Harmony (now Lanesboro) church are lost, so it will never be known for certain whether he remained on the rolls for only three days or for six months.

50. Lucy Mack Smith, Preliminary MS, 46, not in *Biographical Sketches* or *History of Joseph Smith*.

51. Lucy Mack Smith, Preliminary MS, 49; *Biographical Sketches* (1853), 84; *History of Joseph Smith* (1958), 82.

CHAPTER FOUR

MANCHESTER SCRYER

The possibility of finding buried treasure fascinated many in late eighteenth- and early nineteenth-century America. Reports of searching for such riches were widespread in the Palmyra area,[1] and extant accounts show that treasure was generally sought through supernatural means. Locations for buried wealth and lost Spanish mines were sometimes located through dreams. Treasures could also be located by using divining rods, often made from "witch hazel," or by looking in special stones or crystals. Sometimes when a stone was used, a person would place the stone in a hat and then conjure the guardian treasure spirit. After finding a spot where the cache was supposedly hidden, the seekers would draw a magic circle on the ground around the hidden treasure. Sometimes they would maintain absolute silence, but other times they would recite magical charms or religious verses used as charms. Whatever the means, money-diggers needed to overcome the guardian spirit who had enchanted the treasure, otherwise the treasure would slip back into the earth.

In his official history, Joseph Smith downplayed his experience as a money-digger and sought to cast this activity in the context of manual labor. However, Smith was involved in such endeavors for years in two widely separated areas and enjoyed an established reputation as a gifted seer. He was thought to be able to locate lost goods with a special seer stone and magical religious ceremonies.[2]

Joseph was assisted by his father and his older brothers Alvin and Hyrum.[3] In addition neighbors of the Smith family were money diggers, including Willard Chase, Samuel Lawrence, as well as John,

Joshua, and William Stafford.[4] Others in the area also claimed to have special stones, including Sarah or Sally Chase and Joshua and William Stafford.[5] In southern New York and northern Pennsylvania, William Hale, Oliver Harper, and Josiah Stowell also searched for treasures.[6] Financial support was supplied, among others, by Abraham Fish in Manchester and by Asa and Josiah Stowell in Bainbridge.[7]

When Joseph Smith recalled his money-digging activities for his official history, he wrote only about searching for a lost mine in 1825 for Josiah Stowell. But contemporary records suggest that this had been one of the Smith family occupations in the Palmyra/Manchester area since the early 1820s. For example, Joshua Stafford of Manchester recalled that he "became acquainted with the family of Joseph Smith, Sen. about the year 1819 or 20. They then were laboring people, in low circumstances. A short time after this, they commenced digging for hidden treasures, . . . and told marvellous stories about ghosts, hob-goblins, caverns, and various other mysterious matters."[8] Willard Chase, another friend of the family, similarly recalled, "I became acquainted with the Smith family . . . in the year 1820. At that time, they were engaged in the money digging business."[9]

One of the most detailed accounts of this early period was given by William Stafford, a neighbor who lived in Manchester and whose family gave the name to Stafford Road where the Smiths' house still stands.

> I first became acquainted with Joseph, Sen., and his family in the year 1820. They lived, at that time, in Palmyra, about one mile and a half from my residence. A great part of their time was devoted to digging for money: . . . I have heard them tell marvellous tales, respecting the discoveries they had made in their peculiar occupation of money digging. They would say, for instance, that in such a place, in such a hill, on a certain man's farm, there were deposited kegs, barrels and hogheads of coined silver and gold—bars of gold, golden images, brass kettles filled with gold and silver—gold candlesticks, swords, &c, &c.[10]

Joseph Sr. believed he could locate objects that were lost or hidden from sight under the ground. A neighbor, Peter Ingersoll, recalled that "he requested me to walk with him a short distance from his house, for the purpose of seeing whether a mineral rod would work in my hand, saying at the same time he was confident it would. . . . he cut a small witch hazel bush and gave me direction how to hold it."[11]

The younger Joseph learned to work the witch hazel rod from his father. Mrs. S. F. Anderick recalled that Joseph Jr. claimed "he could tell where lost or hidden things and treasures were buried or located with a forked witch hazel." She continued:

> Willard Chase, a Methodist who lived about two miles from uncle's, while digging a well, found a grey smooth stone about the size and shape of an egg. Sallie, Willard's sister, also a Methodist, told me several times that young Jo Smith, who became the Mormon prophet, often came to inquire of her where to dig for treasures. She told me she would place the stone in a hat and hold it to her face, and claimed things would be brought to her view. Sallie let me have it several times, but I never could see anything in or through it. I heard that Jo obtained it and called it a peep-stone, which he used in the place of the witch hazel. Uncle refused to let Jo dig on his farm. I have seen many holes where he dug on other farms.[12]

Willard Chase had employed Joseph Smith to help him dig a well on the Chase property where the seer stone was discovered. Willard was twenty-four years old and Joseph was sixteen. Chase gives details of the discovery from his perspective:

> In the year 1822, I was engaged in digging a well. I employed Alvin and Joseph Smith to assist me; the latter of whom is now known as the Mormon prophet. After digging about twenty feet below the surface of the earth, we discovered a singularly appearing stone, which excited my curiosity. I brought it to the top of the well, and as we were examining it, Joseph put it into his hat, and then his face into the top of his hat. It has been said by Smith, that he brought the stone from the well; but this is false. There was no one in the well but myself. The next morning he came to me, and wished to obtain the stone, alledging that he could see in it; but I told him I did not wish to part with it on account of its being a curiosity, but would lend it. . . . He had it in his possession about two years."[13]

The magical stone is now in the possession of the Mormon church in Salt Lake City.[14]

William Stafford, who helped the Smith father-and-son team with their digging, later recalled how young Joseph used the stone to search for treasure:

> They would say, also, that nearly all the hills in this part of New York, were thrown up by human hands, and in them were large caves, which Joseph, Jr., could see, by placing a stone of singular appearance in his hat, in such a manner as to exclude all light; at which time they pretended he could see all things within and under the earth, —that he could see within the above mentioned caves, large gold bars and silver plates—that he could also discover the spirits in whose charge these treasures were, clothed in ancient dress.

Stafford also recalled that young Joseph "had been looking in his glass" and saw some kegs of gold and silver underneath the earth. He went with both Smiths and the elder Joseph made a circle and said that the treasure was within the circle. Hazel sticks were then put in the ground "around the said circle, for the purpose of keeping off the evil spirits." After putting a steel rod in the center of the circles and digging a trench, the older Smith consulted his son who had been "looking in his stone and watching the motions of the evil spirit." It was determined that they "had made a mistake in the commencem[e]nt of the operation; if it had not been for that, said he, we should have got the money."[15]

The Smiths obtained no gold or silver, but witnesses claimed young Joseph helped find other objects. Martin Harris, who became a close friend of the Smith family, was impressed when Joseph used his stone to find his lost toothpick. He recalls:

> I was at the house of his [Joseph's] father in Manchester, two miles south of Palmyra village, and was picking my teeth with a pin while sitting on the bars. The pin caught in my teeth, and dropped from my fingers into shavings and straw. I jumped from the bars and looked for it. . . . I then took Joseph on surprise, and said to him—I said, "Take your stone." I had never seen it, and did not know that he had it with him. He had it in his pocket. He took it [out] and placed it in his hat—the old white hat—and placed his face in his hat.

I watched him closely to see that he did not look [to] one side; he reached out his hand beyond me on the right, and moved a little stick, and there I saw the pin, which he picked up and gave to me. I know he did not look out of the hat until after he had picked up the pin.[16]

An early 1832 letter written at Canandaigua, New York, south of Manchester, reported that Joseph "had been engaged for some time in company with several others of the same character in digging for money . . . and for a time were supported by a Mr. Fish an illiterate man of some property."[17] Abraham Fish was acquainted with Joseph and his father.[18]

Josiah Stowell was a farmer with substantial holdings in the town of Bainbridge, Chenango County, in southern New York[19] and a member of the local Presbyterian church.[20] In the mid-1820s Stowell organized a money digging company to search for a mine he believed had been hidden by Spaniards in northern Pennsylvania near the home of Isaac Hale.[21] Stowell hired Joseph Smith and his father to help. It was while digging and boarding at the home of Isaac Hale that Smith met his future wife Emma Hale. She was born in July 1804 and was a year and a half older than Smith.

Two of Emma's cousins, Joseph and Hiel Lewis, later recalled how the possibility of a treasure came to light:

We are unable at this time to give precise dates, but some time previous to 1825, a man by the name of Wm. Hale, a distant relative of our uncle Isaac Hale, came to Isaac Hale, and said that he had been informed by a woman named Odle, who claimed to possess the power of seeing under ground, (such persons were then commonly called peepers) that there was great treasures concealed in the hill north-east from his, (Isaac Hale's) house. By her directions, Wm. Hale commenced digging, but being too lazy to work, and too poor to hire, he obtained a partner by the name of Oliver Harper, of [New] York state, who had the means to hire help. But after a short time, operations were suspended for a time.[22]

Josiah Stowell eventually took up the search. In the fall of 1825 he went north to the Manchester area to visit his son Simpson Stowell. While there he heard about the Smiths' ability to locate buried treasure. Reportedly Joseph Jr. told Stowell that he could see the treasure Stowell had been looking for in Harmony through his peep stone even while still in Manchester. He also, according to Stowell's account, "described Josiah Stowel[l]'s house and outhouses" accurately.[23] Stowell was impressed and hired Smith and his father to help locate the treasure.

Oliver Cowdery, who became a friend of the Smith family in 1829, wrote of Stowell's project and of his hiring Joseph Smith:

> This gentleman, whose name is Stowel[l], resided in the town of Bainbridge, on or near the head waters of the Susquehannah river. Some forty miles south, or down the river, in the town of Harmony, Susquehannah county, Pa. is said to be a cave or subterraneous recess. . . . where a company of Spaniards, a long time since, when the country was uninhabited by white settlers, excavated from the bowels of the earth ore, and coined a large quantity of money. . . . Enough, however, was credited of the Spaniard's story, to excite the belief of many that there was a fine sum of the precious metal lying coined in this subterraneous vault, among whom was our employer [Stowell]; and accordingly our brother [Joseph Smith] was required to spend a few months with some others in excavating the earth, in pursuit of this treasure.[24]

In his own history Joseph Jr. also mentioned this work with Stowell:

> In the month of October Eighteen hundred and twenty five I hired with an old Gentleman, by name of Josiah Stoal [Stowell] who lived in Chenango County, State of New York. He had heard something of a silver mine having been opened by the Spaniards in Harmony, Susquahana [sic] County, State of Pen[n]sylvania, and had previous to my hiring with him been digging in order if possible to discover the mine. After I went to live with <him> he took me among the rest of his hands to dig for the silver mine, at which I continued to work for nearly a month without success in our undertaking, and finally I prevailed with the old gentleman to cease digging after it. Hence arose the very prevalent story of my having been a money digger.[25]

Smith's father and mother indicated that he was more than a hired hand for Stowell. Joseph Sr. reportedly told Fayette Lapham that his son went to Harmony, Pennsylvania, "at the request of some one who wanted the assistance of his divining rod and stone in finding hidden treasure, supposed to have been deposited there by the Indians or others."[26] Similarly Lucy recalled that Stowell had sought her son's help because he heard Joseph "possessed certain keys, by which he could discern things invisible to the natural eye."[27]

In other words it was because of Smith's reputation that father and son made the trip of over one hundred miles to Harmony, Pennsylvania, where Stowell employed them to help locate the mine. Smith was now nineteen, and his father fifty-four.

On 1 November 1825, soon after their arrival in Harmony and in anticipation of their discoveries, Stowell's treasure digging company drew up "Articles of Agreement." This agreement stipulated, "if anything of value should be obtained at a certain place in Pennsylvania near a Wm. Hale's, supposed to be a valuable mine of either Gold or Silver and also to contain coined money and bars or ingots of Gold or Silver," each member would receive a share, including a share to Oliver Harper's widow. According to this agreement, Joseph Sr. and his son Joseph (who both signed the agreement) would receive "two elevenths of all the property that may be obtained."[28]

It was while they were away in southern New York that the new land agent in Canandaigua agreed to sell the Smith's delinquent Manchester farm to their neighbor to the south who wanted to add it to his holdings. Only panic-stricken appeals by Lucy and Hyrum Smith to sympathetic neighbors and the return of Joseph Sr. prevented eviction. A kindly Quaker, Lemuel Durfee, bought the land and allowed the Smiths to remain as tenants.[29]

In 1834 Isaac Hale recalled the treasure-seeking venture:

[Joseph] Smith, and his father, with several other "money-diggers" boarded at my house while they were employed in digging for a mine that they supposed had been opened and worked by the Spaniards, many years since. Young Smith gave the "money-diggers" great encouragement, at first, but when they had arrived in digging, to near the place where he had stated an immense treasure would be found—he said the enchantment was so powerful that he could not see. They then became discouraged, and soon after dispersed. This took place about the 17th of November, 1825; and one of the company gave me his note for $12[.]68 for his board, which is still unpaid.[30]

Others in the area also recalled Smith's activities and placed them within the context of religious and supernatural practice. Michael Morse described the treasure forays around Harmony to an interviewer in 1879:

> Joseph came into Harmony with a Mr. Stowell, to dig for treasure - silver in oars [ores] - which was said to have be[e]n mined & hid by Spaniards a long time before. He thinks three different companies had been digging for it in all and that Mr. Stowell with his company were one of the three Says Joseph at that time (about 1825) was a green, awkward, and ignorant boy of about 19 yrs of age Says he <then> made no profession of religion. Said Mr. Stowell was a religious man, as was also Mr. Isaac Hale at whose house Mr. Stowell, Joseph and the other hired men boarded, and that prayers were had of mornings before the company set off to work.[31]

In 1842 Joel K. Noble of Colesville, New York, placed the money digging within the context of occult ritual. He recalled that young Joseph "came here when about 17-18 Y[ears]. of age in the capacity of Glass Looker or fortune tel[l]er."[32] Noble summarized the story of the company's alleged sprinkling the ground with a dog's blood while offering prayers to obtain a buried treasure.[33]

While Joseph Smith was working for Josiah Stowell, he was brought before a court on charges sworn against him by a nephew of Josiah Stowell, Peter G. Bridgman (or Bridgeman). Apparently Bridgman became concerned that his uncle's money was being spent in the pursuit of elusive treasure.[34] Accounts of these charges corroborate Smith's treasure hunting in southern New York and Pennsylvania.

In 1831 Abram W. Benton, a young man about the same age as Joseph Jr., recalled the arrest for disorderly conduct and the judgement of guilt, adding, "considering his youth, (he then being a minor,) and thinking he might reform his conduct, he was designedly allowed to escape. This was four or five years ago."[35] In Noble's 1842 recollection, Smith was charged with vagrancy, condemned, and "whisper came to Jo. off off—took Leg Bail (or Gave [Leg Bail])."[36]

For over a hundred years three different published printings of the actual 1826 court record taken from Albert Neely's docket book have been available as well as an account by William D. Purple. But because the pages from the original docket book had been lost, the authenticity of these published accounts was questioned. However, in 1971 two itemized bills were discovered which had been submitted by Justice Neely and Constable Philip De Zeng to cover costs incurred in the arrest and examination of Joseph Smith, and they confirm many of the details of both the Purple account and the published versions of the record. (For a detailed description of each of these documents, see the Appendix.)

Because of the multiplicity of documents concerning the 20 March 1826 examination of Joseph Smith, it is possible to reasonably reconstruct the order of events as the young glass-looker would have experienced them. When Smith was arrested, he would have been brought before Neely for a preliminary examination, often referred to loosely as a "trial" but specified by Neely on his bill as an "examination." The examination was to determine whether Smith should be released as innocent of the charges or, if the evidence seemed sufficient, actually brought to trial. During the examination Smith's statement was taken (not under oath), and witnesses for and against the accused were sworn in and examined and their statements taken down.[37] Both before and during the examination Joseph remained under guard by Constable De Zeng, who charged the county for "attendance with Prisoner two days & 1 nigh[t]"—the day of the examination and the day and night preceding.[38]

As indicated, Bridgman had sworn out the warrant. Neely's court record begins with the complaint: "State of New York v. Joseph Smith. Warrant issued upon written complaint upon oath of Peter G. Bridgeman, who informed that one Joseph Smith of Bainbridge was a disorderly person and an impostor."[39] New York law collected various types of vagrancy under the broad heading of "Disorderly Persons" and included, along with beggars, prostitutes, and those who neglect their wives and children, "all persons pretending to have skill in physiognomy, palmistry, or like crafty science, or pretending to tell fortunes, or to discover where lost goods may be found."[40] Since Smith had never actually led the diggers to anything of value, Bridgman considered that Joseph was indeed pretending to discover lost items.

According to Neely's court record, as published in *Fraser's Magazine*, Smith first made a statement in his own defense:

> Prisoner examined: says that he came from the town of Palmyra, and had been at the house of Josiah Stowel[l] in Bainbridge most of time since; had small part of time been employed in looking for mines, but the major part had been employed by said Stowel[l] on his farm, and going to school. That he had a certain stone which he had occasionally looked at to determine where hidden treasures in the bowels of the earth were; that he professed to tell in this manner where gold mines were a distance under ground, and had looked for Mr. Stowel[l] several times, and had informed him where he could find these treasures, and Mr. Stowel[l] had been engaged in digging for them. That at Palmyra he pretended to tell by looking at this stone where coined money was buried in Pennsylvania, and while at Palmyra had frequently ascertained in that way where lost property was of various kinds; that he had occasionally been in the habit of looking through this stone to find lost property for three years, but of late had pretty much given it up on account of its injuring his health, especially his eyes, made them sore; that he did not solicit business of this kind, and had always rather declined having anything to do with this business.[41]

Joseph Smith made a passing remark about attending school and Josiah Stowell, Jr., who was almost seventeen years old at the time remembered, "I also went to schoal [school] with him one winter he was a fine likely young man & at that time did not Profess religion."[42]

The next witness called was Josiah Stowell:

> [Stowell] says that prisoner [Joseph Smith] had been at his house something like five months; had been employed by him to work on farm part of time; . . . that prisoner had looked [in his stone] for him sometimes; once to tell him about money buried in Bend Mountain in Pennsylvania, once for gold on Monument Hill, and once for a salt spring; and that he positively knew that the prisoner could tell, and did possess the art of seeing those valuable treasures through the medium of said stone; that he found the [1883 printing: "digging part"] at Bend and Monument Hill as prisoner represented it; that prisoner had looked through said stone for Deacon Attleton for a mine, did not exactly find it, but got a [1883: "piece"] of ore

which resembled gold, he thinks; that prisoner had told by means of this stone where a Mr. Bacon had buried money; that he and prisoner had been in search of it; that prisoner had said it was in a certain root of a stump five feet from surface of the earth, and with it would be found a tail feather; that said Stowel[l] and prisoner thereupon commenced digging, found a tail feather, but the money was gone; that he supposed the money moved down. That prisoner did offer his services; that he [Joseph Smith] never deceived him; that prisoner looked through stone and described Josiah Stowel[l]'s house and outhouses, while at Palmyra at Simpson Stowel[l]'s, correctly; that he had told about a painted tree, with a man's head painted upon it, by means of said stone. That he had been in company with prisoner digging for gold, and had the most implicit faith in prisoner's skill.[43]

Stowell's comment about Smith searching for ore at Monument Hill and looking for salt is confirmed by William R. Hine's recollection that "Asa Stowel[l] furnished the means for Jo to dig for silver ore, on Monument Hill." He also mentions that Smith "and his workmen lived in a shanty while digging for salt. When it rained hard, my wife has often made beds for them on the floor in our house."[44]

Another witness, Jonathan Thompson, also testified in support of Smith's skills in locating treasure:

that prisoner [Joseph Smith] was requested to look for chest of money; did look, . . . that prisoner, Thompson, and Yeomans went in search of it; that Smith arrived at spot first; was at night; that Smith looked in hat while there, and when very dark, and told how the chest was situated. After digging several feet, struck upon something sounding like a board or plank. Prisoner would not look again, pretending that he was alarmed on account of the circumstances relating to the trunk being buried, [which] came all fresh to his mind. That the last time he [Joseph Smith] looked he discovered distinctly the two Indians who buried the trunk, that a quarrel ensued between them, and that one of said Indians was killed by the other, and thrown into the hole beside the trunk, to guard it, as he supposed. Thompson says that he believes in the prisoner's professed skill; that the board which he struck his spade upon was probably the chest, but on account of an enchantment the trunk kept settling away from under them when digging; that notwithstanding they continued constantly removing the dirt, yet the trunk kept about the same distance from them. Says prisoner said that it appeared to him that salt might be found in Bainbridge, and that he is certain that prisoner can divine things by means of said stone. That as evidence of the fact prisoner looked into his hat to tell him about some money witness [Thompson] lost sixteen years ago, and that he described the man that witness supposed had taken it, and the disposition of the money.[45]

Dr. Purple reports that he heard the testimony of Joseph's father, though this testimony is not mentioned in the official record, which only had to "put in writing" as much of the testimony "as shall be material to prove the offence."[46] Purple states that "Joseph Smith, Sr., was present, and sworn as a witness" and that "He swore that both he and his son were mortified that this wonderful power which God had so miraculously given him should be used only in search of filthy lucre, or its equivalent in earthly treasures." According to Purple, Joseph Sr. "trusted that the Son of Righteousness would some day illumine the heart of the boy, and enable him to see His will concerning him."[47]

After hearing the testimony, Justice Neely concluded that there was enough evidence to indicate that the prisoner, Joseph Smith the Glass Looker, had claimed to have the skill to discover lost goods, a misdemeanor under the Vagrant Act, and had not actually found anything. Neely wrote in his court record, "And therefore the Court find the Defendant [Joseph Smith] guilty."[48] He ordered the constable, Philip De Zeng, to notify two other justices and prepare for trial. The material witnesses, three in this instance, were put under recognizances to appear at the forthcoming Court of Special Sessions.[49]

At this point the course of events becomes somewhat difficult to trace. Certainly many people found guilty in a pre-trial hearing do not go to trial. The bills of the four justices have been found, and they show that no Court of Special Sessions was held. When Justice Noble writes that Joseph took "Leg Bail" he was using an early slang expression meaning "to escape from custody."[50] What may have happened is that the three justices discussed the case, and considered that since this was Joseph Smith's first offence, privately made a deal with him. Dr. Purple who was present at the examination recalled that Smith was discharged. Years later Smith's co-worker Oliver Cowdery, probably getting his information from Smith, recalled that "some very officious person complained of him as a disorderly person, and brought him before the authorities of the county; but there being no cause of action he was honorably acquitted."[51] It is true that no penalty was administered.[52]

Whatever the outcome may have been, it is clear from the testimonies recorded at the examination and also from other statements by neighbors and witnesses, both from the Bainbridge-Harmony area and also from the Manchester-Palmyra area nearly one hundred miles away, that young Smith had for several years earned part of his livelihood by hiring out as a glass looker to locate hidden treasures by gazing into his seer stone. It is also evident that Joseph surrounded his activities with a religious atmosphere flavored with the supernatural, although he himself at this time made no profession of religion. He looked into his peepstone to see: hidden mines and treasures under ground; Stowell's house and farm a hundred miles away; a miscreant who stole Thompson's money ten years earlier; the murder of a native American Indian whose spirit was guarding a treasure; and the location of treasures and ghosts or spirits of the dead guardians who moved them around under the ground.

These activities led the two widely separated communities to associate him with divination and necromancy. In fact early adherents of the Mormon faith affirm that Joseph located the gold plates from which he dictated the Book of Mormon by gazing into his seer stone. He also used this stone to obtain the text of the book as well as to receive instructions from God for his early followers.[53]

One valuable discovery which Joseph Smith did make during this period was Emma Hale. Smith told her that as soon as he saw her, he recognized that she was the one who had to be with him to enable him to find the treasure which he had been promised.[54] She was won over, but her father was not. Isaac Hale later stated that "young Smith made several visits at my house, and at length asked my consent to his marrying my daughter Emma. This I refused, and gave him my reasons for so doing; some of which were, that he was a stranger, and followed a business that I could not approve."[55]

Without her father's permission, Emma and Joseph eloped and

were married on 18 January 1827 by Zachariah Tarble, a justice of the peace in Bainbridge. As she later told the story to her son:

> I was visiting at Mr. Stowell's, who lived in Bainbridge, and saw your father there. I had no intention of marrying when I left home; but, during my visit at Mr. Stowell's, your father visited me there. My folks were bitterly opposed to him; and, being importuned by your father, aided by Mr. Stowell, who urged me to marry him, and preferring to marry him to any other man I knew, I consented.[56]

Joseph had turned twenty-one years old; Emma was twenty-two. Since Isaac Hale did not approve of the marriage, the couple lived with Joseph's parents in Manchester. Emma's parents were Methodists and she was probably also a Methodist.[57]

Sometime after their marriage, they hired Peter Ingersoll to help pick up Emma's personal possessions and furniture. Isaac Hale related that "Smith stated to me, that he had given up what he called 'glass-looking,' and that he expected to work for a living, and was willing to do so." Emma's brother Alva reported that "Joseph Smith Jr. told him that [']his (Smith's) gift in seeing with a stone and hat, was a gift from God,' but also states 'that Smith told him at another time that this *'peeping'* was all d—d nonsense. He (Smith) was deceived himself but did not intend to deceive others; — that he intended to quit the business, (of peeping) and labor for his livelihood.'"[58]

Peter Ingersoll described his trip with Smith to Harmony:

> I was hired by Joseph Smith, Jr. to go to Pennsylvania, to move his wife's household furniture up to Manchester, where his wife then was. When we arrived at Mr. Hale's, in Harmony, Pa., from which place he had taken his wife, a scene presented itself, truly affecting. His father-in-law (Mr. Hale) addressed Joseph, in a flood of tears: "You have stolen my daughter and married her. I had much rather have followed her to her grave. You spend your time in digging for money—pretend to see in a stone, and thus try to deceive people." Joseph wept, and acknowledged he could not see in a stone now, nor ever could; and that his former pretensions in that respect, were all false. He then promised to give up his old habits of digging for money and looking into stones. Mr. Hale told Joseph, if he would move to Pennsylvania and work for a living, he would assist him in

getting into business. Joseph acceded to this proposition. . . . Joseph told me on his return, that he intended to keep the promise which he had made to his father-in-law; but, said he, it will be hard for me, for they will all oppose, as they want me to look in the stone for them to dig money: and in fact it was as he predicted.[59]

Joseph now had a wife to support. He promised his father-in-law he would stop crystal-gazing and work hard for a living. About June 1827 Smith's father first told his friend Willard Chase that his son had discovered a hidden record written on plates of gold.

NOTES

1. Newspaper articles mention unnamed people who claimed to have found vast treasures. The *Orleans Advocate* published in Albion, New York, contains the following: "A few days since was discovered in this town, by the help of a mineral stone, (which becomes transparent when placed in a hat and the light excluded by the face of him who looks into it, provided he is fortune's favorite,) a monstrous potash kettle in the bowels of old mother Earth, filled with the purest bullion" (reprinted in *Wayne Sentinel* 3 [27 Dec. 1825]: 2).

2. Wayland D. Hand, "The Quest for Buried Treasure: A Chapter in American Folk Legend[a]ry," in *Folklore on Two Continents: Essays in Honor of Linda Degh* (Bloomington, IN: Trickster Press, 1980), 112-19; D. Michael Quinn, *Early Mormonism and the Magic World View* (Salt Lake City: Signature Books, 1987). As Rodger I. Anderson explains,

> the practice of money digging by no means originated with Smith. Long before Smith's neighbors accused him of hunting for buried money by occult means, the art of magical treasure hunting was already widespread in America. Accounts of men pursuing enchanted treasures with divining rods appear throughout the eighteenth century, and in combination suggest that the practice had very early become ritualized. The treasure was located by a divining rod, immobilized by charms, magic circles, or special steel rods driven into the ground for that purpose, and incantations recited to protect the diggers from "certain malicious Demons who are said to h[a]unt and guard such Places." Any deviation from these prescribed rituals on the part of the treasure hunters, any "Mistake in the Procedure, some rash Word spoken, or some Rule of Art neglected, the Guardian Spirit had Power to sink it deeper into the Earth and convey it

out of their reach" ("Joseph Smith's Early Reputation Revisited," *Journal of Pastoral Practice* 4 [1980]: 77-78; see also Rodger I. Anderson, *Joseph Smith's New York Reputation Reexamined* [Salt Lake City: Signature Books, 1990], 12-13).

3. In January 1859 Martin Harris, an early Mormon convert then residing at Kirtland, Ohio, was interviewed by Joel Tiffany. This account was subsequently published in *Tiffany's Monthly* 5 (Aug. 1859): 163-70, a spiritualist publication at New York City. See also the affidavit of Peter Ingersoll, Palmyra, Wayne County, New York, 2 Dec. 1833, in E. D. Howe, *Mormonism Unvailed* (Painesville [OH]: Printed and Published by the Author, 1834), 233. Philastus Hurlbut (a former member of the Mormon church) visited Palmyra and Manchester townships during November and December 1833 and obtained, besides two general statements, a number of statements from some Joseph Smith family acquaintances. These were subsequently printed in Howe's compilation *Mormonism Unvailed* in 1834. Joseph Smith's biographer Donna Hill wrote, "there is testimony from early Mormons that Joseph had searched for treasure, that to some extent he had accepted the myths which often accompanied belief in buried treasure at that time and that a number of his close friends in the church were 'money-diggers' and rodsmen" (*Joseph Smith: The First Mormon* [Garden City, NY: Doubleday, 1977], 66).

4. *Tiffany's Monthly*, 5 (Aug. 1859): 164; John Stafford in *Saints' Herald* 28 (1 June 1881): 167; and C. R. Stafford, statement of Mar. 1885, in *Naked Truths About Mormonism* 1 (Jan. 1888): 3, original publication in the Yale University Library.

5. Statement of C. R. Smith, Mar. 1885, in *Naked Truths About Mormonism* 1 (Apr. 1888): 1; interview of John Stafford in William H. Kelley papers, Library-Archives, Reorganized Church of Jesus Christ of Latter Day Saints, Independence, Missouri (hereafter RLDS archives); see *Saints' Herald* 28 (1 June 1881): 167.

6. Joseph and Hiel Lewis, "Mormon History", *The Amboy Journal* 24 (30 Apr. 1879): 1; Frederic G. Mather, "The Early Mormons," *Binghamton Daily Republican*, 29 July 1880, see also *Lippincott's Magazine of Popular Literature and Science* (Philadelphia: J.B. Lippincott and Co., 1880), 26:200, 202; *Tiffany's Monthly* 5 (Aug. 1859): 164.

7. Copy of a letter from six leading citizens of Canandaigua, New York, dated Jan. 1832, in answer to a query about Mormons from Rev. Ancil Beach, in the Walter Hubbell papers, Manuscript Division, Department of Rare Books and Special Collections, Princeton University Libraries, Princeton, New Jersey; Statement of W. R. Hine, in *Naked Truths About Mormonism* 1 (Jan.

1888): 2; and A. W. Benton, "Mormonites," *Evangelical Magazine and Gospel Advocate* 2 (9 Apr. 1831): 120.

8. Statement of Joshua Stafford, Manchester, Ontario County, New York, 15 Nov. 1833, in *Mormonism Unvailed*, 258.

9. Affidavit of Willard Chase, before Justice of the Peace, Frederick Smith, 11 Dec. 1833, in *Mormonism Unvailed*, 240.

10. Affidavit of William Stafford, Manchester, New York, 8 Dec. 1833, in *Mormonism Unvailed*, 237.

11. Affidavit of Peter Ingersoll, 2 Dec. 1833, in *Mormonism Unvailed*, 232. In a letter of Jesse Smith to "Hiram" Smith written on 17 June 1829, Jesse wrote concerning a person who discussed the Smith family, "he says your father has a wand or rod like Jannes & Jambres who withstood Moses in Egypt—that he can tell the distance from India to Ethiopia" (copy of letter in Joseph Smith Letterbook 2:60, in archives, historical department, Church of Jesus Christ of Latter-day Saints, Salt Lake City, Utah, hereafter LDS archives). Fayette Lapham, who interviewed Joseph Sr., said that Smith "believed that there was a vast amount of money buried somewhere in the country; that it would some day be found; that he himself had spent both time and money searching for it, with divining rods, but had not succeeded in finding any, though sure that he eventually would" ("The Mormons," *Historical Magazine* 7 [May 1870]: 306).

12. Statement of Mrs. S. F. Anderick, 1887, in *Naked Truths About Mormonism* 1 (Jan. 1888): 2. See William W. Phelps to E. D. Howe, 15 Jan. 1831, in *Mormonism Unvailed*, 273. Benjamin Saunders said, "I have seen Sally (Sarah) Chase peep or look in her seer stone a many a time. She would look for any thing. I have had it in my hand" (W. H. Kelley Collection, "Miscellany 1795-1948," RLDS archives). Sallie (named Sarah) was born on 20 October 1800 to Clark and Phebe Chase. Her father died in 1821. The records of the Clark Chase family are found in William E. Reed, *The Descendants of Thomas Durfee of Portsmouth, R.I.* (Washington, D.C.: Gibson Bros., 1902), 213-14, and George Grant Brownell, comp., *Genealogical Record of the Descendants of Thomas Brownell 1619 to 1910* (Jamestown, NY, 1910), 200.

13. Affidavit of Willard Chase, 11 Dec. 1833, in *Mormonism Unvailed*, 240-41. Smith later borrowed the stone and returned it at Chase's insistence. The stone was subsequently borrowed by Hyrum Smith and never returned. Joseph in his examination before Justice Albert Neely on 20 March 1826 said that he "had occasionally been in the habit of looking through the stone to find lost property for 3 years" or since about 1823. Fayette Lapham learned from Joseph Sr. that after the stone was found when working on a well "Joseph spent about two years looking into this stone, telling fortunes, where

to find lost things, and where to dig for money and other hidden treasure" (*Historical Magazine* 7 [May 1870]: 306). On Joseph Smith's use of seer stones, see Richard Van Wagoner and Steven Walker, "Joseph Smith: 'The Gift of Seeing,'" *Dialogue: A Journal of Mormon Thought* 15 (Summer 1982): 49-68. For additional information on seer stones, see Quinn, *Early Mormonism and the Magic World View*, 38-50, 122-23, 143-48, 194-204.

14. Quinn, *Early Mormonism and the Magic World View*, 196.

15. Affidavit of William Stafford, 8 Dec. 1833, in *Mormonism Unvailed*, 237-39.

16. *Tiffany's Monthly* 5 (Aug. 1859): 164. Lucy Harris, Martin's wife, stated, "About a year previous to the report being raised that Smith had found gold plates, he became very intimate with the Smith family, and said he believed Joseph could see in his stone any thing he wished" (*Mormonism Unvailed*, 255).

17. Copy of a letter from six leading citizens of Canandaigua, New York, dated Jan. 1832, in answer to a query about Mormons from Rev. Ancil Beach, in the Hubbel papers, Princeton University Libraries, Princeton, New Jersey.

18. Mr. Fish is Abraham Fish of Manchester, New York, a neighbor of the Smith family. He lived south of the Smith/Durfee farm. That Fish was illiterate is evidenced in the Nathan Pierce Docket Book when he signed his name with an "X" identified as "his mark." He was born about 1773 and died on 17 July 1845 at the age of seventy-two (*Wayne Sentinel* [23 July 1845], 2).

The probate of the will of Lemuel Durfee, Sr., lists "One note signed by Joseph Smith [Sr.] and Abraham Fish, thirty-seven dollars and fifty cents" with interest of $1.42 (Probate Papers, Surrogate's Court, Wayne County Courthouse, Lyons, New York). After Durfee's death on 8 August 1829 (*Wayne Sentinel* 6 [14 Aug. 1829]: 3), Durfee's son, also named Lemuel, brought suit against Joseph Smith, Sr. and Abraham Fish on 19 January 1830 for $39.92, which was eventually paid (Docket Book of Nathan Pierce, Town Hall of Manchester, Manchester, New York). Pierce was a justice of the peace in Manchester where Joseph Sr. was residing and Durfee was a resident of Palmyra.

A receipt dated 10 March 1827 received by the younger Joseph from the Thayer store in Palmyra reads: "Palmyra, 10th March 1827, Recd of Joseph Smith Jr Four dollars which is credited to the account of A. Fish" and signed J & L Thayer. Joel and Levi Thayer were the owners of the store (Joseph Smith Collection, under Receipts, in LDS archives).

19. Josiah Stowell was married to Miriam Bridgman. They had eight children, four sons and four daughters: Simpson (or Simson; also listed as Simeon), b. 29 July 1791; Martha b. 10 Sept. 1793; Horace b. 10 Mar. 1796;

Miranda b. 6 Sept. 1798; Thomas b. 28 Sept. 1800; Rhoda b. 11 Mar. 1805; Miriam (Mary) b. 22 May 1807; and Josiah b. 16 Apr. 1809. See William Henry Harrison Stowell, *Stowell Genealogy* (Rutland, VT: Tuttle Co., 1922), 229-30. Josiah Stowell's name is in the 1820 census of Bainbridge, Chenango County, New York, microfilm #193721, 158 (LDS Family History Library). Stowell's name is also in the civil Docket Book of Zechariah Tarble in a civil case against him dated 4 Aug. 1823. Written across the entry in the docket book is: "Recd October 26th 1825 [unclear word] Damages in full on this Judgment. Otis Loveland" (Justice Docket Book of Zechariah Tarble, 17 June 1822 - 7 March 1826; Bainbridge Town Hall, Bainbridge, New York).

20. Stowell was a deacon in the First Presbyterian church in Bainbridge. He was assessed on 416 acres in Bainbridge in 1826. See Assessment Roll, 29 July 1826, Bainbridge Town Hall, Bainbridge, New York, copy and typescript in our possession (18). The total valuation was $2,085.

21. Stowell "became infatuated with the idea that he must go in search of hidden treasures, which he believed were buried in the earth" (James H. Smith, *History of Chenango and Madison Counties, New York* [Syracuse, NY: Published by D. Mason & Co., 1880], 153). This was based on the 1877 recollection of William D. Purple. The name "Isaiah Stowel" in the text should be Josiah Stowell.

22. *The Amboy Journal* 24 (30 Apr. 1879): 1.

23. See Stowell's 1826 testimony in Charles Marshall, "The Original Prophet. By a Visitor to Salt Lake City," *Fraser's Magazine* 7 (Feb. 1873): 229.

24. *Messenger and Advocate* 2 (Oct. 1835): 201. This account may have been written in response to Isaac Hale's 1834 affidavit, which is mentioned in the article. Although Cowdery's letter claims Smith worked for Stowell as "a common laborer" (200), Smith's mother indicated he was hired because Stowell had heard Joseph saw things which the natural eye could not (see n27).

25. Manuscript History, Book A-1: 7-8, LDS archives; JS-H 1:56, PGP; Dean C. Jessee, comp., *The Papers of Joseph Smith* (Salt Lake City: Deseret Book Co., 1989), 1:282. Joseph's account records that he worked "for nearly a month," Lucy's book has "by the month," and Oliver Cowdery's account "a few months." Much of Lucy's printed history is similar in wording to the Joseph Smith account published in the *Times and Seasons* 3 (2 May 1842): 772. In the *Elder's Journal* Joseph responded to a question of whether he had been a money digger with this answer: "Yes, but it was never a very profitable job for him, as he only got fourteen dollars a month for it" (1 [July 1838]: 43, Far West, Missouri; see B. H. Roberts, ed., *History of the Church of Jesus Christ of*

Latter-day Saints [Salt Lake City: Deseret Book Co., 1959], 3:29). It is not known whether the fourteen dollars was in addition to his room and board.

26. "The Mormons," *Historical Magazine* 7 (May 1870): 307.

27. Lucy Mack Smith, *Biographical Sketches of Joseph Smith the Prophet, and His Progenitors for Many Generations* (Liverpool: Published for Orson Pratt by S. W. Richards, 1853), 91-92; *History of Joseph Smith By His Mother, Lucy Mack Smith* (Salt Lake City: Bookcraft, 1958), 91-92.

28. *Daily Tribune*, 23 Apr. 1880, 4, Salt Lake City, from the *Susquehanna Journal*, 20 Mar. 1880.

29. Lemuel Durfee purchased it on 20 December 1825 (Deed Liber 44:232-34, Ontario County Records Center and Archives, Canandaigua, New York). The Smith family eventually lost the farm.

30. Affidavit of Isaac Hale, 20 Mar. 1834, in *Susquehanna Register, and Northern Pennsylvanian* 9 (1 May 1834): 1, original newspaper in the Susquehanna County Historical Society, Montrose, Pennsylvania. The testimonies from the *Register* were reprinted in *The New York Baptist Register* 11 (13 June 1834): 68, original in Colgate University Archives. Also published in Howe, *Mormonism Unvailed*, 263.

31. William W. Blair Journal, 8 May 1879, RLDS archives. Blair interviewed Michael Morse in Amboy, Illinois. In his journal Blair wrote Morse's first name as "Gabriel" rather than Michael. Blair also wrote to the editor of the *Saints' Herald* about what he learned from Michael Morse. See *Saints' Herald* 26 (15 June 1879): 190, letter dated 22 May 1879.

32. Letter of Joel King Noble to Jonathan B. Turner, 8 Mar. 1842, in answer to an inquiry from Professor Turner of Illinois College in Jacksonville, Illinois. Located in the Turner Collection of the Illinois State Historical Library, Springfield, Illinois.

33. Ibid.William R. Hine, who lived in Colesville at the time, stated that Joseph "claimed to receive revelations from the Lord through prayer, and would pray with his men, mornings and at other times." *Naked Truths About Mormonism* 1 (Jan. 1888): 2. Cf. similar statements by Henry A. Sayer (ibid., 1:3) and Joseph Rogers (ibid., 1 [Apr. 1888]: 1). Joseph's use of sacrifice in his Palmyra diggings is referred to in William Stafford's testimony (*Mormonism Unvailed*, 239); Pomeroy Tucker, *The Origin, Rise and Progress of Mormonism* (New York: D. Appleton & Co., 1867), 24-25; Stephen S. Harding's letter in Thomas Gregg, *The Prophet of Palmyra* (New York: John B. Alden, 1890), 56; C. R. Stafford's statement in *Naked Truths About Mormonism* 1 (Jan. 1888): 3. The same ritual in the Pennsylvania diggings is recorded in Emily C. Blackman, *History of Susquehanna County, Pennsylvania* (Philadelphia: Claxton, Remsen & Haffelfinger, 1873), 580; and in Frederick Mather's interviews in

Lippincott's Magazine 26 (Aug. 1880): 200. See also *Binghamton Daily Republican*, 29 July 1880.

34. Within a month after swearing out the warrant, this crusading twenty-two-year-old was licensed as an exhorter by the Methodists and within three years helped establish the West Bainbridge Methodist church. Upon his death in 1872 his fellow ministers characterized him as "an ardent Methodist, and any attack upon either the doctrines or the polity of the M.E. Church, within his field of labor, was sure to be repelled by him with a vigorous hand" (*Minutes*, Wyoming Annual Conference, Methodist Episcopal Church [1872], 34). Bridgman served as one of the original trustees of the West Bainbridge (now North Afton) Methodist church, organized 17 February 1829 ("Incorporation of Religious Societies," 107, Chenango County Office Building).

35. Letter written by A. W. Benton of South Bainbridge, New York, dated Mar. 1831, in *Evangelical Magazine and Gospel Advocate* 2 (9 Apr. 1831): 120, Utica, New York. Dr. Abram Benton, according to the family Bible record, was born on 16 July 1805. He was later received into the Medical Society in October 1830 (see James H. Smith, *History of Chenango and Madison Counties, New York*, 100, 144). For a while he lived on the east bank in South Bainbridge just north of the bridge (Chenango County Deeds RR:587). About 1838 he moved to Sterling, Illinois, and then to Fulton, where he died on 9 March 1867.

36. Noble to Turner, 8 Mar. 1842. The letter arrived too late to be included in Turner's book, *Mormonism in All Ages*, 1842 (see correspondence from Absalom Peters, 1 Jan. and 6 July 1842, regarding the printing, in another Turner Collection in the Illinois State Historical Survey Library, Urbana). Noble after 1850 moved to Hartland Township, Huron County, Ohio, where he died on 19 February 1874.

37. "The examination of the prisoner should not be upon oath" (*A New Conductor Generalis: Being a Summary of the Law Relative to the Duty and Office of Justices of the Peace, Sheriffs, Coroners, Constables, Jurymen, Overseers of the Poor* [Albany: Published by E. F. Backus, 1819], 142.

38. Cf. Constable Redfield's 1829 bill, 19 May re: Jacob Lee, for "keeping him part of two days & one night and attending the Examination."

39. *Fraser's Magazine* 7 (Feb. 1873): 229. Peter Bridgman was a nephew of Josiah and Mariam Bridgman Stowell (Burt Nichols and Joseph Clark Bridgman, *Genealogy of the Bridgman Family* [Hyde Park, MA, 1894), 129, 116, 118-19).

40. *Laws of the State of New York, Revised and Passed . . .*, 2 vols. (Albany: H.C. Southwick & Co., 1813), revisers William P. Van Ness and John Wood-

worth, 1:114, 410, usually cited as Revised Laws, or R.L. See *Conductor Generalis* (1819), 108; also *Revised Statutes* (1829), 1:638.

41. *Fraser's Magazine* 7 (Feb. 1873): 229.

42. Josiah Stowell, Jr. to J. S. Fullmer, 17 Feb. 1843, LDS archives, published in *LDS Church News* (12 May 1985), 10.

43. *Fraser's Magazine* 7:229; Daniel S. Tuttle, "Mormons," *New Schaff-Herzog Encyclopedia* (New York: Funk and Wagnalls, 1883), 2: 1,576.

44. W. R. Hine, in *Naked Truths About Mormonism* 1 (Jan. 1888): 2. Hine stated,

> Jo Smith, who became the Mormon prophet, and his father came from Palmyra, or Manchester, N.Y., and dug for salt two summers, near and in sight of my house. The old settlers used to buy salt from an Indian squaw, who often promised to tell the whites where the salt spring was, but she never did. Jo Smith claimed to be a seer. He had a very clear stone about the size and shape of a duck's egg, and claimed that he could see lost or hidden things through it. He said he saw Captain Kidd sailing on the Susquehanna River during a freshet, and that he buried two pots of gold and silver. He claimed he saw writing cut on the rocks in an unknown language telling where Kidd buried it, and he translated it through his peepstone. I have had it many times and could see in it whatever I imagined.

The *Oxford Gazette* in a brief history of Bainbridge stated:

> There is an opinion prevalent among the oldest settlers of the town, of the existence of salt springs near the river, in the southern part of this town. This belief is founded upon the testimony of many of the Indians, who were in the habit of borrowing kettles of many families in the neighborhood, and returning them encrusted with pure salt, of an excellent quality; but no promises could ever induce them to disclose this important secret—and many attempts have been made to discover this hidden treasure, but without success, as the Indians through jealousy, would never permit any person to accompany them in their excursions, and were careful to erase every trace which might lead to the discovery (*Oxford Gazette* 9 [28 Apr. 1824]).

45. *Fraser's Magazine* 7:229-30. Purple was impressed by Thompson's detailed description of their search:

> many years before a band of robbers had buried on his

[Thompson's] flat a box of treasure, and as it was very valuable they had by a sacrifice placed a charm over it to protect it, so that it could not be obtained except by faith, accompanied by certain talismanic influences. So, after arming themselves with fasting and prayer, they sallied forth to the spot designated by Smith. . . . Mr. Stowell went to his flock and selected a fine vigorous lamb, and resolved to sacrifice it to the demon spirit who guarded the coveted treasure. Shortly after the venerable Deacon [Josiah Stowell] might be seen on his knees at prayer near the pit, while Smith, with a lantern in one hand to dispel the midnight darkness might be seen making a circuit around the pit, sprinkling the flowing blood from the lamb upon the ground, as a propitiation to the spirit that thwarted them. They then descended the excavation, but the treasure still receded from their grasp, and it was never obtained (W. D. Purple, "Joseph Smith, the Originator of Mormonism," *Chenango Union* 30 [3 May 1877]: 3).

Martin Harris remembered the time when the treasure seekers "took Joseph to look in the stone for them, and he did so for a while, and then he told them the enchantment was so strong that he could not see, and they gave it up" (*Tiffany's Monthly* 5 [Aug. 1859]: 164). Mrs. S. F. Anderick mentioned that Joseph induced many farmers "to dig nights for chests of gold, when the pick struck the chest, someone usually spoke, and Jo would say the enchantment was broken, and the chest would leave" (*Naked Truths About Mormonism* 1 [Jan. 1888]: 2).

46. *Laws of New York* (1813), 2:507.

47. Purple, "Joseph Smith, the Originator of Mormonism," *Chenango Union* 30 (3 May 1877): 3.

48. *Fraser's Magazine* 7: 230.

49. "A bond or recognizance, 25," *Conductor Generalis* (1819), 482. "The fees of a Justice for his services in apprehending, binding, committing, &c for crimes and misdemeanors, are—for every oath, 12 1/2 cents; warrant, 19; recognizance, 25; mittimus, 19; which are audited and allowed by the board of supervisors as county charges" (Thomas G. Waterman, *The Justice's Manual: or, A Summary of the Power and Duties of Justices of the Peace in the State of New-York* [Binghamton, NY: Printed by Morgan & Canoll, 1825], 199). On defendant and witness recognizances see *Revised Statutes* (1829), 2:707, Sec. 8; 709 Sec. 21.

50. Eric Partridge, *A Dictionary of Slang and Unconventional English* (New York: Macmillan Co., 1967 ed.), 476.

51. *Messenger and Advocate* 2 (Oct. 1835): 201. See Jessee, *Papers of Joseph Smith*, 1:95.

52. Edwin Brown Firmage and Richard Collin Mangrum have written:

> Dr. Purple's account suggests that Smith was discharged. The trial [examination] record indicates Smith was found guilty but mentions no sentence. Noble's letter and Benton's article agree that Smith was condemned, but Noble suggests Smith jumped bail and left. Benton, however, suggests that the court took into account Smith's age and hoped his conduct might be reformed, and therefore "he was designedly allowed to escape." In any case, it seems no sanction was imposed, and the court did not pursue the matter any further (*Zion in the Courts: A Legal History of the Church of Jesus Christ of Latter-day Saints, 1830-1900* [Urbana: University of Illinois Press, 1988], 382n1).

See also Gordon A. Madsen, "Joseph Smith's 1826 Trial: The Legal Setting," *Brigham Young University Studies* 30 (Spring 1990): 91-108. Madsen shows no knowledge that the proceedings were a pre-trial examination.

Dale L. Morgan concluded: "From the point of view of Mormon history, it is immaterial what the finding of the court was on the technical charge of being 'a disorderly person and an impostor;' what is important is the evidence adduced, and its bearing on the life of Joseph Smith before he announced his claim to be a prophet of God" (John Phillip Walker, ed., *Dale Morgan on Early Mormonism: Correspondence and A New History* [Salt Lake City: Signature Books, 1986], 373n44).

53. Joseph Jr. himself commented in 1841 that "every man who lived on the earth was entitled to a seer stone, and should have one, but they are kept from them in consequence of their wickedness, and most of them who do find one make an evil use of it: he showed us his seer stone" ("The History of Brigham Young," *The Deseret News* 8 [10 Mar. 1858]: 3; also in *Latter-day Saints' Millennial Star* 26 [20 Feb. 1864]: 118).

After Smith's death, Brigham Young is recorded as saying that "the seer stone which Joseph Smith first obtained He got in an Iron kettle 15 feet under ground. He saw it while looking in another seers stone which a person had. He went right to the spot & dug & found it" (Scott G. Kenney, ed., *Wilford Woodruff's Journal* [Midvale, UT: Signature Books, 1984], 5: 382-83, entry of 11 Sept. 1859). See also *Historical Magazine* 7 (May 1870): 306.

On 6 May 1849 the Quorum of the Twelve discussed Joseph Smith's first seer stone and other items. According to the minutes of the meeting: "evening in conversation upon many little incidents connected with finding the

Plates, preserving them from the hand of the wicked, & returning them again to Cumorah, who did it &c, also the gift of seeing & how Joseph obtained his first seer stone. Treasures known to exist in the earth of money &, records" (quoted in Van Wagoner and Walker, "Joseph Smith: 'The Gift of Seeing,'" 68n83; see also 63, and Journal History of the Church of Jesus Christ of Latter-day Saints, 6 May 1849, LDS archives, microfilm copies at Harold B. Lee Library, Brigham Young University, Provo, Utah and Marriott Library, University of Utah, Salt Lake City).

54. *Historical Magazine* 7 (May 1870): 307.

55. Isaac Hale, *Susquehanna Register* 9 (1 May 1834): 1; Howe, *Mormonism Unvailed*, 263.

56. *Saints' Herald* 26 (1 Oct. 1879): 289. This interview was conducted by her son Joseph Smith III in February 1879.

57. Mary Audentia [Smith] Anderson, *Ancestry and Posterity of Joseph Smith and Emma Hale* (Independence, MO: Herald House, 1929), 302.

58. Alva Hale, *Susquehanna Register* 9 (1 May 1834): 1, emphasis in original; Howe, *Mormonism Unvailed*, 268.

59. Affidavit of Peter Ingersoll, Palmyra, Wayne County, New York, 2 Dec. 1833, Howe, *Mormonism Unvailed*, 234-35.

CHAPTER FIVE

THE TREASURE

By the summer of 1827, when newlyweds Joseph and Emma Smith[1] were living with Joseph's family in Manchester, New York, people began to hear from the Smith family about a treasure Joseph had found. They told the story of a book written on plates of gold which had been buried in the ground in a Manchester hill (later called the Hill Cumorah) about two miles southeast from their home. This glacial drumlin had been, according to one scholar, "the site of treasure digging both before and after Joseph Smith's receiving the golden plates."[2]

This chapter attempts to recover from available sources the earliest versions of this saga. Certainly no single account gives a complete picture of events pieced together years later. But important patterns and similarities recur among the various early accounts. In contrast to the account which was later told, the earliest versions linked the finding of the plates with the practice of searching for buried treasure. They also linked obtaining the plates with magical rituals traditionally associated with winning treasure from its guardian spirits.

Willard Chase was a neighbor and friend of the Smith family. He had known them since 1820 and later recalled that the family followed the money-digging business "until the latter part of the season of 1827." That June, Joseph Smith, Sr., told Chase a remarkable story, whose beginnings went back more than three years:

That some years ago, a spirit[3] had appeared to Joseph his son, in a vision, and informed him that in a certain place there was a record on plates of gold, and that he was the person that must obtain them, and this he must do in the following manner: On the 22d of September, he must repair to the place where was deposited this manuscript, dressed in black clothes, and riding a black horse with a switch tail, and demand the book in a certain name, and after obtaining it, he must go directly away, and neither lay it down nor look behind him.[4] They accordingly fitted out Joseph with a suit of black clothes and borrowed a black horse.

Chase reportedly was told that Smith in fact went to the stone box in which the book of gold was deposited and removed the book:

but fearing some one might discover where he got it, he laid it down to place back the top stone, as he found it; and turning round, to his surprise there was no book in sight. He again opened the box, and in it saw the book, and attempted to take it out, but was hindered. He saw in the box something like a toad, which soon assumed the appearance of a man, and struck him on the side of his head.

Smith tried to take the book again but was again struck by the spirit. On asking "why he could not obtain the plates," he was told that he had not obeyed the orders of the spirit. He was then instructed to bring his oldest brother Alvin:

come one year from this day, and bring with you your oldest brother, and you shall have them. This spirit, he said, was the spirit of the prophet who wrote this book, and who was sent to Joseph Smith, to make known these things to him. Before the expiration of the year, his oldest brother died; which the old man said was an accidental providence!

When Smith returned a year later, the spirit asked about his brother. Learning he was dead, the spirit "commanded him to come again, in just one year, and bring a man with him. On asking who might be the man, he was answered that he would know him when he saw him."

According to Chase's account, filtered through his and Joseph Sr.'s perspectives, Joseph Jr. first decided that the next year he should bring Samuel Lawrence, another treasure seeker and seer in the Manchester area:

Joseph believed that one Samuel T. Lawrence was the man alluded to by the spirit, and went with him to a singular looking hill, in Manchester, and shewed him where the treasure was. Lawrence asked him if he had ever discovered any thing with the plates of gold; he said no: he then asked him to look in his stone to see if there was any thing with them. He looked, and said there was nothing; he told him to look again, and see if there was not a large pair of specks with the plates; he looked and soon saw a pair of spectacles, the same with which Joseph says he translated the Book of Mormon.

Lawrence told him it would not be prudent to let these plates be seen for about two years, as it would make a great disturbance in the neighborhood. Not long after this, Joseph altered his mind, and said L[awrence]. was not the right man, nor had he told him the right place.[5]

One hundred miles to the south, a resident of Colesville for whom Smith worked briefly, recounted a very similar story. Joseph Knight, whose recollections were written sometime between 1835 and 1847, when Knight died, also told of the spirit requesting that Joseph bring Alvin to the hill. Knight does not mention Lawrence, but his account adds the identity of a third person Smith felt compelled by the spirit personage to take to the hill in order to obtain the treasure—his future wife Emma Hale:

From thence he [Joseph Smith] went to the hill where he was informed the Record was and found no trouble for it appear[e]d plain as tho[ugh] he was acquainted with the place it was so plain in the vision that he had of the place. He went and found the place and opened it and found a plane Box. He oncovered it and found the Book and took it out and laid [it] Down By his side and thot he would Cover the place over again thinkinking [sic] there might be something else here. But he was told to take the Book and go right away. And after he had Covered the place he turned round to take the Book and it was not there and he was astonished that the Book was gone. He thot he would look in the place again and see if it had not got Back again. He had heard people tell of such things. And he opened the Box and Behold the Book was there. He took hold of it to take it out again and Behold he Could not stur the Book any more then he Could the mountain. He exclaimed "why Cant I stur this Book?" And he was answer[e]d, "you have not Done rite; you should have took the Book and a gone right away. You cant have it now." Joseph says, "when can I have it?" The answer was the 22nt Day of September next if you Bring the right person with you. Joseph says, "who is the right Person?" The answer was "your oldest Brother."

But before September Came his oldest Brother Died. Then he was Disap[po]inted and did not [k]now what to do. But when the 22nt Day of September Came he went to the place and the personage appear[e]d and told him he Could not have it now. But the 22nt Day of September nex[t] he mite have the Book if he Brot with him the right person. Joseph says, "who is the right Person?" The answer was you will know. Then he looked in his glass and found it was Emma Hale, Daughter of old Mr Hail [Hale] of Pensylvany, a girl that he had seen Before, for he had Bin Down there Before with me.[6]

About 1830 Fayette Lapham visited the Smith family with a friend, Jacob Ramsdell, and talked with Joseph Sr. about finding the buried record. Lapham's narrative, which was published in 1870, is very similar to the versions related by Chase and Knight—including the details about bringing Alvin and then Emma to the hill in order to placate the guardian spirit:

He [Joseph] then told his father that, in his dream, a very large and tall man appeared to him, dressed in an ancient suit of clothes, and the clothes were bloody. And the man said to him that there was a valuable treasure, buried many years since, and not far from that place; and that he had now arrived for it to be brought to light, for the benefit of the world at large; and, if he would strictly follow his directions, he would direct him to the place where it was deposited, in such a manner that he could obtain it. He then said to him, that he would have to get a certain coverlid, which he described, and an old-fashioned suit of clothes, of the same color, and a napkin to put the treasure in. . . . when he had obtained it, he must not lay it down until he placed it in the napkin. . . . Joseph mounted his horse. . . . Taking up the first article, he saw the others below: laying down the first, he endeavored to secure the others; but before he could get hold of them, the one he had taken up slid back to the place he had taken it from.

Smith was struck down and fell on his back. The personage then told him that

> when the treasure was deposited there, he was sworn to take charge of and protect that property, until the time should arrive for it to be exhibited to the world of mankind; and, in order to prevent his making an improper disclosure, he was murdered or slain on the spot, and the treasure had been under his charge ever since. He said to him [Joseph] that he had not followed his directions; and, in consequence of laying the article down before putting it in the napkin, he could not have the article now; but that if he would come again one year from that time, he could have them.
>
> The year passed over before Joseph was aware of it, so the time passed by; but he went to the place of deposit, where the same man appeared again, and said he had not been punctual in following his directions, and, in consequence, he could not have the article yet. Joseph asked when he could have them; and the answer was, "Come in one year from this time, and bring your oldest brother with you; then you may have them." During that year, it so happened that his oldest brother died; but, at the end of the year, Joseph repaired to the place again, and was told by the man who still guarded the treasure, that, inasmuch as he could not bring his oldest brother, he could not have the treasure yet; but there would be another person appointed to come with him in one year from that time, when he could have it.

Smith was then told about an important person he soon would meet:

> Joseph asked, "How shall I know the person?" and was told that the person would be known to him at sight. During that year, Joseph went to the town of Harmony, in the State of Pennsylvania, at the request of some one who wanted the assistance of his divining rod and stone in finding hidden treasure, supposed to have been deposited there by the Indians or others. While there, he fell in company with a young woman; and, when he first saw her, he was satisfied that she was the person appointed to go with him to get the treasure he had so often failed to secure.[7]

In 1879 Hiel and Joseph Lewis, cousins of Emma Hale Smith, recorded their recollections. According to the brothers, Joseph had told, probably in early 1828 in Harmony, Pennsylvania, how he discovered the plates. In addition to other details, the brothers recalled the importance of their cousin Emma to Smith's narrative:

> He [Joseph] said that by a dream he was informed that at such a place in a certain hill, in an iron box, were some gold plates with curious engravings, which he must get and translate, and write a book; that the plates were to be kept concealed from every human being for a certain time, some two or three years; that he went to the place and dug till he came to the stone that covered the box, when he was knocked down; that he again attempted to remove the stone, and was again knocked down; this attempt was made the third time, and the third time he was knocked down.
>
> Then he exclaimed, "Why can't I get it?" or words to that effect; and then he saw a man standing over the spot, which to him appeared like a Spaniard, having a long beard coming down over his breast to about here, (Smith putting his hand to the pit of his stomach) with his (the ghost's) throat cut from ear to ear, and the blood streaming down, who told him that he could not get it alone; that another person whom he, Smith, would know at first sight, must come with him, and then he could get it. And when Smith saw Miss Emma Hale, he knew that she was the person, and that after they were married, she went with him to near the place, and stood with her back toward him, while he dug up the box, which he rolled up in his frock.[8]

Smith's mother, Lucy Mack Smith, added her own recollections about the gold record to her autobiography. She dates Joseph's first trip to the nearby hill just before Alvin's death in 1823 and emphasizes Alvin's place in these events. She thus indirectly suggests why Joseph may have felt the guardian spirit required Alvin's presence at the hill:

> <He vis[i]ted the place where the plates were laid and> thinking he could keep every commandment given him <supposed> that it would be possible for him to take them from their place and carry them home. But said the divine messenger you must take them into your hands and go straight to the house without delay <and put them [in] immediately and lock them up>.
>
> Accordingly when the time arrived he went to the place ap-

pointed and removed the moss and grass from the surface of the rock and then pryed up the first stone according to the directions which he had received. He then discovered the plates laying on 4 pillars in the inside of the box. He put forth his hand <and> took them up <but> when he lifted them from their place the thought flashed across his mind that there might be something more in the box that would be a benefit to him in a pecuniary point of view. In the excitement of the moment he laid the record down in order to cover up the box least some one should come along and take away whatever else might be deposited there. When he turned again to take up the record it was gone but where he knew not nor did he know by what means it was taken away. He was much alarmed at this. <He> kneeled down <&> asked the Lord why it was that the record was taken from him. The angel appeared to him and told him that he had not done as he was commanded in that he laid down the record in order to secure some imaginary treasure that remained.

After some further conversation Joseph was then permit[t]ed to raise the stone again and there he beheld the plates the same as before. He reached forth his hand to take them but was <thrown> to the ground. When he recov<ered the angel was gone and he arose and went to the house>.[9]

According to his mother, Joseph was instructed that "when you get the record take it immediately into the house and lock it up as soon as possible."[10] She adds that Alvin told Joseph that they would "have a fine long evening <and> all set down and hear you talk." Joseph told the family about the plates and asked them not to discuss what he said outside their family. She then describes how in the evenings the Smith family would meet and listen to Joseph's religious teachings. They also heard Joseph tell stories of the continent's former civilizations.[11]

Alvin, his mother remembers, was especially interested in the record. On his death bed he told Joseph, "I want you to be a good boy & do everything that lays in your power to obtain the record. Be faithful in receiving instruction and keeping every commandment that is given you."[12] According to Lucy, "Alvin had ever manifested a greater zeal and anxiety if it were possible than any of the rest with regard to the record which had been shown to Joseph and he always showed the most intense interest concerning the matter. With this before our minds we could not endure to hear or say one word upon that subject, for the moment that Joseph spoke of the record it would immediately bring Alvin to <our> minds."[13] Lucy continues, "but none were more engaged than the one whom we were doomed [to] part with, for Alvin was never so happy as when he was contemplating the final suc[c]ess of his brother in obtaining the record. And now I fancied I could hear him with his parting breath conjureing his brother to continue faithful that he might obtain the prize which the Lord had promised him."[14]

Clearly the gold plates story had been repeated outside the Smith family before September 1827, and no doubt seemed familiar to those who heard it and were acquainted with stories about the treasure-digging activities of the Smith family. A number of accounts have survived describing how Smith obtained possession of the gold plates. According to his mother's detailed account, on 20 September 1827 Joseph Knight and his friend Josiah Stowell arrived at the Smith family house.[15] Knight had heard that Joseph was to get the record on 22 September. This was why he was at the Smith home before Joseph went to get the plates,[16] and "they remained with us untill the 22."[17]

Early on the morning of the 22nd, Joseph and Emma left the Smith home "taking Mr. Knight's horse and wagon" without his knowledge to travel to the hill about two miles away.[18] When they arrived at the hill, Joseph left Emma with the wagon while he went to the side of the hill. Joseph said he then took the plates out of a box in the ground and hid them in a fallen treetop, concealing them with the bark of the tree.[19] He returned to Knight's wagon, where Emma was waiting, and they started back to the house.

Meanwhile at the Smith home, according to Lucy, "When the male part of the family sat down to breakfast Mr. Smith enquired for Joseph, <for no one but myself knew where he was> as no one knew where he had gone but myself. I told him that I thought I would not call Joseph, that I would have him set down with his wife." Lucy asked her husband to cover her son's absence—"do let him eat with his wife this morning."[20]

Joseph Knight soon discovered his "Horse and Carriage was

gone."[21] Lucy remembered that "Mr. Knight came in quite disturbed. Why, Mr. Smith, said he, my horse is gone. I can't find him on the premises and I want to start home in half an hour. Never mind the horse, said I, Mr. Knight does not know all the nooks and corners in the pasture. I will call William (this <was> my 5th son), he will soon bring him. This satisfied him for a little while but he soon made another discovery, his waggon was gone, & now he concluded that the Horse and waggon had gone together and some rogue had gone with them both." Knight evidently went out to look for them, and "while he was absent Joseph returned."[22] Knight recalled, "after a while he [Joseph] Came home and he turned out the Horse. All Come into the house to Brackfirst [breakfast]. But no thing said about where they had Bin [been]."[23]

The plates were now, according to Joseph,[24] hidden in a fallen treetop, but a better place to deposit them was needed. According to Lucy, Joseph "asked my advice what it was best to do about getting a chest." They decided to have one made but lacked the money to pay for it until

> The next day <Mr. Warner> came to him and requested <Joseph> to go with him to a widows house <in Macedon by the name of Wells>, that she wanted <a wall in a well and as she wanted some labor done>, would pay him the money for it. <He accompanied> Mr. Warner to Macedon <according to> Mrs. Wells <request. This> woman [n]one of the family had ever seen or heard of before although she sent purposely for Joseph. We considered it a provision of Providence to enable us to pay the money we were owing the cabinet maker.[25]

The story now went abroad from the Smith family that Joseph had obtained some gold plates which had been buried under the ground. Since Joseph and his father had been involved with a treasure-seeking group, his former partners wanted their share of the find. As Martin Harris explained, "The money-diggers claimed that they had as much right to the plates as Joseph had, as they were in company together. They claimed that Joseph had been [a] traitor, and had appropriated to himself that which belonged to them. For this reason Joseph was afraid of them."[26]

According to Lucy, Joseph Sr. was informed that a group of "10 or 12 men were club[b]ed together with one Willard Chase a Methodist class leader at their head," and they had sent for an unnamed conjuror "to divine the place where the record was deposited by magic art." "Accordingly," she continued, "the morning after we heard of their plans Mr. Smith went over a hill that <lay> east of <us> to see what he could discover among the neighbors there. At the first house he came to he found the conjurer, Willard Chase and the company all together. This was the house of one Mr. Laurence."[27] Joseph Knight later wrote: "I will say there [was] a man near By By the name Samuel Lawrance. He was a Seear [Seer] and had Bin [been] to the hill and knew about the things in the hill and he was trying to obtain them."[28]

While Joseph Jr. was working and living in Macedon, helping Mrs. Wells with her well, Emma took a stray horse that had been on the Smiths' premises two days (according to Lucy) and rode to Macedon. Joseph came up out of the well because he had perceived that Emma was coming to see him. She informed him that the money-diggers claimed to have located where he had hidden his golden book. Joseph looked in his peep-stone and said to Emma that the plates were safe. Joseph promised Mrs. Wells that he would come back when he could, then mounted a horse "in his linen frock" (smock or work apron), and rode back home with Emma.[29]

Joseph then walked by himself to where he had hidden the gold plates on or near the hill. Several people remember the story they heard of how he brought the plates back to the Smith house. According to Lucy's version,

> he took the plates from their [hiding] place and wrapping them in his linen frock put them under his arm and started for the house. After walking a short distance in the road, he concluded it would be safer to go across through the woods. In a moment he struck through the timber where there was a large windfall to cross. He had not proceeded far in this direction till, as he was jumping over a log, a man spran[g] up and gave him a heavy blow with a gun. Joseph <leveled> him to the ground.[30]

Smith claimed he knocked down several men as he ran home, arriving out of breath. When all the commotion settled, Smith showed those in attendance his dislocated thumb, which his father put back in place.[31] Smith then "related to our guests [Joseph Knight and Josiah Stowell] the whole history of the record."

After this Smith went to Willard Chase's house and talked with him. Chase recalled the story that Smith told him, which is similar to the accounts of Smith's mother and his friend Joseph Knight

> That on the 22d of September, he arose early in the morning, and took a one horse wagon, of some one that had stayed over night at their house, without leave or license; and, together with his wife, repaired to the hill which contained the book. He left his wife in the wagon, by the road, and went alone to the hill, a distance of thirty or forty rods from the road; he said he then took the book out of the ground and hid it in a tree top, and returned home. He then went to the town of Macedon to work. After about ten days, it having been suggested that some one got his book, his wife went after him; he hired a horse, and went home in the afternoon, staid long enough to drink one cup of tea, and then went for his book, found it safe, took off his frock, wrapt it round it, put it under his arm and run all the way home, a distance of about two miles. He said he should think it would weigh sixty pounds, and was sure it would weigh forty. On his return home, he said he was attacked by two men in the woods, and knocked them both down and made his escape, arrived safe and secured his treasure. — He then observed that if it had not been for that stone, (which he acknowledged belonged to me,) he would not have obtained the book.[32]

Martin Harris, a wealthy farmer of Palmyra who knew the Smiths as money-diggers, heard about the find. Lucy Smith said that Harris was aware of the existence of the gold plates for sometime: "here let me mention that no one knew anything of this buisness [sic] <from us> except one confidential friend of My Husband's to whom he named it some 2 or 3 years before."[33] However, Harris said he heard about the gold plates "about the first of October, 1827." He remembered that

> The first time I heard of the matter, my brother Presarved [Preserved] Harris, who had been in the village of Palmyra, asked me if [I] had heard about Joseph Smith, jr., having a golden bible. My

thoughts were that the money-diggers had probably dug up an old brass kettle, or something of the kind. I thought no more of it. This was about the first of October, 1827.

He also recalled being told by the Smith family how Joseph obtained the gold plates. (The horse and wagon which Harris remembered belonging to Stowell, as we know, belonged to Joseph Knight):

> After this, on the 22nd of September, 1827, before day, Joseph took the horse and wagon of old Mr. Stowel[l], and taking his wife, he went to the place where the plates were concealed, and while he was obtaining them, she kneeled down and prayed. He then took the plates and hid them in an old black tree top which was hollow. Mr. Stowel[l] was at this time at old Mr. Smith's, digging for money.
> . . .
> When Joseph had obtained the plates he communicated the fact to his father and mother. The plates remained concealed in the tree top until he got the chest made. He then went after them and brought them home. While on his way home with the plates, he was met by what appeared to be a man, who demanded the plates, and struck him with a club on his side, which was all black and blue. Joseph knocked the man down, and then ran for home, and was much out of breath. When he arrived home, he handed the plates in at the window, and they were received from him by his mother. They were then hidden under the hearth in his father's house. But the wall being partly down, it was feared that certain ones, who were trying to get possession of the plates, would get under the house and dig them out.

Harris recalled that the above events occurred before he talked with Joseph:

> A day or so before I was ready to visit Joseph, his mother came over to our house and wished to talk with me. I told her I had no time to spare, she might talk with my wife, and, in the evening when I had finished my work I would talk with her. When she commenced talking with me, she told me respecting his bringing home the plates, and many other things, and said that Joseph had sent her over and wished me to come and see him.

Harris "waited a day or two," had breakfast, and then "told my

folks I was going to the village, but went directly to old Mr. Smith's."
While there Harris requested Smith "to tell me the story, which he
did as follows. He said: 'An angel had appeared to him, and told him
[Joseph] it was God's work.'" According to Harris, the angel "told him
he must quit the company of the money-diggers."[34]

Harris discussed Smith's story with the Reverend John A. Clark.
Clark later recalled, "According to Martin Harris, it was after one of
these night excursions, that Jo, while he lay upon his bed, had a
remarkable dream. An angel of God seemed to approach him, clad
in celestial splendor."[35]

Almost all who heard versions of the story remembered in particular Smith's interaction with this messenger or spirit associated
with the gold records. Abigail Harris remembered a visit by Smith's
parents, "They told me that the report that Joseph, jun. had found
golden plates, was true, and that he was in Harmony, Pa. translating
them—that such plates were in existence, and that Joseph, jun. was to
obtain them, was revealed to him by the spirit of one of the Saints
that was on this continent, previous to its being discovered by Colum-
bus."[36]

Henry Harris heard about the gold plates from Joseph Smith and
remembered Smith's interaction with an angel and his use of the seer
stone:

> After he pretended to have found the gold plates, I had a conversa-
> tion with him, and asked him where he found them and how he
> come [sic] to know where they were. He said he had a revelation
> from God that told him they were hid in a certain hill and he looked
> in his stone and saw them in the place of deposit; that an angel
> appeared, and told him he could not get the plates until he was
> married, and that when he saw the woman that was to be his wife,
> he should know her, and she would know him.[37]

Benjamin Saunders, who was thirteen years old at the time,
remembered hearing the story at his home:

> I heard <Joe> tell my Mother and Sister how he procured the plates.
> He said he was directed by an angel where it was. He went in the
> night to get the plates. When he took the plates there was something
> down near the box that looked some like a toad that rose up into a

man which forbid him to take the plates. He found a big pair of spectacles <also with the plates>. As he went home some one tried to get the plates away from him. He said he knock[ed] the man down and got away. Had two or three skirmishes on the way. I saw his hand all swel[l]ed up and he said it was done in hitting the enemy.[38]

During the time Smith reportedly had the gold plates in Manchester, they were said to have been hidden in several places. Several accounts have survived which detail the help of Alvah Beeman. Lucy Smith remembered that Beeman "came from the village <of Livonia>, a man in whom we reposed much confidence. . . . it was resolved that a portion of the hearth should be taken up and the plates buried under the same." This was just before a "large company of men came rushing up to the house armed with guns" looking for the gold plates.[39] Martin Harris mentioned "old Mr. Beman" as one of the treasure seekers who had been "digging for money supposed to have been hidden by the ancients."[40] The gold plates were eventually "put into an old Ontario glass-box." Martin Harris said, "Old Mr. Beman sawed off the ends, making the box the right length to put them in, and when they went in he said he heard them jink [clink], but he was not permitted to see them. He told me so."[41]

Beeman's daughter Mary related what she heard about her father and the gold plates:

> Father became acquainted with Father Joseph Smith, the Father of the Prophet, he frequently would go to Palmira to see Father Smiths and his family, during this time Brother Joseph Smith came in possession of the plates which contained the Book of Mormon. Soon as it was noised around that there was a golden Bible found (for that was what it was called at that time) the minds of the people became so excited and it arose at such a pitch that a mob collected together to search the house of Father Smith to find the records. My Father was there at the time and assisted in concealing the plates in a box in a secluded place where no one could find them.[42]

After being hidden under the hearth, they reportedly were placed in the Smith's cooper's shop.[43] Finally the plates were "nailed up in a box and the box put into a strong cask made for the purpose, the cask was then filled with beans and headed up."[44] The barrel-making skills of the Smiths may have been useful here.

Fearing the hostile money-diggers around Manchester, Emma's family allowed her and her husband to move back home to Harmony, Pennsylvania. Her brother Alva helped transport the couple and their barrel of beans to the Hale property where Joseph started dictating the text of his book. In 1829, after the dictation was completed and the type was being set, Smith wrote a letter from Harmony to Oliver Cowdery about their stay in southern New York and Pennsylvania: "the people are all friendly to <us> except a few who are in opposition to ev[e]ry thing unless it is some thing that is exactly like themselves and two of our most formadable persacutors are now under censure and are cited to a tryal [trial] in the church for crimes which if true are worse than all the Gold Book business."[45]

Emma's father Isaac later remembered his daughter's and son-in-law's stay at his home:

> I was informed they had brought a wonderful book of Plates down with them. I was shown a box in which it is said they were contained, which had, to all appearances, been used as a glass box of the common sized window-glass. I was allowed to feel the weight of the box, and they gave me to understand, that the book of plates was then in the box—into which, however, I was not allowed to look.[46]

In the spring of 1828 Martin Harris arrived at Harmony to assist Smith as a scribe during the process of translating. Surviving accounts of the translation process suggest that Smith worked without directly using the plates—this despite all of the difficulty in obtaining, hiding, and bringing the plates along. When it came to translating the crucial plates, they were no more present in the room than was John the Beloved's ancient "parchment," the words of which Joseph also dictated at the time.[47] The accounts emphasize Smith's continued use of a seer stone.[48]

Isaac Hale's summary of the process suggests his incredulity: "The manner in which he [Joseph] pretended to read and interpret, was the same as when he looked for the money-diggers, with the stone in his hat, and his hat over his face, while the Book of Plates were at the same time hid in the woods!"[49] David Whitmer of Fayette, New

York, an early disciple of Joseph Smith who became acquainted with him in 1829 while the book was still being dictated, recalled in 1881: "He [Joseph] did not use the plates in the translation, but would hold the interpreters to his eyes and cover his face with a hat, excluding all light, and before his eyes would appear what seemed to be parchment" on which he would see the characters on the plates and the translation. Joseph would then read the words that he saw to his scribe.[50] In an 1885 interview, Whitmer said that Joseph used a seer stone "placed in a hat into which he buried his face, stating to me and others that the original Character[s] appeared upon parchment and under it the translation in english which [enabled him] to read it readily."[51]

It is not clear from the early accounts whether Smith used a single seer stone or, as in one tradition, a pair of stones or spectacles. In Smith's 1832 account he mentions there were spectacles "to read the Book."[52] Joseph Knight, who visited Smith in Harmony, wrote,

> Now the way he translated was he put the urim and thummim into his hat and Darkned his Eyes then he would take a sentance and it would appe[a]r in Brite Roman Letters. Then he would tell the writer and he would write it. Then that would go away [and] the next sentance would Come and so on. But if it was not Spelt rite it would not go away till it was rite, so we see it was marvelous. Thus was the hol [whole] translated.[53]

The biblical term "Urim and Thummim" in Knight's account seems to be a later term used to apply to the seer stone. Lucy Smith remarked, "Joseph kept the urim and thum[m]im constantly about his person," even having it with him while he was working down in a well.[54] It was by the "Urim and Thummim," according to Lucy, that Joseph received a commandment that he should baptize Oliver Cowdery and that Cowdery should baptize him.[55] At one time an intimation "was given through the urim and thum[m]im" as Joseph "one morning applied the latter to his eyes to look upon the record, instead of the words of the book [of Mormon] being given him, he was commanded to write a letter to one David Whitmore [Whitmer]."[56]

Accounts also differ about what supposedly happened to the

gold plates.[57] David Whitmer told an interviewer in 1884 that the plates "were taken away by the angel to a cave, which we saw by the power of God while we were yet in the Spirit."[58] William Smith said in 1841 that Joseph "was directed by a vision to bury the plates again in the same manner; which he accordingly did."[59] Brigham Young, who joined the Mormon church in 1832, spoke of Joseph Smith and Oliver Cowdery going to the Hill Cumorah and "the hill opened, and they walked into a cave." Orson Pratt referred to "the grand repository of all the numerous records of the ancient nations of the western continent," which "was located in another department of the hill."[60]

Taken together, these earliest accounts about the gold plates place the event within the larger context of buried treasure hunting. Smith reported that he obtained the gold plates from the ground where they had been hidden for 1,400 years. Like his earlier attempts to locate lost objects and valuable treasures in the earth, he located the plates by looking in the stone.[61] He removed his find from its depository and laid it down. After laying it down, however, it suddenly disappeared and went back into the box. This is similar to another treasure dig he participated in, with the guardian standing by and protecting the item.

The guardian spirit is a consistent focus of these earliest stories. Whether the guardian of the plates was spirit or angel, its purpose was to watch over the buried box and its contents. Smith went to great lengths to obey the spirit's commands. He wore special clothes. He was given a simple command not to lay the plates down. When he did, the spirit struck him and kept him from obtaining the treasure. Because he did not do as he was instructed, Joseph was told to come in another year and bring his brother Alvin with him. Later he looked into the stone and learned he was to bring Emma Hale.

Many aspects of the story told in New York and Pennsylvania were later revised, especially details which linked the gold plates and treasure hunting.[62] In the 1832 retelling of the gold plates story, Smith was not given elaborate tasks to break the spell but was simply informed by the angel that in "due time thou shalt obtain them."[63] By the time of Smith's 1838-39 account, he was instructed from the very start that there would be a four-year waiting period: "I made an attempt to take them out but was forbidden by the messenger and was again informed that the time <for> bringing them forth had not yet arrived, neither would untill four years from that time."[64]

NOTES

1. Joseph Knight wrote that Joseph Smith "looked in his glass and found it was Emma Hale" who was the right person to bring to the hill to obtain the book (manuscript in archives, historical department, Church of Jesus Christ of Latter-day Saints, Salt Lake City, Utah (hereafter LDS archives); see Dean C. Jessee, ed., "Joseph Knight's Recollection of Early Mormon History," *Brigham Young University Studies* 17 [Autumn 1976]: 31; Jessee added minimal punctuation and editing to facilitate reading).

Smith told Henry Harris "that an angel appeared, and told him he could not get the plates until he was married" (E. D. Howe, *Mormonism Unvailed* [Painesville (OH): Printed and Published by the Author, 1834], 252). William R. Hine said, "Jo told Emma he had a revelation about the plates, but that he could not obtain them until he had married her" (*Naked Truths About Mormonism* 1 [Jan. 1888]: 2, original in the Yale University Library; see also Fayette Lapham, *Historical Magazine* 7 [May 1870]: 307; and Joseph and Hiel Lewis, *The Amboy Journal* 24 [30 Apr. 1879]: 1).

2. Ronald W. Walker, "The Persisting Idea of American Treasure Hunting," *Brigham Young University Studies* 24 (Fall 1984): 435.

3. Smith evidently did not give the messenger a name while he was in New York. In his 1838-39 history he mentioned that the personage who appeared to him stated "his name was Nephi" (Manuscript History, Book A-1: 5; also in duplicate Book A-2: 6, both in LDS archives). In other sources the person who buried the gold plates and appeared to Smith is named "Moroni," son of Mormon. In the manuscript history above the name "Nephi" has been added the name "Moroni" with a footnote added after Smith's death giving three references where the name was published as "Moroni" (*Messenger and Advocate* 1 [Apr. 1835]: 112; 1835 D&C 50:2 [p. 180], name added to the 1830 text in 1835 [see LDS D&C 27:5 and RLDS D&C 26:2a]; *Elders' Journal* 1 [July 1838]: 42-43, Far West, Missouri; Andrew F. Ehat and Lyndon W. Cook, eds., *The Words of Joseph Smith: The Contemporary Accounts of the Nauvoo Discourses of the Prophet Joseph* [Provo, UT: Religious Studies Center, 1980], 13).

Some historians consider this reference to "Nephi" as a scribal error:

The contradictions in regard to the name of the angelic messenger who appeared to Joseph Smith occurred probably through the mistakes of clerks in making or copying documents, and, we think, should be corrected, and the corrections be published for general information, at as early a date as may be found convenient. From careful research we are fully convinced that Moroni is the correct name. This also was the decision of the former historian, George A. Smith (Orson Pratt, Sr., and Joseph F. Smith to John Taylor, 18 Dec. 1877, 4-5, LDS archives).

4. It is noteworthy that no scriptural passages were cited in Smith's 1832 account of the messenger's visit, unlike his later account. In Oliver Cowdery's description published in the 1835 *Messenger and Advocate*, the angel quoted many biblical verses. In Smith's 1838-39 narrative history, passages of scripture appear but are revised with new emphasis.

5. Affidavit of Willard Chase, Manchester, Ontario County, New York, 11 Dec. 1833, in Howe, *Mormonism Unvailed*, 240, 242-43.

6. Jessee, "Joseph Knight's Recollection," 30-31. Joseph Knight, Jr., recalled the following: "I think it was in November [1826] he [Smith] made known to my Father and I, that he had seen a vision, that a personage had appeared to him and told him where there was a gold book of ancient date buried and if he would follow the directions of the Angel he would get it. We were told it in secret. I being the youngest son, my two elder brothers [Nahum and Newel] did not believe in such things. my Father and I believed what he told us" ("Joseph Knight's incidents of History from 1827 to 1844," comp. Thomas Bullock, from loose sheets in Joseph Knight Jr.'s possession, 16 Aug. 1862, LDS archives, as cited in *They Are My Friends: A History of the Joseph Knight Family, 1825-1850* [Provo, UT: Grandin Book Co., l986], 214).

7. *Historical Magazine* 7 (May 1870): 306-307.

8. *The Amboy Journal* 24 (30 Apr. 1879): 1.

9. Lucy Mack Smith, Preliminary Manuscript (MS), "History of Lucy Smith," 50-51, LDS archives (page numbering corresponds with a typed transcript in LDS archives and with the page numbers in the photocopy of the manuscript); Lucy Mack Smith, *Biographical Sketches of Joseph Smith the Prophet, and His Progenitors for Many Generations* (Liverpool: Published for Orson Pratt by S. W. Richards, 1853), 85-86, hereafter *Biographical Sketches*; Lucy Mack Smith, *History of Joseph Smith By His Mother, Lucy Mack Smith* (Salt Lake City: Bookcraft, 1958), 83-84, hereafter *History of Joseph Smith*.

William Smith remembered that Joseph had told the family concerning his first attempt to receive the plates:

When he went to get the plates he found them as he was told he should. He took them from the stone box in which they were found, and placed them on the ground behind him, when the thought came into his mind that there might be a treasure hidden with them. While stooping forward to see, he was overpowered, so that he could not look farther. Turning to get the plates, he found they had gone; and on looking around found that they were in the box again; but he could not get them (*Saints' Herald* 31 [4 Oct. 1884]: 643).

10. Lucy Mack Smith, Preliminary MS, 47; not in *Biographical Sketches* or *History of Joseph Smith*.

11. Lucy Mack Smith, Preliminary MS, 47-50; *Biographical Sketches* (1853), 83-85; *History of Joseph Smith* (1958), 81-83.

12. Lucy Mack Smith, Preliminary MS, 52; *Biographical Sketches* (1853), 88; *History of Joseph Smith* (1958), 87.

13. Lucy Mack Smith, Preliminary MS, 55; *Biographical Sketches* (1853), 89-90; *History of Joseph Smith* (1958), 89.

14. Lucy Mack Smith, Preliminary MS, 115; not in *Biographical Sketches* or *History of Joseph Smith*.

15. Lucy Mack Smith, Preliminary MS, 66; *Biographical Sketches* (1853), 99; *History of Joseph Smith* (1958), 102; and Jessee, "Joseph Knight's Recollection," 32. Martin Harris said that Josiah Stowell "was at this time at old Mr. Smith's digging for money" (*Tiffany's Monthly* 5 [Aug. 1859]: 165). According to Knight, it was Stowell who took Joseph and his new wife to Manchester after their marriage (Jessee, "Joseph Knight's Recollection," 32).

16. Joseph Knight wrote that "He [Joseph] had talked with me and told me the Conversation he had with the personage which told him if he would Do right according to the will of God he mite obtain [the plates] the 22nt Day of Septem[b]er Next and if not he never would have them" (Jessee, "Joseph Knight's Recollection," 32).

17. Lucy Mack Smith, Preliminary MS, 66; *Biographical Sketches* (1853), 99; *History of Joseph Smith* (1958), 102. Lucy's narration later has Joseph Knight and Josiah Stowell still at their home after Joseph locked up the plates in a chest. Knight wrote, "I went to Rochester on Buisness [sic] and return[e]d By Palmyra to be there about the 22nt of September. I was there several Days" (Jessee, "Joseph Knight's Recollection," 32).

18. Lucy Mack Smith, Preliminary MS, 66; *Biographical Sketches* (1853), 100; *History of Joseph Smith* (1958), 102.

19. Here we follow Martin Harris (*Tiffany's Monthly* 5 [Aug. 1859]: 165) and Willard Chase (*Mormonism Unvailed*, 216) that the hiding place was in a fallen tree top. As to the type of tree, Lucy Smith said that Joseph hid the plates "in a cavity in a birch log" (Preliminary MS, 72), and Martin Harris

mentioned that they were hidden "in an old black oak tree top" (*Tiffany's Monthly* 5 [Aug. 1859]: 165, see also 166).

20. Lucy Mack Smith, Preliminary MS, 66-67; *Biographical Sketches* (1853), 100; *History of Joseph Smith* (1958), 103.

21. Jessee, "Joseph Knight's Recollection," 33.

22. Lucy Mack Smith, Preliminary MS, 67; *Biographical Sketches* (1853), 100-101; *History of Joseph Smith* (1958), 103.

23. Jessee, "Joseph Knight's Recollection," 33.

24. Affidavit of Willard Chase, in Howe, *Mormonism Unvailed*, 246. Joseph Sr. asked Emma "if she knew aught of the record, whether Joseph had taken them out or where they were. She said She did not know" (Lucy Mack Smith Preliminary MS, 69-70; *Biographical Sketches* [1853], 103; *History of Joseph Smith* [1958], 106).

25. Lucy Mack Smith, Preliminary MS, 68; *Biographical Sketches* (1853), 101; *History of Joseph Smith* (1958), 104. Lucy stated, "there was not a shilling in the house."

26. *Tiffany's Monthly* 5 (Aug. 1859): 167. David Whitmer in a newspaper interview said: "I had conversations with several young men who said that Joseph Smith had certainly golden plates, and that before he attained them he had promised to share with them, but had not done so, and they were very much incensed with him" (*Kansas City Daily Journal*, 5 June 1881; reprinted in the *Deseret Evening News*, 11 June 1881; *Saints' Herald*, 28 [1 July 1881]: 197; and *Latter-day Saints' Millennial Star* 43 [4 July 1881]: 422). See also Milton V. Backman, Jr., *Eyewitness Accounts of the Restoration* (Orem, UT: Grandin Book, 1983), 230, and Lyndon W. Cook, ed., *David Whitmer Interviews: A Restoration Witness* (Orem, UT: Grandin Book, 1991), 60.

27. Lucy Mack Smith, Preliminary MS, 68-69; *Biographical Sketches* (1853), 102; *History of Joseph Smith* (1958), 105.

28. Jessee, "Joseph Knight's Recollection," 32. Exactly when Joseph Sr. went to the Lawrence home is not known. Lucy has the visit after Joseph recovered the plates, and this is the account followed in our reconstruction. Knight has the visit to the Lawrence home occurring the night of 21 September. He wrote, "Now Joseph was some affraid of him [Samuel Lawrence] that he mite [might] be a trouble to him. He therefore sint [sent] his father up to Sams, as he Called him, near night to see if there was any signs of his going away that night" (Jessee, "Joseph Knight's Recollection," 32-33). This would make sense if the group meeting at the Lawrence home knew about the 22 September date.

29. Lucy Mack Smith, Preliminary Ms, 70-71; *Biographical Sketches* (1853), 104; *History of Joseph Smith* (1958), 107. Lucy makes a point that the stray horse

had "a large hickory withe around his neck as it was ac[c]ording to law to put a withe round the neck of a stray horse before turning him into an inclosure."

30. Lucy Mack Smith, Preliminary MS, 72; *Biographical Sketches* (1853), 104-105; *History of Joseph Smith* (1958), 108. This is the only account that mentions a gun. Martin Harris understood that he was struck by a club (*Tiffany's Monthly* 5 [Aug. 1859]: 166).

31. Lucy Mack Smith, Preliminary MS, 73; *Biographical Sketches* (1853), 106; *History of Joseph Smith* (1958), 109. The story at this point is taken from Lucy Smith's account. Benjamin Saunders said, "I saw his hand all swel[l]ed up" (Benjamin Saunders interview, 1884, in the W. H. Kelley Collection, "Miscellany 1795-1948," 23, Library-Archives, Reorganized Church of Jesus Christ of Latter Day Saints, Independence, Missouri, hereafter RLDS archives). During the scuffles Smith was struck on his side (*Tiffany's Monthly* 5 [Aug. 1859]: 166; *The Reflector* 2 [14 Feb. 1831]: 101, Palmyra, New York; *Historical Magazine* 7 [May 1870]: 307).

Orson Pratt wrote in 1840 concerning this part of the story:

> And after having obtained those sacred things, while proceeding home through the wilderness and fields, he was waylaid by two ruffians, who had secreted themselves for the purpose of robbing him of the records. One of them struck him with a club before he perceived them; but being a strong man, and large in stature, with great exertion he cleared himself from them, and ran towards home, being closely pursued until he came near his father's house (Dean C. Jessee, ed., *The Papers of Joseph Smith* [Salt Lake City: Deseret Book, 1989], 1:400).

Orson Hyde further stated when he published his German pamphlet in 1842, "on one occasion he [Joseph] was beaten by two men with clubs so violently, that he still bears the scars on his body to this day" (ibid., 1:425). In 1844 it was reported that "*Joseph Smith was knocked down with a handspike,* and afterwards healed *almost instantly*" (*Times and Seasons* 5 [2 Sept. 1844]: 635, emphasis in original).

Josiah Stowell was still at the Smith home at the end of September. Martha L. Campbell wrote, referring to Stowell, "If I understood him right he was the first person that took the plates out of your hands the morning you brought them in" (letter dated 19 Dec. 1843, LDS archives; see Larry C. Porter, "A Study of the Origins of the Church of Jesus Christ of Latter-day Saints in the States of New York and Pennsylvania, 1816-1831," Ph.D. diss., Aug. 1971, Brigham Young University, 365).

32. Affidavit of Willard Chase, in Howe, *Mormonism Unvailed,* 245-46.

33. Lucy Mack Smith, Preliminary MS, 68; *Biographical Sketches* (1853), 102; *History of Joseph Smith* (1958), 104-105. Lucy further stated, "The reader will notice, that on a preceeding page I spoke of a confidential friend to whom Mr. Smith [Joseph Sr.] mentioned the existence of the record 2 or 3 years before it came forth. This was no other than Martin Harris" (Preliminary MS, 76; *Biographical Sketches* [1853], 109; *History of Joseph Smith* [1958], 114).

Norton Jacob heard Lucy speak in Nauvoo, Illinois: "mother Smith, Joseph's mother, addressed the congregation about an hour, speaking of the history of herself and family in bringing forth the Book of Mormon. She said it was eighteen years ago last Monday since she commenced preaching the gospel being called upon by Joseph to go and tell Martin Harris and family that he had got the plates and he wanted him to take an alphabet of the characters and carry them to the learned men to decypher" ("The Life of Norton Jacob," 8 Oct. 1845, typescript, 15, Utah State Historical Society, Salt Lake City). See *Times and Seasons* 6 (1 Nov. 1845): 1,013-14; B. H. Roberts, ed., *History of the Church of Jesus Christ of Latter-day Saints* (Salt Lake City: Deseret Book, 1959), 7:470-72; and "Lucy Mack Smith Speaks to the Nauvoo Saints," *Brigham Young University Studies* 32 (Winter/Spring 1992): 279.

Martin Harris mentioned that he knew members of the Smith family as treasure seekers and that he (Harris) "had a revelation the summer before, that God had a work for me to do" (*Tiffany's Monthly* 5 [Aug. 1859]: 163).

34. *Tiffany's Monthly* 5 (Aug. 1859): 164-69. In 1829, after the text of the Book of Mormon had been written, Martin Harris traveled to Rochester, New York, to try to obtain a printer and binder. *The Gem*, a newspaper in Rochester, published the following account of Harris and the story that he told.

A man by the name of Martin Harris, was in this village a few days since endeavouring to make a contract for printing a large quantity of a work called the Golden Bible. He gave something like the following account of it. "In the autumn of 1827 a man named Joseph Smith of Manchester, in Ontario County, said that he had been visited by the spirit of the Almighty in a dream, and informed that in a certain hill in that town, was deposited a Golden Bible, containing an ancient record of divine origin. He states that after a third visit from the same spirit in a dream, he proceeded to the spot, removed earth, and there found the Bible, together with a large pair of spectacles. He had also been directed to let no mortal see them under the penalty of immediate death, which injunction he steadfastly adheres to. The treasure consisted of a number of gold plates, about 8 inches long, 6 wide, and one eighth of an inch thick, on which were engraved hieroglyphics. By placing the spectacles in a hat and looking into it, Smith interprets the characters into the English language" (*The Gem, of Literature and Science* 1 [5 Sept. 1829]: 70; for a similar account see the *Rochester Daily Advertiser and Telegraph* 3 [31 Aug. 1829], which reprinted the article from the *Palmyra Freeman*, about Aug. 1829).

35. *The Episcopal Recorder* 18 (5 Sept. 1840), Philadelphia, Pennsylvania, letter dated 24 Aug. 1840; cf. *Gleanings by the Way* (Philadelphia: W. J. & J. K. Simon; New York: Robert Carter, 1842), 225; Milton V. Backman, Jr., *Eyewitness Accounts of the Restoration*, 211. Oliver Cowdery wrote to William W. Phelps that Joseph had previously been acquainted with the place where the record was deposited (*Messenger and Advocate* 1 [Feb. 1835]: 80, Kirtland, Ohio).

36. Statement of Abigail Harris, 28 Nov. 1833, in Howe, *Mormonism Unvailed*, 253.

37. Statement of Henry Harris, in Howe, *Mormonism Unvailed*, 252.

38. Benjamin Saunders interview (1884), 22-24, RLDS archives.

39. Lucy Mack Smith, Preliminary MS, 74-75; *Biographical Sketches* (1853), 108; *History of Joseph Smith* (1958), 112.

40. *Tiffany's Monthly* 5 (Aug. 1859): 164. Alvah (or Alva) Beeman (also spelled Beman and Beaman) was born on 22 May 1775. Joseph Knight wrote, "Beeman took out his [divining] Rods and hild [held] them up and they pointed Dow[n] to the h[e]arth whare they ware hid. 'There,' says Beeman, 'it is under that h[e]arth'" (Jessee, "Joseph Knight's Recollection," 34). Since Lucy Smith and Mary A. Noble said that Alvah Beeman helped hide the plates in the hearth, perhaps he was just demonstrating the power of his rods.

41. *Tiffany's Monthly* 5 (Aug. 1859), 167. Joseph B. Noble (son-in-law of Alvah Beeman) wrote that Beeman "was permit[t]ed to handle the Plates with a thin cloth covering over them" (Journal of Joseph B. Noble, LDS archives).

42. Journal of Mary Adeline Beeman Noble, written after Sept. 1834, LDS archives.

43. Lucy Mack Smith, Preliminary MS, 75; *Biographical Sketches* (1853), 108; *History of Joseph Smith* (1958), 113.

44. Lucy Mack Smith, Preliminary MS, 79; *Biographical Sketches* (1853), 113; *History of Joseph Smith* (1958), 118. Also Martin Harris in *Tiffany's Monthly* 5 (Aug. 1859): 170. Orson Pratt wrote in 1840 that the plates were put "into a barrel of beans" (Jessee, *Papers of Joseph Smith*, 1:401).

45. Copy of letter of Joseph Smith to Oliver Cowdery, 22 Oct. 1829, transcribed in 1832 into Joseph Smith's Letterbook 1, 9, LDS archives; Dean C. Jessee, comp., *The Personal Writings of Joseph Smith* (Salt Lake City: Deseret Book Co., 1984), 227.

46. Affidavit of Isaac Hale, 20 Mar. 1834, in *The Susquehanna Register, and Northern Pennsylvanian* 9 (1 May 1834): 1; reprinted in Howe, *Mormonism Unvailed*, 264.

47. BC 6 (Apr. 1829); LDS and RLDS D&C 7. A relatively recent study observes:

> The plates could not have been used directly in the translation process. The Prophet, his face in a hat to exclude exterior light, would have been unable to view the plates directly even if they had been present during transcription. A mental picture of the young Joseph, face buried in a hat, gazing into a seer stone, plates out of sight, has not been a generally held view since the early days of the Church. The view raises some difficult questions. Why, for example, was such great care taken to preserve the plates for thousands of years if they were not to be used directly in the translation process? (Richard Van Wagoner and Steven Walker, "Joseph Smith: 'The Gift of Seeing,'" *Dialogue: A Journal of Mormon Thought* 15 [Summer 1982]: 53).

48. On the method that the Book of Mormon was said to have been translated, see, under various titles, James E. Lancaster in *Saints' Herald* 109 (15 Nov. 1962): 798-802, 806, 817; reprinted in *John Whitmer Historical Association Journal* 3 (1983): 51-61; *Restoration Studies III* (Independence, MO: Herald Publishing House, 1986), 220-31; and Dan Vogel, ed., *The Word of God: Essays on Mormon Scripture* (Salt Lake City: Signature Books, 1990), 97-112. James Lancaster wrote, "An examination of the eyewitness testimony produces the following consensus on the method of translation of the Book of Mormon: . . . the plates were not used in the translating process and often were not even in sight during the translation" (*Restoration Studies III*, 226).

49. *Susquehanna Register* 9 (1 May 1834): 1; reprinted in Howe, *Mormonism Unvailed*, 265.

50. *Kansas City Daily Journal* (5 June 1881), 1; reprinted in the *Deseret Evening News*, 11 June 1881; *Saints' Herald* 28 (1 July 1881): 198; *Latter-day Saints' Millennial Star* 43 (4 July 1881): 423; and Cook, *David Whitmer Interviews*, 62.

51. Interview of David Whitmer by Zenas H. Gurley, Jr., 14 Jan. 1885, typescript, LDS archives. The bracketed words "enabled him" came from

Autumn Leaves 5 (1892): 453, Lamoni, Iowa. See also Cook, *David Whitmer Interviews*, 157-58.

52. Jessee, *Papers of Joseph Smith*, 1:9.

53. Jessee, "Joseph Knight's Recollection," 35. Regarding the Urim and Thummim, see Kenneth Sowers, Jr., "The Mystery and History of the Urim and Thummim," *Restoration Studies II* (Independence, MO: Herald Publishing House, 1983), 75-79. Concerning the seer stone in a hat, see J. L. Traughber, Jr., "Testimony of David Whitmer," *Saints' Herald* 26 (15 Nov. 1879): 341; and David Whitmer, *An Address to All Believers in Christ* (Richmond, MO: author, 1887), 12, 30, 37.

54. Lucy Mack Smith, Preliminary MS, 71; *Biographical Sketches* (1853), 103; *History of Joseph Smith* (1958), 107.

55. Lucy Mack Smith, Preliminary MS, 101; *Biographical Sketches* (1853), 131; *History of Joseph Smith* (1958), 142. See also BC 15:6-7; LDS D&C 18:7; RLDS D&C 16:2b.

56. Lucy Mack Smith, Preliminary MS, 105; *Biographical Sketches* (1853), 135; *History of Joseph Smith* (1958), 147.

57. Folklore has it that Joseph returned the gold plates into a cave in the Hill Cumorah in Manchester, New York. For a collection of these stories, see Paul Thomas Smith, "A Preliminary Draft of the Hill Cumorah Cave Story Utilizing Seven Secondary Accounts and Other Historical Witnesses," Mar. 1980, privately circulated.

58. Interview of David Whitmer by Edmund C. Briggs, in *Saints' Herald* 31 (21 June 1884): 396.

59. William Smith interview, *The Congregational Observer* 2 (3 July 1841): 1.

60. Brigham Young in *Journal of Discourses* 19:38, 17 June 1877; quoted in *The Contributor* 3 (Feb. 1882): 137; *The Juvenile Instructor* 31 (1 Sept. 1896): 514; and Daniel H. Ludlow, ed., *Encyclopedia of Mormonism: The History, Scripture, Doctrine, and Procedure of the Church of Jesus Christ of Latter-day Saints* (New York: Macmillan Publishing Co., 1992), 3:1,427-28. Young remembered that "Joseph Smith said that Cave Contained tons of Choice Treasures & records" (Scott G. Kenney, ed., *Wilford Woodruff's Journals* [Salt Lake City: Signature Books, 1984], 6:509, entry of 11 Dec. 1869). Orson Pratt's comments are in the *Latter-day Saints' Millennial Star* 28 (7 July 1866): 417.

61. Interview of Martin Harris, *Tiffany's Monthly* 5 (Aug. 1859): 163, 169.

62. Rodger I. Anderson commented on why such details were omitted from Smith's historical accounts:

His earlier story of the mobile plates which vanished and reappeared so mysteriously was not mentioned because of its similarity to the elusive treasures he was accused of hunting; the spirit's command to bring Alvin to the hill and after Alvin's death, Emma, was deleted because it smacked more of ritualistic magic than religion "pure and undefiled"; and Joseph Knight's recollection that Smith had "looked in his glass" to find the right person was discarded because of its resemblance to the glass looking charge he had been convicted of in 1826. Smith had learned from bitter experience that not all regarded such activities as divine ("Joseph Smith's Early Reputation Revisited," *Journal of Pastoral Practice* 4 [1980]: 98; see also Rodger I. Anderson, *Joseph Smith's New York Reputation Reexamined* [Salt Lake City: Signature Books, 1990], 47).

63. Jessee, *Papers of Joseph Smith*, 1:8.

64. Manuscript History, Book A-1:7, LDS archives; JS-H 1:53, PGP; Jessee, *Papers of Joseph Smith*, 1:281.

CHAPTER SIX

SMITH FAMILY ACTIVITIES

After the Smith family joined Joseph Sr. in Palmyra village, New York, they first lived on Main Street. Pomeroy Tucker, who was personally acquainted with the Smith family at this period, recalled:

> At Palmyra, Mr. Smith, Sr., opened a "cake and beer shop," as described by his signboard, doing business on a small scale, by the profits of which, added to the earnings of an occasional day's work on hire by himself and his elder sons, for the village and farming people, he was understood to secure a scanty but honest living for himself and family. . . . Mr. Smith's shop merchandise consist[ed] of gingerbread, pies, boiled eggs, root-beer.[1]

Pomeroy Tucker described the family's Manchester cabin as "a small, one-story, smoky log-house, which they had built prior to removing there. This house was divided into two rooms, on the ground-floor, and had a low garret, in two apartments. A bedroom wing, built of sawed slabs, was afterwards added."[2]

Tucker also recalled the family's economic activities during this period:

> The chief application of the useful industry of the Smiths during their residence upon this farm-lot, was in the chopping and retailing of cord-wood, the raising and bartering of small crops of agricultural products and garden vegetables, the manufacture and sale of black-ash baskets and birch brooms, the making of maple sugar and molasses in the season for that work, and in the contin-

117

ued business of peddling cake and beer in the village on days of public doings.[3]

The male members of the Smith family hired out to others in the community. John H. Gilbert, a resident of Palmyra, recalled "Hyrum Smith was a common laborer, and worked for any one as he was called on."[4] Orsamus Turner remembered young Joseph bringing "little jags of wood" to the village and obtained an odd job at Seymour Scovell's store.[5]

Coopering or making barrels, the essential containers for all sorts of goods and commodities at the time, was a Smith family trade. Asael Smith, the grandfather, was a cooper.[6] Mrs. Anderick recalled that Joseph Sr. and his son Hyrum "worked some at coopering."[7] Besides making barrels, they also made related items such as slipwood chairs, baskets, and birch brooms.

Christopher M. Stafford remembered, "Old Jo claimed to be a Cooper but worked very little at anything. He was intemperate. Hyrum worked at cooperage. . . . I exchanged work with Jo but more with his brother Harrison, who was a good, industrious boy."[8] Other neighbors agreed that Samuel Harrison was an asset to the family. "Harrison was a good worker for one day or a month," said Hyram Jackaway.[9]

Benjamin Saunders, another neighbor living near the Smiths, remembered them as "good workers by days work. They were coopers by trade. Did not like to make steady business of it. <They were> Big hearty fellows. Their morals were good. The old man sometimes would drink until he felt quite happy at our log rollings and raisings: but he was not quarrelsome. He was not a bad man."[10] Isaac Butts mentioned that old Joseph "taught me to mow. I worked with old and young Jo at farming."[11]

According to his mother, Alvin Smith was the one who took charge of acquiring materials and beginning construction of a frame house for the family. However, after the house was raised, Alvin became sick. Because their own doctor was away, they called a doctor from the next town who over Alvin's objection gave him a large dose of calomel (mercurous chloride), a toxic compound used as a digestive remedy. The calomel had to be followed by a powerful purgative for removing it promptly from the body. When this did not work, Alvin realized he was dying. On his death bed he called Hyrum to his side and told him, as Lucy later recalled, "I must die and now I want to say a few things to you that you must remember. I have done all that I could to make our dear Parents comfortable. I now want you to go on and finish the House, take care <of> them in their old age, and do not ever let them work hard any more."[12] Joseph Sr. was fifty-two and Lucy was forty-eight years old when their son died.

At the autopsy performed by Dr. Robinson and the Smiths' own doctor, Dr. McIntire, the calomel was found untouched in the upper bowel, surrounded by gangrene.[13] Thereafter, according to Lucy, Robinson "spoke long and earnestly to the younger physicians upon the danger of administering powerful medicines without a thorough knowledge of <the practice of> physick." He expressed regret that as fine a youth as "ever trod the streets of Palmyra" was "murdered, as it were, by him at whose hand relief was expected." Apparently another person grieved at Alvin's death—"a lovel[y] young woman who was engaged to be married to my son."[14] Alvin's death was a shock and heartbreak to the whole family.

Work on the house continued until it was habitable, and the family moved in. This frame house was an improvement over the log cabin, which later became Hyrum's home. The Smith family would reside on the Manchester portion of the Stafford Road for seven years.

Work during this period included treasure seeking for the older male members. "There was a company there in that neighborhood," Martin Harris later recalled, "who were digging for money . . . Of this company were old Mr. Stowel[l] — I think his name was Josiah — also old Mr. Beman, also Samuel Lawrence, George Proper, Joseph Smith, jr., and his father, and his brother Hiram Smith."[15] Alvin helped young Joseph dig the well on the Chase farm in 1822 when they discovered a seer stone.[16] Lucy Smith described treasure-seeking activities as balancing other family occupations such as farming:

> I shall change my theme for the present, but let not my reader suppose that because I pursue another topic for a season that we stopt our labor and went <at> trying to win the faculty of Abrac,

drawing Magic circles or sooth saying to the neglect of all kinds of bus<i>ness. We never during our lives suffered one important interest to swallow up every other obligation but whilst we worked with our hands we endeavored to remmember [sic] the service of & the welfare of our souls.[17]

About two years after the Smith family settled on their hundred-acre farm, Lucy, Hyrum, Samuel, and Sophronia joined the local Western Presbyterian Church of Palmyra. As a result, family activities during the mid-1820s included some church going. As William Smith recalled in 1883:

My mother, who was a very pious woman and much interested in the welfare of her children, both here and hereafter, made use of every means which her parental love could suggest, to get us engaged in seeking for our souls' salvation, or (as the term then was) "in getting religion." She prevailed on us to attend the meetings, and almost the whole family became interested in the matter, and seekers after truth.[18]

Participating family members would have taken part in the instruction, confession of faith, membership vows, baptism, and welcome by the elders and congregation which constituted active membership in the church.

The family was given a reprieve of sorts during this period after Zechariah Seymour, the land agent who collected their mortgage payments, died in July 1822. But the Evertson heirs in New York City hired John Greenwood, a lawyer, to replace Seymour and conferred to him power of attorney in May 1824. Lucy wrote, "<at this time> we received intelligence of the arrival of a new land agent for the Ever[t]son Land, of which our farm was a portion. This caused us to bethink ourselves of the remmaining [sic] payment which was still due and which we would be under the necessity of making <prior> to obtaining the deed <which> our bonds called for." The death of Seymour prevented their final payment on the land. According to Lucy, her husband "sent Hyrum to the new Agent at Canandaguia [sic] to inform him that the money should be forthcoming as soon as the 25th of <Dec>[em]ber [1825] which the Agent said would answer every purpose and agreed to retain the land untill that time."[19]

About this time Joseph Jr. sent his brother Hyrum to borrow back the seer stone from Willard Chase. As Chase recalled it:

> I believe, some time in 1825, Hiram Smith (brother of Joseph Smith) came to me, and wished to borrow the same stone, alledging that they wanted to accomplish some business of importance, which could not very well be done without the aid of the stone. I told him it was of no particular worth to me, but merely wished to keep it as a curiously, and if he would pledge me his word and honor, that I should have it when called for, he might take it; which he did and took the stone. I thought I could rely on his word at this time, as he had made a profession of religion.[20]

Soon thereafter Joseph Sr. and his namesake were hired by Josiah Stowell to come south with him and help him dig for treasure near Harmony, Pennsylvania.[21] They were there until about 17 November 1825, after which they returned to Bainbridge.

Lucy remembered that Mr. Stoddard, a neighbor, had been "the principle workman on the house" and had offered to purchase their home but was flatly refused by the Smiths.[22] Squire Stoddard had bought the Evertson land south of the Smith farm on 2 November 1825.[23] He told the land agent that the elder Smith and young Joseph had both left town and that Hyrum was cutting the sugar maple trees for fire wood and doing damage to the farm. He offered to buy the farm for cash, and since the Smiths were in default, Greenwood agreed and gave Stoddard the deed. Afterward Stoddard and two friends went to the Smiths and asked them to leave the property.

Panic ensued. The family sent for Joseph Sr., and he hurried north to Manchester. As Lucy told the story,

> Hyrum went straightway to Dr. Robinson, (an old Friend <of ours who lived in Palmira)>. . . . [he] sat down and wrote [about] the charecter [sic] of <my> family our industry and faithful exertion's to obtain a home in <the> forest, where we had set[t]led ourselves, with many commendations ca[l]culated to beget confidence in us as to buisness [sic] transactions. This he took in his own hands and went through the village and in an hour there was attached to the paper the names of 60 subscribers. He then sent the same by the hand of Hyrum to the land Agent in Canandaguia [sic].

Greenwood was enraged that he had been misled by Stoddard and sent a messenger to re-obtain the deed.[24]

The Smiths then turned to a friend who directed them to Lemuel Durfee. Durfee, his son Lemuel, and Joseph Sr. went to Canandaigua, where Durfee paid $1,135 on 20 December 1825 for the farm.[25] Stoddard "gave up the deed to Mr. Durfy [Durfee] . . . who now came into posses[s]ion of the Farm. With this Gentleman," said Lucy, "we were now to s[t]ipulate as renters." Durfee allowed the Smiths to remain in the frame house and on the farm. According to Lucy, Durfee "gave us the privileage [sic] of the place one year with this provision that Samuel our 4th son was to labor for him 6 months."[26]

Almost one year after the family became renters, the *Wayne Sentinel* announced, "MARRIED - In Manchester . . . Mr. Hiram Smith, to Miss Jerusha Barden." They were married on 2 November 1826.[27] Jerusha was twenty-one years old, and Hyrum was twenty-six. Lucy heartily approved, noting in her history, "My oldest son [Hyrum] . . . Married him a wife that was one of the most excellent of Women."[28] Two months later Joseph Jr. married Emma Hale in Bainbridge on 18 January 1827, bringing her back to live in the family home in Manchester. That same year, Sophronia married Calvin Stoddard on 30 December.[29]

Young Joseph was often hired by Martin Harris to work "on his farm, and that they had hoed corn together many a day, Brother Harris paying him fifty cents per day. Joseph, he [Harris] said, was good to work and jovial and they often wrestled together in sport, but the Prophet was devoted and attentive to his prayers."[30]

Samuel Harrison Smith worked for the elder Durfee in 1827, according to one of Durfee's account books: "April the 16 day the year 1827 S. Harrison Smith Son of Joseph Smith began to Work for me by the month. [He] is to Work 7 Months for the use of the place Where Said Joseph Smith Lives."[31]

Hyrum continued working as a cooper and with his father and brothers for local farmers including Lemuel Durfee. They apparently took their wages in credits toward their purchases. In Durfee's account book for 1827 he noted:

> Joseph [Sr.] and Hiram Smith Dr [debit] to three barrels of Cider at 9/ per barrel May the Last 1827 [9 shillings per barrel]
>
> June the 26 day Joseph Smith Dr. to Veal hind Quarter 23 pound $0.69 also one fore Quarter Wt. 22 pounds $=55 55
>
> august Credit by Joseph Smith by mo[w]ing three days & Joseph Smith Ju Jnr. two days mowing & Hiram Smith one day mowing even
>
> Sept. first to two barrels of Cider racked of[f] to Joseph & Hiram Smiths at 9/ per barrel $2=25[32]

Hyrum Smith was now living in the log house with his wife Jerusha, who was expecting their first child. Hyrum had previously joined the Masonic Lodge in Palmyra and was listed as a member of the Mount Moriah Masonic Lodge No. 112 for the period June 1827 to June 1828. Levi Daggett, Pomeroy Tucker, and other respected citizens were also members of the lodge.[33] Hyrum was still attending the Palmyra Presbyterian church.[34] Hyrum and Jerusha's first child, a girl named Lovina, was born on 16 September 1827.[35]

Joseph Jr.'s interest in prehistoric America affected family life during these years. Lucy recalled the recitals about the land's ancient inhabitants which Joseph began recounting during his teenage years:

> In the course of our evening conversations Joseph would give us some of the most ammusing [sic] recitals which could be immagined. He would de[s]cribe the ancient inhabitants of this continent, their dress, thier [sic] man[n]er of traveling, the animals [upon] which they rode, The cities that were built by them, the structure of their buildings, with every particular, of their mode of warfare [and] their religious worship - as particularly as though he had spent his life with them.[36]

The family became directly involved in Joseph's passion after the gold plates were retrieved from the fallen treetop where he reported leaving them the first night. According to Lucy, her son Don Carlos was sent to Hyrum's home to let him know that Joseph needed a chest:

> Carlos went into Hyrum's house he found him at tea with 2 of his wife's sisters, Carlos touched his brother's shoulder just as he was raising his cup to his mouth. Without waiting to hear a word of the

child's errand Hyrum dropped his cup & sprang from the table and
ketched [caught] up the chest, turned it upside down and leaving
the contents on the [floor] left the House in an instant with the chest
on his shoulder. The young ladies were much surprized at his
singular behaviour and protested to his wife (who was bedfast her
oldest daughter Lovina being but 4 days) that her husband was
positively crazy. She laughed heartily, O! not in the least said she.
[Hyrum] has just thought of something that he has neglected and
it's just like him to fly off in a tangent when he thinks of anything
that way.[37]

Before Joseph deposited the artifact in the chest, he permitted
the family to feel and handle the plates. William Smith remembered
that he "did not see them [the plates] uncovered but I handled them
and hefted them while [they were] wrapped in a tow frock." He
mentioned that his "Father and my brother Samuel saw them as I did
while in the frock. So did Hyrum and others of the family."[38] Joseph
then locked the record in the box and with the family's help hid it
under the brick hearth in the west room of the house. This hearth
surrounded the fireplace where the Smith family discussed the events
of the day and where Joseph talked to his family about his adventures.
It was probably in this room that he related to Josiah Stowell and
Joseph Knight "the whole history of the record, which interested
them very much." They listened and believed "all that was told them"
by Joseph.[39]

Still concerned about the safety of the plates, Joseph took the box
from the hearth and carried it out to the "cooper shop across the
road." He put the box under the floor of the shop. The money-diggers
located it there and smashed the box to pieces but did not find the
plates.[40] According to Martin Harris, Joseph had taken the plates out
of the box and hidden them in the loft under some flax.[41] Alvah
Beeman, a friend of the family, helped make a new container from a
wooden box made to hold window glass, and Joseph worked "with
his Father on the Farm in order to be near the treasure that was
commit[t]ed to his care."[42]

Lucy Smith went to the Harris home just north of the village of
Palmyra and invited Harris's wife and daughter to come and see the
container. Harris recalled, "My daughter said, they were about as

much as she could lift. They were now in the glass-box, and my wife said they were very heavy. They both lifted them."

Martin arrived later but found that Joseph had gone to Peter Ingersoll's farm to get some flour. Harris talked with Emma and the Smith family and said that Joseph "found them [the plates] by looking in the stone found in the well of Mason Chase [brother of Willard]. The family had likewise told me the same thing."

While at the Smith home, Harris hefted the plates and thought that they weighed about forty or fifty pounds. Harris told Joseph that if this was the Lord's work, "you can have all the money necessary to bring it before the world." He then went home, prayed, and was "satisfied that it was the Lord's work" and that he "was under a covenant to bring it forth."[43]

Although several people felt the plates under a cloth before they were put in a box or held the box while it was in a pillow case, others were dissatisfied and determined to see the actual plates. As a result Joseph and Emma went to her parents' home in Harmony to work on the translation of the plates away from the curious. Harris paid off Joseph's debts and gave him $50 for the journey.

Alva Hale, Emma's brother, came north to Manchester to move their belongings. The box containing the plates was put into a barrel of beans for the trip. Before leaving, Joseph arranged with Harris to come to Harmony and pick up an alphabet transcribed from the Egyptian characters said to be on the gold plates. Harris wanted copies of the writing on the plates verified by experts. According to Lucy, when Harris went to Harmony a few months later to get the copy, "Hyrum went with him."[44]

Meanwhile the life and work of the Smiths in Manchester went on as before. Lemuel Durfee noted in his account book:

> May the 13th Joseph [Sr.] & [Samuel] Harrison Smith Dr. [debit] to three barrels of Cider the Liqure at $3=38
> June the 18 day the year 1828 Credit By Hiram & Har[r]ison Smiths a hoeing one Day a piece
> June the 20 day Joseph & Harrison Smiths Dr. to the Liqure of three barrels of Cider at 9/0 per barrel $3=38
> July 7 day Credit by J. Smith & Rockwell by hoeing three days
> July 20 Jos. Smith & Harrison Cr. by Work binding Wheat one

day of william and three days of Harrison Work

    august 7 Credit <by> Rockwell to two days Mowing for me by Harrison Smith by three days a Mowing for me [45]

Early in 1829 Lucy and Joseph Sr. went south to visit Joseph and Emma and to meet Emma's parents, Isaac and Elizabeth Hale. They found all was well in Harmony.

Because Hyrum Smith was one of the trustees of the local school, he was responsible for hiring teachers. Lyman Cowdery applied but soon encountered a scheduling conflict and recommended his brother Oliver, who was hired.[46] While teaching, Oliver boarded with the Smith family, where he heard the story of Joseph and the ancient record. Oliver decided that as soon as the school term was ended, he would like "the priviledge of writing for Joseph," who was still in Harmony. Lucy remembered, "The time was now drawing to a close. We now began to make preparations to remove our family and effects to the log house <which> was now occupied by Hyrum" and his family.[47] Thus the extended Smith family crowded into the old cabin. "In April," related Lucy, "all Mr. Cowdray's affairs being arranged according to his mind," he left for Pennsylvania with Samuel Harrison. They arrived on 5 April 1829, and Cowdery became a scribe for Joseph's religious history. Thereafter the writing of the manuscript of the Book of Mormon progressed more rapidly. Cowdery was reportedly shown the plates in a vision before he left Manchester.[48]

In May Hyrum visited Joseph to see how the translation was coming. While there Joseph received revelation directed to Hyrum personally:

whosoever will thrust in his sickle and reap, the same is called of God. . . . Seek not for riches but for wisdom, and behold the mysteries of God shall be unfolded unto you, and then shall you be made rich; behold he that hath eternal life is rich. . . . Keep my commandments, and assist to bring forth my work according to my commandments, and you shall be blessed. Behold thou has a gift, or thou shalt have a gift, if thou wilt desire of me in faith, with an honest heart, believing in the power of Jesus Christ, or in my power which speaketh unto thee: for behold it is I that speaketh: behold I am the light which shinneth in darkness, and by my power I give these words unto thee. . . . Behold I command you, that you need not suppose that you are called to preach until you are called: wait a little longer, until you shall have my word, my Rock, my church, and my gospel, that you may know of a surety my doctrine . . . Yea, cleave unto me with all your heart, that you may assist in bringing to light those things of which have been spoken: Yea, the translation of my work: be patient until you shall accomplish it. . . . Behold thou art Hyrum, my son; seek the kingdom of God and all things shall be added according to that which is just.[49]

During June Hyrum, who had not attended the Presbyterian church at Palmyra for the past eight months, visited Fayette, New York, where Joseph rebaptized him for the remission of his sins.[50] A copyright was secured for the Book of Mormon in the name of Joseph Smith on 11 June,[51] and Joseph and Oliver began thinking about starting a new church.[52]

After his return to Manchester, Hyrum received a letter from Cowdery, written to strengthen Hyrum's resolve. Cowdery said he was "feeling anxious for your steadfastness in the great cause of which you have been called to advocate."[53] A few days later Hyrum received correspondence with a very different thrust from his Uncle Jesse Smith, who was living in Stockholm, New York:

Again you say, if you are decieved [sic] God is your decieve[r] [sic], Blasphemous wretch - how dare you utter such a sentence, how dare you harbor such a thot - aye, you never did think so, but being hardened in iniquity, you make use of the holy name of Jehovah! for what, why to cover your neferious [sic] designs & impose on the credulity of your Grandfather, one of the oldest men on the earth, Blackness of darkness! . . . You state your father cannot write by reason of a nervous affection this is a poor excuse, worse than none, he can dictate to others and they can write, If he knows not what to write, he can get your Brother's spectacles he would then be as able to dictate a letter, as Joe is to decipher hieroglyphics, if more should be wanting he can employ the same scoundrel of a scribe, and then not only the matter but manner and style would be correct.[54]

On 27 June another daughter, named Mary, was born to Hyrum and Jerusha.[55]

On 23 August 1829, Martin Harris made an indenture between himself and Egbert Grandin, editor of the *Wayne Sentinel*, "in consid-

eration of the sum of three thousand dollars" for typesetting, printing, and binding the Book of Mormon. This was secured by a mortgage for "the same tract of land or farm upon which the said Martin
Harris now resides" and was to be paid in eighteen months.[56]

Oliver Cowdery squeezed into the log home, where the entire
Smith family was living, and began making a copy of the manuscript
of the Book of Mormon for the printer to use in typesetting. According to Lucy, "Peter Whitmer was commanded to remain at our house
to assist in guarding the writings."[57]

Most of the typesetting was done by twenty-seven-year-old John
H. Gilbert, who recalled years later:

> When the printer was ready to commence work, [Martin] Harris was
> notified, and Hyrum Smith brought the first installment of manu-
> script, of 24 pages, closely written on common foolscap paper — he
> had it under his vest, and [his] vest and coat closely buttoned over
> it. At night Smith came and got the manuscript, and with the same
> precaution carried it away. The next morning with the same watch-
> fulness, he brought it again, and at night took it away. This was kept
> up for several days. . . . After working a few days, I said to [Hyrum]
> Smith on his handing me the manuscript in the morning; "Mr.
> Smith, if you would leave this manuscript with me, I would take it
> home with me at night and read and punctuate it." His reply was,
> "We are commanded not to leave it." A few mornings after this,
> when Smith handed me the manuscript, he said to me: — "If you will
> give your word that this manuscript shall be returned to us when
> you get through with it, I will leave it with you." I assured Smith that
> it should be returned all right when I got through with it. For two
> or three nights I took it home with me and read it, and punctuated
> it with a lead pencil. . . . Martin Harris, Hyrum Smith and Oliver
> Cowdery were very frequent visitors to the office during the printing
> of the Mormon Bible.[58]

Thomas B. Marsh described visiting the Grandin printing office:

> I returned back westward and found Martin Harris at the printing
> office, in Palmyra, where the first sixteen pages of the Book of
> Mormon had just been struck off, the proof sheet of which I
> obtained from the printer and took with me. As soon as Martin
> Harris found out my intentions he took me to the house of Joseph

Smith, sen. . . . Here I found Oliver Cowdery, who gave me all the information concerning the book I desired. After staying there two days I started for Charleston, Mass., highly pleased with the information I had obtained concerning the new found book.[59]

Stephen S. Harding remembered that during the summer of 1829 he went to the *Wayne Sentinel* office and to the Smiths' residence in Manchester, which he described as "a log house, not exactly a cabin. Upon our arrival, I was ushered into the best room in company with the others." Oliver Cowdery read from the Book of Mormon manuscript. When Harding returned to the printing office a few weeks later, he was given a copy of a proof sheet that included the title page.[60]

Solomon Chamberlain also stopped in Palmyra and visited the Smith family:

I soon arrived at the house, and found Hyrum walking the floor; as I entered the room, I said peace be to this house; he looked at me and said "I hope it will be peace." I then said is there any one here that believes in visions and revelations. He [Hyrum] said yes, we are a visionary house. I then said I will give you one of my pamphlets, (which was visionary and of my own composition). . . .[61]

* * *

They then called the people together, which consisted of five or six men who were out at the door. Father Smith was one and some of the Whitmer's. They then sat down and read my pamphlet. Hyrum read first, but was so affected he could not read it, He then gave it to a man, which I learned was Christian Whitmer, he finished reading it. I then opened my mouth and began to preach to them, in the words that the angel had made known to me in the vision, that all Churches and Denominations on the earth had become corrupt, and [that] no Church of God [was] on earth but that he would shortly raise up a Church, that would never be confounded nor brought down and be like unto the Apostolic Church. They wondered greatly who had been telling me these things, for said they we have the same things wrote down in our house, taken from the Gold record, that you are preaching to us.[62]

Chamberlain continued:

and if you are a visionary house, I wish you would make known some of your discoveries, I think I can bear them. Then they began to make known to me, that they had obtained a gold record, and had just finished translating it. Here I staid, and they instructed me in the manuscripts of the Book of Mormon; after I had been there two days, I went with Hyrum and some others to [the] Palmyra printing office, where they began to print the Book of Mormon; and as soon as they had printed sixty-four pages I took them and started for Canada.[63]

During the last week of October, Martin Harris and Hyrum Smith went to Fayette to visit the Whitmers. Oliver Cowdery wrote to Joseph, "Hyram and Martin went out to Fayette last week they had a joyful time and found all in as good health as could be expected."[64]

A free-thinking Palmyra lawyer, whose office was located in the center of town on Main Street as early as 1812, began in September 1829 a satirical paper called *The Reflector*. Abner Cole presented his commentary on village life under the pen name of Obadiah Dogberry. He arranged to use the press of the *Wayne Sentinel* on evenings and Sundays to print his paper.[65] He had probably heard much talk around town about Joseph Smith's new Bible and was intrigued by the sheets containing pages of the Book of Mormon that he found around the printing office.

Lucy Smith remembered that in January 1830 on "One Su[n]day <afternoon> Hyrum became very uneasy, he told Oliver that his peculiar feellings [sic] led him to believe that something <going> was [sic; was going] wrong at [the] printing Office." Oliver and Hyrum went to Grandin's printing establishment and found Abner Cole "at work printing a paper which seemed to be a <weekly> periodical." Hyrum discovered that Cole was printing portions of the Book of Mormon in his paper. Thus *The Reflector* became the first publication to print extracts from the text of the Book of Mormon even before its issuance in March 1830.[66]

"Mr. Cole, said he [Hyrum], what right have <you> to print the book of Mormon in this way, do you not know that we have secured a copy right." Lucy continued, "Hyrum <&> Oliver returned immediately home and after counciling with Mr. Smith it was considered neces[s]ary that Joseph should be sent for. Accordingly My husband set out as soon as possible for Penn."[67] Joseph made a trip north from Harmony to talk to Cole and told him to desist from publishing any more from his book. The last issue of *The Reflector* containing any text from the forthcoming Book of Mormon was an "Extra," dated 22 January 1830.

The Smiths struggled to maintain control over the printing and sale of the book. Joseph Sr. signed the following agreement with Martin Harris:

> I hereby agree that Martin Harris shall have an equal privilege with me & my friends of selling the Book of Mormon of the Edition now printing by Egbert B. Grandin until enough of them shall be sold to pay for the printing of the same or until such times as the said Grandin shall be paid for the printing the aforesaid Books or copies. Manchester January the 16th 1830 Joseph Smith Sr.
> Witness Oliver H. P. Cowdery[68]

There were thirty-seven galley sheets printed for the 1830 Book of Mormon. With two unnumbered pages containing the Testimony of the Three and Eight Witnesses, the book contained a total of 590 pages. The cost of printing each book, including binding, was about sixty cents. With 5,000 copies printed, the total cost was $3,000. Martin Harris was assured of having enough books to sell to recover his investment in the printing.

An old debt incurred by Joseph Sr. resulted in legal action against him three days after he signed the agreement with Harris. When Lemuel Durfee's estate was inventoried, it included a note signed by Joseph Sr. and by Abraham Fish with an "x" for $36.50 plus interest. On 19 January Durfee's son entered a plea before Justice Nathan Pierce against Smith and Fish, and the two signed a consent for judgment. It was turned over to Constable S. Southworth for collection and resolved in September.[69]

About September 1828, Lucy as well as Hyrum and Samuel Harrison had stopped attending the Palmyra Presbyterian Church and partaking of the sacrament of the Lord's Supper.[70] By spring 1830 the pastor and elders of the church had become concerned:

> March 3d 1830 Session met pursuant to notice - opened with prayer
> Present Revd Alfred E. Campbell Moderr [Moderator]

Henry Jessup
Geo Beckwith
David White   Elders
Pelatiah West
Newton Foster
   . . . Resolved that the Revd A. E. Campbell and H Jessup
be a committee to visit Hiram Smith Lucy Smith and Samuel Harri-
son Smith and report at the next meeting of session
   Closed with prayer -
Recorded from the Moderators minutes
          [Signed] Geo. N. Williams Clk [Clerk]

A week later the session met again and received the report of
their committee's visit: "The committee appointed to visit Hiram
Smith Lucy Smith and Samuel Harrison Smith reported that they had
visited them and received no satisfaction. They acknowledged that
they had entirely neglected the ordinances of the church for the last
eighteen months and that they did not wish to unite with us any-
more." The session accordingly cited them to appear before it in two
weeks to answer the charge of "Neglect of public worship and the
sacrament of the Lord's Supper for the last eighteen months."[71]

Lucy remembered the visit from three men, one of whom she
called "Deacon Beckwith." George Beckwith had been appointed to
be the advocate to manage their defense and either went with the
committee or on his own to do what he could to bring them back to
the church. Lucy reported her firm resistance to Deacon Beckwith's
pleas:

No sir, said I, it is <of> no use; you cannot effect any thing by all
that you can say - he then bid me farewell and went out to see
Hyrum. They asked him if he really did believe that his brother had
got the record which he pretended to have. Hyrum <testified boldly
to the truth>, told him that if he would take the book of Mormon
when it was finished [being printed and bound] and read it asking
God for a witness to the truth of [it] he would receive what he
desired and now, said he [Hyrum], Deacon Beckwith just try it and
see if I do not tell you [the] truth.[72]

Beckwith remained unconvinced.
When the Smiths did not appear before the session on the

appointed day, they were cited to appear five days later. Pelatiah West was appointed to serve the citation and be sure they received it. The Palmyra session records for the trial read:

> March 29th 1830 Session met pursuant to adjournment
> Opened with prayer
> Present Revd Alfred E. Campbell Modr
>> Geo Beckwith
>> Newton Foster
>> Pelatiah West   Elders
>> Henry Jessup
>
> The persons before cited to wit. Hiram Smith Lucy Smith and Samuel Harrison Smith not appearing and the Session having satisfactory evidence that the citations were duly served Resolved that they be censored for their contumacy Resolved that George Beckwith manage their defense. The charge in the above case being fully sustained by the testimony of Henry Jessup, Harvey Shel, Robert W. Smith and Frederick U. Sheffield (see minutes of testimony, on file with the clerk) the Session after duly considering the matter were unanimously of opinion that Hiram Smith, Lucy Smith and Samuel Harrison Smith ought to be Suspended. Resolved that Hiram Smith, Lucy Smith and Samuel Harrison Smith be and they hereby are suspended from the Sacrament of the Lord's Supper.
> Closed with prayer - Adjourned
> Recorded from the minutes of the Moderator.
>> [Signed] Geo. N. Williams Clk[73]

As this was occurring, the Book of Mormon was being sold.[74] Eight days later the Church of Christ was organized at the Manchester loghouse on 6 April 1830. With Joseph Jr. in Harmony, Hyrum was a central figure in the new church in the Palmyra area. For example, in August 1830 Hyrum was visited by Parley P. Pratt, who later recalled:

> I accordingly visited the village of Palmyra, and inquired for the residence of Mr. Joseph Smith. I found it some two or three miles from the village. As I approached the house at the close of the day I overtook a man who was driving some cows, and inquired of him for Mr. Joseph Smith, the translator of the "Book of Mormon." He informed me that he now resided in Pennsylvania; some one hun-

dred miles distant. I inquired for his father, or for any of the family. He told me that his father had gone [on] a journey; but that his residence was a small house just before me; and, said he, I am his brother. It was Mr. Hyrum Smith. . . . He welcomed me to his house.[75]

Pratt left for a few days but soon returned to Hyrum's house:

I now returned immediately to Hyrum Smith's residence, and demanded baptism at his hands. I tarried with him one night, and the next day we walked some twenty-five miles to the residence of Mr. Whitmer, in Seneca County. Here we arrived in the evening, and found a most welcome reception. . . . I found the little branch of the church in this place [Fayette] full of joy, faith, humility and charity. We rested that night, and on the next day, being about the 1st of September, 1830, I was baptized by the hand of an Apostle of the Church of Jesus Christ, by the name of Oliver Cowdery. This took place in Seneca Lake, a beautiful and transparent sheet of water in Western New York. A meeting was held the same evening, and after singing a hymn and prayer, Elder Cowdery and others proceeded to lay their hands upon my head in the name of Jesus, for the gift of the Holy Ghost. After which I was ordained to the office of an Elder in the Church.[76]

Parley P. Pratt left Fayette but returned to Manchester in October 1830 after baptizing his brother Orson. Parley recalled:

I now took leave, and repaired again to the western part of New York, and to the body of the Church. On our arrival, we found that brother Joseph Smith, the translator of the Book of Mormon, had returned from Pennsylvania to his father's residence in Manchester, near Palmyra, and here I had the pleasure of seeing him for the first time. . . . On Sunday we held meeting at his house; the two large rooms were filled with attentive listeners, and he invited me to preach. . . . We repaired from the meeting to the water's edge, and, at his request, I baptized several persons.[77]

One of those baptized at this time was Ezra Thayer. He recalled that his half brother and a nephew also heard Hyrum preach before Joseph returned:

I had a half brother living with me and a nephew, and they took my horses and went to meeting, to hear Hyrum preach while I was gone. . . . My half brother said that Hyrum said that Joseph had seen an angel. My nephew said that there was something in it, and that I had better go and hear him. . . . The next Sunday I went and there was a large concourse of people around his father's house, so that they extended to the road, filling up the large lot. . . . Hyrum began to speak. . . . Joseph was then in Harmony, Pa., and the next Sunday he came to his father's house, and we assembled to see him. . . . He then asked me what hindered me from going into the water, as Oliver Cowdery's mother was going to be baptized. . . . Then we started to the water. . . . We were baptized just below the mill. . . . Parley P. Pratt baptized us.[78]

In August 1830, about the time Parley Pratt visited Hyrum, the census was taken of those living in the Smith family house in Manchester. It had been a decade since the previous census and the families of both Joseph Sr. and Hyrum were listed as one household.[79] The ages of the male family members were: 10-15, 1 (Don Carlos); 15-20, 1 (William); 20-30, 2 (Hyrum and Samuel Harrison), and 50-60, 1 (Joseph Sr.). Females members were: under 5, 2 (Lovina and Mary, daughters of Hyrum and Jerusha); 5-10, 1 (Lucy); 20-30, 1 (Jerusha); 30-40, 1 (not identified), and 50-60, 1 (Lucy Mack Smith). Catherine (age seventeen) was not listed.

By August growing financial complications would shortly result in the family quitting the area entirely. On the day after the founding of the Mormon church, 7 April 1830, Hyrum Smith signed a note for shoeing horses with Levi Daggett of Palmyra. When this was not repaid, Daggett brought suit before Nathan Pierce, a justice of the peace in Manchester.[80] A summons was served by Constable Southworth on 8 June, the day before the first church conference in Fayette. Ten days later another summons was issued. On the 28th Joseph Sr. appeared on his son's behalf. The Docket Book reads:

28th June 1830 Joseph <Smith> father of the Defendant appeared and the Case was called and the plaintif[f] declared for a note and account Note dated 7th April 1830 for $20.07 on Interest and on account for Shoeing horses of ballance due on account $0.69 Joseph Smith sworn and saith that his Son the Defendant engaged him to Come down at the return of the summons and direct the Justice to enter Judgment against the defendant for the amount of the note & account Judgment for the plaintif for twenty one dollars seven cents $21.07

August came and Daggett still had not been paid. Thus on 14 August Pierce issued an execution:

> THESE are therefore to command you to levy on the goods and chattels of the said defendant (except such as are by law exempted from execution) the amount of the said judgment, and bring the money before me, on the *13th-* day of *September* 1830 at my office in the town of *Manchester*. . . . And if no goods or chattels can be found, or not sufficient to satisfy this execution, then you are hereby commanded to take the body of the said defendant and convey *him* to the common Jail of the county aforesaid.[81]

Constable Nathan Harrington collected $12.81 from Hyrum and after court costs paid Daggett $9.94 of the amount owed him on 13 September. This was not quite half of the debt. On 27 September the execution was renewed by Justice Pierce with additional fees and again the threat of jail. After nearly a month Harrington came with the execution to collect the remainder and found neither Hyrum nor anything of value. He wrote on the execution: "No property to be found Nor Boddy [sic] and I return this Execution October the 26 1830."[82] Hyrum had left for Colesville.

In these hard times, when people heard that their neighbors were going to move they wanted hard cash.[83] Lucy commented concerning Hyrum's leaving the house about October 1830: "Hyrum was flying from his home, and why I knew not." She mentioned, "Hyrum had settled up his business, for the purpose of being at liberty to do whatever the Lord required of him." Thus Hyrum, his wife, and their two daughters were to "go immediately to Colesville." Lucy notes that this was a Wednesday and "Hyrum had not been long absent when the neighbors called one after another and enquired where Hyrum was gone. I told each one that he was in Colesville." A few days later a young gentleman came to the house and asked "if Mr. Hyrum Smith was at home. I told [him], as I had others, that he was in Colesville. The young man said that Mr. H. Smith was owing Dr. Mackintire, who was then absent, a small sum of money." Lucy told him that the debt was to be paid in corn and beans and arranged for them to be delivered the next day.[84]

About the same time Hyrum left for Colesville an elderly Quaker came to the house with a note owed by Joseph Sr. and demanded payment. According to Lucy, the man offered to forfeit the note if Smith would burn the copies of the Book of Mormon, but he received neither payment nor satisfaction. A constable was ordered to arrest Smith and take him to the Canandaigua Jail, where he became "an imprisoned debtor." Samuel Harrison visited his father in the jail. Lucy reported that her "husband [was] confined in the same dungeon with a man committed for murder." The elder Smith remained at the jail yard "until he was released, which was thirty days."[85] The man mentioned by Lucy was Eli Bruce. Bruce had been convicted on charges dealing with the abduction and murder of William Morgan, reportedly by Masons. In his diary Bruce recorded:

> *November 5th* — Not so much pain in my head as yesterday. Had a long talk with the father of *the Smith*, (Joseph Smith,) who, according to the old man's account, is the particular favorite of Heaven! To him Heaven has vouchsafed to reveal its mysteries; he is the herald of the latter-day glory. The old man avers that he is commissioned by God to baptize and preach this new doctrine. He says that our Bible is much abridged and deficient; that soon the Divine will is to be known to all, as written in the *new Bible*, or *Book of Mormon*.[86]

Samuel helped move the family to Waterloo, near the Whitmer's farm in Fayette. There were still threats from creditors. Joseph Jr., who had since moved to Kirtland, Ohio, warned Hyrum that David Jackaway was planning to arrest his father. "I <have> had much Concirn about you but I always remember you in <my> prayers Calling upon God to keep <you> Safe in spite <of> men or devils. I think <you> had better Come into this Country immediately for the Lord has Commanded us that we should Call the Elders of this Chursh [sic] to gether unto this plase as soon as possable." In a postscript he wrote, "Harrison [Smith] and O[r]son Prat[t] arrived here on Feb. 27th. They left our folks well. David Jackways has threatened to take father with a supreme writ in the spring. You had <bet[t]er> Come to Fayette and take father along with you. Come in a one horse wagon if you Can. Do not Come threw [sic] Buf[f]alo for th[e]y will lie in wait for you. God protect you. I am Joseph."[87]

In Colesville Hyrum, his wife, and two daughters stayed with Newel and Sally Knight.[88] Hyrum was appointed to preside over the Colesville branch of the church, and, according to Knight, they spent their time

> in the villages around, preaching the gospel wherever we could find any who would listen to us, either in public or private. A few believed and were baptized, among whom was Emer Harris, brother to Martin Harris. . . . On the 14th of October, Brother Hyrum Smith and I held a meeting at my uncle Hezekiah Peck's. Brother Hyrum had great liberty of speech, and the Spirit of the Lord was poured out upon us in a miraculous manner. There was much good instruction and exhortation given, such as was calculated to encourage and strengthen the Saints in this their infantile state. At this meeting, four persons came forward and manifested their desire to forsake all, serve their God in humility, and obey the requirements of the gospel. . . . After laboring for some time in this vicinity, we returned to my home, found our wives well and in the enjoyment of the Spirit of the Lord. We also found Brother Orson Pratt awaiting us, who had been called by the prophet to labor with us in the ministry.[89]

That December Orson Pratt arrived from Fayette with a letter from Joseph Smith and John Whitmer. Later that month Pratt and Hyrum traveled from Colesville to Fayette to attend the third church conference on 2 January 1831.[90] Previous to the conference Joseph Jr. received a revelation that the whole church should move to Ohio.[91]

When Hyrum left Colesville for the last time in March 1831, leadership of the branch transferred to Newel Knight. Hyrum and family probably went to Fayette to get his father, then moved all to the new gathering place at Kirtland, Ohio, where the Smith family began anew.[92]

NOTES

1. Pomeroy Tucker, *The Origin, Rise, and Progress of Mormonism* (New York: D. Appleton & Co., 1867), 12. James Gordon Bennett in his diary, entry for 7 Aug. 1831, recorded: "Old Smith [Joseph Sr.] . . . made gingerbread and buttermints &c&c" (in Leonard J. Arrington, "James Gordon Bennett's

1831 Report on 'The Mormonites,'" *Brigham Young University Studies* 10 [Spring 1970]: 355). This was published as "the manufacture of gingerbread" in *The Morning Courier & Enquirer* (New York), 31 Aug. 1831. It was reprinted in such publications as the *Christian Register*, 24 Sept. 1831, and the *Hillsborough Gazette* (Hillsborough, Ohio), 29 Oct. 1831.

2. Tucker, *Origins, Rise, and Progress of Mormonism*, 13. Tucker continued, "Subsequently this property was purchased by Mr. Smith on contract."

3. Ibid., 14.

4. Memorandum dated 8 Sept. 1892, Palmyra, New York, in Wilford C. Wood, *Joseph Smith Begins His Work*, 2 vols. (Salt Lake City: Deseret News Press, 1958), Vol. 1, introductory pages. "Hyrum, another son, helped his father at the trade of a cooper" (Frederic G. Mather, *Lippincott's Magazine of Popular Literature and Science* 26 [1880]: 198).

5. O[rsamus]. Turner, *History of the Pioneer Settlement of Phelps and Gorham's Purchase, and Morris' Reserve* (Rochester: William Alling, 1851), 213-14.

6. Richard L. Anderson, *Joseph Smith's New England Heritage: Influences of Grandfathers Solomon Mack and Asael Smith* (Salt Lake City: Deseret Book Co., 1971), 92, 94, 193nn136-37; and Pearson H. Corbett, *Hyrum Smith: Patriarch* (Salt Lake City: Deseret Book Co., 1963), 14.

7. Statement of Mrs. S. F. Anderick, 1887, in *Naked Truths About Mormonism* 1 (Jan. 1888): 2, original publication in the Yale University Library.

8. Statement of C. M. Stafford, 1885, in *Naked Truths About Mormonism* 1 (Apr. 1888): 1.

9. William H. Kelley Notebook, Mar. 1881 [p. 12], Library-Archives, Reorganized Church of Jesus Christ of Latter Day Saints, Independence, Missouri (hereafter RLDS archives).

10. Interview of Benjamin Saunders, William H. Kelley Collection "Miscellany 1795-1948" (1883-85), [19-20], RLDS archives.

11. Statement of Isaac Butts in *Naked Truths About Mormonism* 1 (Jan. 1888): 2.

12. Lucy Mack Smith, Preliminary Manuscript (MS), "History of Lucy Smith," 52, archives, historical department, Church of Jesus Christ of Latter-day Saints, Salt Lake City, Utah (hereafter LDS archives); the page numbering corresponds with a typed transcript in LDS archives and with the page numbers in the photocopy of the manuscript; Lucy Mack Smith, *Biographical Sketches of Joseph Smith the Prophet, and His Progenitors for Many Generations* (Liverpool: Published for Orson Pratt by S.W. Richards, 1853), 88 (hereafter *Biographical Sketches*); Lucy Mack Smith, *History of Joseph Smith By His Mother*,

Lucy Mack Smith (Salt Lake City: Bookcraft, 1958), 87 (hereafter *History of Joseph Smith*).

13. Lucy Mack Smith, Preliminary MS, 54; *Biographical Sketches* (1853), 89; *History of Joseph Smith* (1958), 88.

14. Lucy Mack Smith, Preliminary MS, 54. This portion of the manuscript was crossed out with an X, evidently to alert the compiler not to include it in the final version.

15. *Tiffany's Monthly* 5 (Aug. 1859): 164. Pomeroy Tucker wrote, "Smith's father and elder brothers generally participated in the manual labors of these diggings" (*Origin, Rise, and Progress of Mormonism*, 23).

16. Willard Chase, in E. D. Howe, *Mormonism Unvailed* (Painesville [OH]: Printed and Published by the Author, 1834), 240-41. Willard, a son of Clark Chase (1770-1821), was on born 1 February 1798. His brother Mason was born on 19 November 1795 (Wm. E. Reed, *The Descendants of Thomas Durfee of Portsmouth, R.I.* [Washington, D.C.: Gibson Bros., 1902], 213-14, and George Grant Brownel, comp., *Genealogical Record of the Descendants of Thomas Brownell 1619 to 1910* [Jamestown, NY: 1910], 200). Martin Harris stated, "Joseph had a stone which was dug from the well of Mason Chase, twenty-four feet from the surface" (*Tiffany's Monthly* 5 [Aug. 1859]: 163).

17. Lucy Mack Smith, Preliminary MS, 46. Not in *Biographical Sketches* or *History of Joseph Smith*. Abrac derives from Abracadabra and Abraxas, both of which were used on magic amulets. Members of the Masonic Lodge of the eighteenth century claimed they knew "the way of obtaining the faculty of *Abrac*" (James Hardie, *The New Free-Mason's Monitor* [New York: n.p., 1818], 203). The *Ontario Phoenix* of 25 Aug. 1830 reprinted the following from the *Boston Free Press* on this subject: "A VERY ANCIENT MASONIC CHARM, or the way of winning the Faculty of Abrac, - is meant the chimerical virtues ascribed to the magical term - ABRACADABRA, written or repeated in a particular manner, and is thought to be efficacious in curing agues, and preventing FITS and other masonic diseas[e]s." John E. Thompson concluded, "It is very clear what Lucy meant by the 'faculty of Abrac.' She meant precisely what both the Masonic and Anti-Masonic writers of her day meant, not merely the ability to know all that is to be known about magic, but rather the ability to use that knowledge for specific magical ends" ("'The Facultie of Abrac:' Masonic Claims and Mormon Beginnings," in *The Masons, the Mormons and the Morgan Incident* [Ames, IA: Iowa Research Lodge No. 2 AF&AM (1984)], 2).

18. *William Smith on Mormonism* (Lamoni, IA: Printed at Herald Steam Book and Job Office, 1883), 6.

19. Lucy Mack Smith, Preliminary MS, 57; *Biographical Sketches* (1853), 92-93; *History of Joseph Smith* (1958), 93.

20. Willard Chase, in Howe, *Mormonism Unvailed,* 241.

21. An 1825 agreement was signed by Stowell, Joseph Smith, Sr., Joseph Smith, and others. It was published in the Salt Lake *Daily Tribune,* 23 Apr. 1880, 4. Statement of Isaac Hale in *Susquehanna Register, and Northern Pennsylvanian* 9 (1 May 1834): 1; Howe, *Mormonism Unvailed,* 263.

22. Lucy Mack Smith, Preliminary MS, 57; *Biographical Sketches* (1853), 91; *History of Joseph Smith* (1958), 91.

23. Deed Liber 44:219-21, Ontario County Records Center and Archives, Canandaigua, New York.

24. Lucy Mack Smith, Preliminary MS, 60-62; *Biographical Sketches* (1853), 95-97; *History of Joseph Smith* (1958), 96-98.

25. Deed Liber 44:232-34, Ontario County Records Center and Archives, Canandaigua, New York. Lucy stated in her manuscript they were told that "if Hyrum could raise $1000 by Saturday at 10 o'clock in the evening they would give up the deed" (Preliminary MS, 61; *Biographical Sketches* [1853], 96; *History of Joseph Smith* [1958], 97).

26. Lucy Mack Smith, Preliminary MS, 63-64. Not in *Biographical Sketches* or *History of Joseph Smith.*

27. *Wayne Sentinel* 4 (24 Nov. 1826): 3. See photo of Hyrum Smith's Bible in *Ensign* 14 (Jan. 1984): 33, "November the 2d 1826."

28. Lucy Mack Smith, Preliminary MS, 58; *Biographical Sketches* (1853), 93; *History of Joseph Smith* (1958), 94.

29. Bible of Joseph and Emma Smith; see photo in *Ensign* 11 (Mar. 1981): 62 and 14 (Jan. 1984): 33; "Genealogy of President Joseph Smith Junior," in Manuscript History A-1:9 [separate section] (see Dean C. Jessee, ed., *The Papers of Joseph Smith* [Salt Lake City: Deseret Book, Co., 1989], 1:18). The Smith-Cowdery Bible purchased in 1829, and used for Joseph Smith's revision of the Bible, contained the following under "Marriages," "Joseph Smith Junr Emma Hale was married Jan 18 1827 Bainbridge, Chenango County State of New York" (RLDS archives). In Lucy Smith's Preliminary Manuscript, Joseph's and Hyrum's marriages are placed previous to the Smiths becoming renters on the farm. For Calvin and Sophronia's marriage date, see Record in Family Bible, photo in our possession. The original Calvin Stoddard Bible was in the possession of Charles Boyd of Chicago, Illinois, in 1968. Lucy's 1853 book has the marriage date as 2 December 1827 (40).

30. Edward Stevenson in *Latter-Day Saints' Millennial Star* 48 (21 June 1886): 389. Stevenson heard this from Martin Harris on their journey from Ohio to Utah territory in 1870.

31. Lemuel Durfee Account Book (1813-29), 15, Ontario County Historical Society, Canandaigua, New York.

32. Lemuel Durfee Account Book, 41-42, location of original in the King's Daughters Library, Palmyra, New York, in 1973, present location unknown, copy in our possession. This is a separate account book and should not be confused with a similar ledger cited in note 31.

33. "Return of Mount Moriah Lodge No. 112 held in the town of Palmyra in the County of Wayne and State of New York from June 4th AL 5827 [1827] to June 4th AL 5828 [1828]," Grand Lodge Free and Accepted Masons of the State of New York, Library and Museum, New York City. Also the Nauvoo, Illinois, Lodge listed Hyrum as having previously been a Mason in New York, entry of 30 Dec. 1841: "Hyrum Smith, Mount Moriah, No. 112, N.Y." in Mervin B. Hogan, ed., *Founding Minutes of Nauvoo Lodge, U.D.* (Des Moines, IA: Research Lodge No. 2 [1971]), 8. See Richard L. Anderson, *Investigating the Book of Mormon Witnesses* (Salt Lake City: Deseret Book, 1981), 149nn28-29.

34. "Records of the Session of the Presbyterian Church in Palmyra," 2 (10 Mar. 1830): 11, microfilm, film #900, reel 59, Harold B. Lee Library, Brigham Young University, Provo, Utah.

35. Lucy Mack Smith, *Biographical Sketches* (1853), 42; *History of Joseph Smith* (1958), 352. See photo of the "Family Record" in Hyrum Smith's family Bible in *The Friend* 18 (Jan. 1988): 35, entry: "Lovina Smith the Daughter of Hyrum & Jerusha Smith was Born September 16th 1827." This Bible is dated to the Kirtland, Ohio, period. Lovina was born in Manchester. See George Albert Smith Family Papers, Special Collections, Marriott Library, University of Utah, Salt Lake City.

36. Lucy Mack Smith, Preliminary MS, 49-50; *Biographical Sketches* (1853), 85; *History of Joseph Smith* (1958), 83.

37. Lucy Mack Smith, Preliminary MS, 73; *Biographical Sketches* (1853), 105-106; *History of Joseph Smith* (1958), 109. Lucy has Lovina being four days old. She should have been eleven days old (or more), as Joseph did not bring the record immediately home.

38. "Wm. B. Smith's last Statement," *Zion's Ensign* 5 (13 Jan. 1894): 6; reprinted in the *Deseret Evening News* 27 (20 Jan. 1894): 11; *Latter-day Saints' Millennial Star* 56 (26 Feb. 1894): 132. Ten years earlier William Smith wrote, "I was permitted to lift them [the plates] as they laid in a pillow-case; but not to see them" (*William Smith on Mormonism*, 12).

39. Lucy Mack Smith, Preliminary MS, 73; *Biographical Sketches* (1853), 106; *History of Joseph Smith* (1958), 109.

40. Lucy Mack Smith, Preliminary MS, 75; *Biographical Sketches* (1853), 109; *History of Joseph Smith* (1958), 113.

41. Martin Harris who was interviewed in 1859 reported, "After they had been concealed under the floor of the cooper's shop for a short time, Joseph was warned to remove them. He said he was warned by an angel. He took them out and hid them up in the chamber of the cooper's shop among the flags [flax]. That night some one came, took up the floor, and dug up the earth, and would have found the plates had they not been removed" (*Tiffany's Monthly* 5 [Aug. 1859]: 167).

42. Lucy Mack Smith, Preliminary MS, 74; *Biographical Sketches* (1853), 107; *History of Joseph Smith* (1958), 111.

43. *Tiffany's Monthly* 5 (Aug. 1859): 168-70. Edward Stevenson wrote, "Martin's Wife had hefted them & felt them under cover as had Martin" (Interview of Martin Harris by Edward Stevenson, 4 Sept. 1870, LDS archives). Willard Chase, a younger brother of Mason Chase, talked with Joseph about the same time that Harris asked the family how the plates were found. Chase recalled, "He then observed that if it had not been for that stone, (which he acknowledged belonged to me,) he would not have obtained the book" (*Mormonism Unvailed*, 246). In the preface to the 1830 Book of Mormon, Joseph wrote: "I would also inform you that the plates of which hath been spoken, were found in the township of Manchester, Ontario county, New-York."

44. Lucy Mack Smith, Preliminary MS, 80; *Biographical Sketches* (1853), 114; *History of Joseph Smith* (1958), 119.

45. Lemuel Durfee Account Book, 43-44, see n32.

46. Lucy Mack Smith, Preliminary MS, 97; *Biographical Sketches* (1853), 128; *History of Joseph Smith* (1958), 138. Mrs. S. F. Anderick recalled: "Hyrum was the only son sufficiently educated to teach school. I attended when he taught in the log school-house east of uncle's [Earl Wilcox]. He also taught in the Stafford District. He and Sophronia were the most respected of the family" (21 Dec. 1887, in *Naked Truths About Mormonism* 1 [Jan. 1888]: 2). William and Oliver Cowdery were evidently living in the township of Arcadia, Wayne County. See list of letters unclaimed at the Newark Post Office, 1 Oct. 1827, in the *Lyons Advertiser* 6 (17 Oct. 1827). For Lyman Cowdery, see list of unclaimed letters at the Palmyra Post Office, *Wayne Sentinel* 5 (11 July 1828): 3.

47. Lucy Mack Smith, Preliminary MS, 99; *Biographical Sketches* (1853), 129; *History of Joseph Smith* (1958), 139-40. The earlier reading "we had formerly lived in" is crossed out in the manuscript. There were two log homes that the Smiths had lived in prior to residing in the frame house. The first

one was in Palmyra, to which they did not return, and the other one was built by the Smiths in Manchester. Lucy Mack Smith, William Smith and Pomeroy Tucker each mention a cabin being built on land in Manchester.

The Smith family's place of residency after their move to the log house of Hyrum and his family is referred to in every case as Manchester. All of the Smiths' legal and personal documents dating from 1829-30 are dated at Manchester. This includes Joseph Smith's revelations; letters written by Oliver Cowdery while living with the Smith family; law suits against Joseph Sr. and Hyrum; the 1830 census; and the 1830 Manchester assessment roll where Hyrum Smith is taxed for fifteen acres on Lot 1.

There is no evidence of Hyrum Smith residing in Palmyra since the highway road tax lists do not include his name on any road district for 1827 or 1828. The road leading from the south boundary of the Corporation of the Village of Palmyra to the town line in 1828 was in Road District 1 and was Stafford Road. There were only six men over twenty-one years of age in this road district (Palmyra Highway Tax Record, Palmyra, New York, Copies of Old Village Records, 1793-1867, microfilm #812869, LDS Family History Library, Salt Lake City; microfilm 900, reel #60 at Harold B. Lee Library, Brigham Young University, Provo, Utah).

48. Lucy Mack Smith, Preliminary MS, 98, 100; *Biographical Sketches* (1853), 129-30; *History of Joseph Smith* (1958), 139, 141. See agreement dated 6 Apr. 1829 signed by Joseph Smith and Isaac Hale in the presence of Oliver H. Cowdery and Samuel H. Smith, LDS archives. On 7 September 1834 Oliver Cowdery wrote, "On Monday the 6th, I assisted him [Joseph] in arranging some business of a temporal nature" (*Messenger and Advocate* 1 [Oct. 1834]: 14, Kirtland, Ohio). Manuscript History, Book A-1: 13, LDS archives, has the date of arrival as "the fifth day of April." This was published in the *Times and Seasons* 3 (1 July 1842): 832 as "the fifteenth day of April."

Joseph wrote concerning Cowdery's vision that the "Lord appeared unto a young man by the name of Oliver Cowd[e]ry and shewed unto him the plates in a vision and also the truth of the work . . . now my wife had writ[t]en some for me to translate and also my Brother Samuel H. Smith" (Joseph Smith's 1832 account, 6, LDS archives, in Jessee, *Papers of Joseph Smith*, 1:10).

49. BC 10:2-5, 8-9, 11; also in LDS D&C 11:4, 7, 9-11, 15-16, 19, 23; and RLDS D&C 10:1b, 3b, 4c-5, 8a-b, 9b, 11a. Compare BC 10:1-4 with similar wording in BC 5:1-4 (for Oliver Cowdery, Apr. 1829), BC 11:1-3 (for Joseph Knight, May 1829), and BC 12:1-3 (for David Whitmer, June 1829).

50. Manuscript History Book A-1: 23; Jessee, *Papers of Joseph Smith*, 1:294. There were three baptisms performed before Hyrum was baptized. Oliver Cowdery, Joseph Smith, and Samuel Harrison Smith were baptized in May

1829. In June 1829, David Whitmer, Peter Whitmer, Jr., and probably John Whitmer were baptized. If John Whitmer is included, the total number of baptisms at this time is seven. In the Manuscript History there are two general statements concerning baptism: (1) "From this time forth many became believers, and were baptized" (Book A-1: 23; Jessee, *Papers of Joseph Smith*, 1:294). Cf. *History of the Church of Jesus Christ of Latter-day Saints*, ed. B. H. Roberts, (Salt Lake City: Deseret Book, 1959), 1:51; (2) "almost daily we administered the ordinance of Baptism for the remission of sins" (Book A-1: 26; Jessee, *Papers of Joseph Smith*, 1:299). Cf. *History of the Church* 1:59.

There are no records that support numerous baptisms previous to 6 April 1830, despite David Whitmer's statement in 1887, "There were six elders and about seventy members before April 6th" (*An Address to All Believers in Christ*, [Richmond, MO: author, 1887], 33). See also *Saints' Herald* 29 (15 June 1882): 189, where Whitmer said "there were about forty or fifty members in the Church when organized on April 6th, 1830."

51. The copyright is documented in three places: (1) a certificate held by Joseph Smith, now in LDS archives; (2) the original entry in vol. 116, Copyright Records, New York Northern District, Sept. 1826 - May 1831, entry 107, by Richard R. Lansing, Clerk, now in the Library of Congress, Washington, D.C.; and (3) a copy written in the printer's manuscript for the 1830 Book of Mormon, RLDS archives.

52. BC 15:1, "instructions relative to building up the church of Christ, according to the fulness of the gospel" (Fayette, New York, June 1829). See also vv 27-43; LDS D&C 18; RLDS D&C 16. Cf. with "A Commandment from God unto Oliver," in Robert J. Woodford, "The Historical Development of the Doctrine and Covenants," Ph.D. diss., Brigham Young University, 1974, 1:287-90.

53. Cowdery to Hyrum Smith, 14 June 1829, transcribed in 1832 into letterbook, located in Joseph Smith's Letterbook 1:5, LDS archives.

54. Jesse Smith to Hyrum Smith, 17 June 1829, located in Joseph Smith's Letterbook, 2:59-61, LDS archives. The letter was copied into the letterbook in 1839.

55. Lucy Mack Smith, *Biographical Sketches* (1853), 42; *History of Joseph Smith* (1958), 352; see Pearson H. Corbett, *Hyrum Smith: Patriarch*, 57, 103. See photo of the "Family Record" in Hyrum Smith's family Bible in *The Friend* 18 (Jan. 1988): 35, entry: "Mary Smith was Born June 27th 1829."

56. Mortgages, Liber 3:325, Wayne County Courthouse, Lyons, New York.

57. Lucy Mack Smith, Preliminary MS, 111; *Biographical Sketches* (1853), 145; *History of Joseph Smith* (1958), 159. Both the printer's and the original

manuscripts were used for the typesetting of the Book of Mormon. See Stanley R. Larson, "A Study of Some Textual Variations in the Book of Mormon Comparing the Original and the Printer's Manuscripts and the 1830, the 1837, and the 1840 Editions," M.A. thesis, Brigham Young University, 1974, 264; "Book of Mormon Manuscript Fragments Examined," *Ensign* 22 (Apr. 1992): 74; and Royal Skousen, "Piecing Together the Original Manuscript," *Brigham Young University Today* 46 (May 1992): 23-24.

58. Memorandum, 8 Sept. 1892, Palmyra, New York, in Wilford C. Wood, *Joseph Smith Begins His Work*, 2 vols. (Salt Lake City: Deseret News Press, 1958), Vol. 1, introductory pages. John Gilbert also wrote: "Hyrum Smith was the only one of the family I had any acquaintance with, and that very slight" (Gilbert to James T. Cobb, 16 Mar. 1879); also, "Hyrum Smith brought to the office 24 pages of manuscript on foolscap paper, closely written and legible, but not a punctuation mark from beginning to end. This was about the middle of August, 1829, and the printing was completed in March, 1830. It was some weeks after this before the binder was able to deliver any copies" (Gilbert to Cobb, 10 Feb. 1879). Both of Gilbert's letters are in the Schroeder Collection, Manuscript and Archives Division, New York Public Library, New York City.

59. "History of Thos. Baldwin Marsh," *Deseret News* 8 (24 Mar. 1858): 18, Fillmore City, Utah Territory. Marsh's sixteen pages would be one galley sheet (eight pages printed on each side) that evidently was given away to a number of persons who visited the printing office. Marsh's account continued: "From this time for about one year I corresponded with Oliver Cowdery and Joseph Smith, jun., and prepared myself to move west." Cowdery wrote to Joseph: "My dear Brother I cannot hardly feel to close this letter as yet without informing you that we received one from Mr. Marsh from Boston, Massachusetts dated the 25th Oct. he informs us that he wishes to hear from us and know of our wellfare he says he has talked considerable to some respecting ou[r] work with freedom but others could not because they had no ears" (Oliver Cowdery to Joseph Smith, Manchester, 6 Nov. 1829, copy transcribed in 1832 into Joseph Smith's Letterbook 1:8, LDS archives). See *Ensign* 13 (Dec. 1983): 47, for a photograph.

60. Letter of Stephen S. Harding, dated Feb. 1882, in Thomas Gregg, *The Prophet of Palmyra* (New York: John B. Alden, 1890), 41, 48, 52. Harding mentioned that after the candle had burned "Mother Smith loaded a clay pipe with tobacco, which she ground up in her hands" (43). Cf. Tucker, *Origin, Rise, and Progress of Mormonism*, 284. For a photograph of the title page Harding was given, and on which Joseph Smith was identified as "author and

proprietor," see *Church History in the Fulness of Times* (Salt Lake City: Church of Jesus Christ of Latter-day Saints, 1989), 64.

61. Account of Solomon Chamberlain, published in "The John Taylor Nauvoo Journal," *Brigham Young University Studies* 23 (Summer 1983): 45, copied into Taylor's diary in the spring of 1845. One pamphlet which contained some background material on Chamberlain was titled *A Sketch of the Experience of Solomon Chamberlin* (Lyons, New York, 1829), copy at the Harold B. Lee Library, Brigham Young University.

62. Larry C. Porter, "Solomon Chamberlain—Early Missionary," *Brigham Young University Studies* 12 (Spring 1972): 316-17, dated 11 July 1858.

63. "John Taylor Nauvoo Journal," 45-46. Chamberlain would have picked up four galley sheets of sixteen pages each for the total of sixty-four pages.

64. Cowdery to Joseph Smith, 6 Nov. 1829, Joseph Smith Letterbook 1:8, LDS archives.

65. Abner Cole was born about 1782. Orsamus Turner mentioned that he was "an early lawyer of Palmyra" (*History of the Phelps and Gorham's Purchase*, 186). Cole was a justice of the peace in Palmyra in 1814 and 1815 (Old Village Records, Palmyra, New York, entries for Apr. 1814 and Apr. 1815). In 1818 he was a village constable. He is listed as a resident of Palmyra in the 1820 and the 1830 censuses. He was in Road District 26, the same one on which Joseph Smith, Sr., is listed, for 1816-21 (Palmyra Highway Tax Records, typed copy). In 1820 he had property in Palmyra (49 1/2 acres) and one hundred acres in Manchester. He published two newspapers. *The Reflector* was published in Palmyra from 2 September 1829 to 16 December 1829. A "New Series" continued with the issue of 22 December 1829 and the last known issue was dated 19 March 1831. Cole moved to Rochester and started another newspaper, the *Liberal Advocate*, using the same pen name, Obadiah Dogberry. The masthead, like that of the Palmyra *Reflector*, included the quote from Alexander Pope: "Know then thyself, presume not God to scan! The proper study of mankind is man." The *Liberal Advocate* ran from 23 February 1832 through 22 November 1834. Cole died 13 July 1835, and a local newspaper reported his death: "In this city, on the 13th inst Abner Cole, Esq. Editor of the 'Liberal Advocate'" (*Rochester Daily Democrat*, 15 July 1835).

For additional material on "Obadiah Dogberry" (Abner Cole), see M. Hamlin Cannon, "Contemporary Views of Mormon Origins (1830)," *The Mississippi Valley Historical Review* 31 (June 1944): 261-66; Russell R. Rich, "The Dogberry Papers and the Book of Mormon", *Brigham Young University Studies* 10 (Spring 1970): 315-20; and Joseph W. Barnes, "Obediah Dogberry Rochester Freethinker," *Rochester History* 36 (July 1974): 1-24.

66. Lucy Mack Smith, Preliminary MS, 118; *Biographical Sketches* (1853), 148; *History of Joseph Smith* (1958), 164. Lucy recalled the newspaper as "Dogberry paper [on] Winter Hill." In fact, *The Reflector* was issued from "his 'Bower' on Winter Green Hill" and was printed on the press of E. B. Grandin. See *The Reflector* 1 [2 Sept. 1829]: 1.

67. Lucy Mack Smith, Preliminary MS, 119; *Biographical Sketches* (1853), 149; *History of Joseph Smith* (1958), 165.

68. In Simon Gratz Autograph Collection, Case 8, Box 17 (American Miscellaneous), under Smith, Joseph, Sr., Historical Society of Pennsylvania, Philadelphia. Used by permission. Photographs have been also published in *Ensign* 13 (Dec. 1983): 44; and *Church History in the Fulness of Times*, 65. The *Ensign* published this comment: "In this agreement (which, incidentally, points out the role of the Prophet's father, Joseph Smith, Sr., in the publication of the Book of Mormon), the elder Smith agrees that the first profits from the sale of the book were to go toward the payment of the printer, thus relieving Martin Harris of the full burden of payment" (*Ensign* 13 [Dec. 1983]: 44). Compare this with the text of the agreement.

69. Probate Papers, Box 053, filed by executors Oliver Durfee and Lemuel Durfee, Jr., filed on 22 Jan. 1830, Surrogate's Court, Wayne County Courthouse, Lyons, New York. For collection process, see Nathan Pierce Docket Book, 1827-30, Manchester Town Office, 25. The signature of Joseph Smith, Sr., appears to be different from the one in the Simon Gratz Autograph Collection. This could be accounted for by the "nervous affection" Jesse Smith mentions, by the quill he used to sign his name, or by his using a different angle when signing.

70. "Records of the Session of the Presbyterian Church in Palmyra," 2 (10 Mar. 1830): 11.

71. Ibid., 11-12.

72. Lucy Mack Smith, Preliminary MS, 117; *Biographical Sketches* (1853), 147; *History of Joseph Smith* (1958), 162. In the 1853 edition it reads: "Hyrum. 'I will tell you what I will do, Mr. Beckwith, if you do get a testimony from God, that the book is not true, I will confess to you that it is not true.'" Lucy stated in her manuscript that one of the men said that they had "belonged to our church a whole year." This is clearly an error on her part.

73. "Records of the Session of the Presbyterian Church in Palmyra" 2:13.

74. Copies of the Book of Mormon were ready for sale by 26 March 1830. See *Wayne Sentinel* 7 (26 Mar. 1830): 3. It was first sold for fourteen shillings ($1.75), and later the cost was reduced to ten shillings ($1.25). Cf. Tucker, *Origin, Rise, and Progress of Mormonism*, 55. Henry Harris recalled talking with Martin Harris: "After the Book was published, I frequently bantered him for

a copy. He asked fourteen shillings a piece for them; I told him I would not give so much; he told me [they] had had a revelation that they must be sold at that price. Sometime afterwards I talked with Martin Harris about buying one of the Books and he told me they had had a new revelation, that they might be sold at ten shillings a piece" (*Mormonism Unvailed*, 252). Sylvia Walker remembered that the price of the Book of Mormon was lowered: "The Mormons said the price of the 'Book of Mormon' was established at $1.75 by revelation. It did not sell well and they claimed to receive another to sell it at $1.25" (*Naked Truths About Mormonism* 1 [Apr. 1888]: 1).

75. *The Autobiography of Parley Parker Pratt*, ed. Parley P. Pratt, Jr. (New York: Published for the Editor and Proprietor by Russell Brothers, 1874), 38-39; 1961 ed., 37-38. Pratt recalled, "He [Hyrum] invited me to his home, where I saw mother Smith and Hyrum Smith's wife, and sister Rockwell, the mother of Orin Porter Rockwell" (discourse delivered on 7 Sept. 1856, *Journal of Discourses* 5:194). In *Biographical Sketches* (1853) is written, "as Joseph was about commencing a discourse one Sunday morning, Parley P. Pratt came in . . . The following day he was baptized and ordained. . . . After Joseph ordained Parley, he went home again to Pennsylvania, for he was only in Manchester on business" (157). This account is in error as Joseph was in Harmony at the end of August and first part of September. Pratt remembered being baptized about the first of September. Also, it was Cowdery who ordained Parley to the office of Elder, not Smith. Compare with 1958 edition (176), where the part about Joseph ordaining Parley is deleted.

76. *Autobiography of Parley Parker Pratt* (1874), 42-43; 1961 ed., 41-42. That Joseph Smith was still in Harmony, see Book of Commandments 28, "given in Harmony, Pennsylvania, September 4, 1830" (60) and the reverse side of the deed of land from Isaac Hale to his son-in-law, dated 6 Apr. 1829, noting that payment was received in full "Harmony August 26th 1830" (Joseph Smith Collection, LDS archives). The Indenture was made on 25 August 1830 and witnessed by John Whitmer. The Manuscript History, Book A-1: 53, says, "during the last week in August we arrived at Fayette" (Jessee, *Papers of Joseph Smith*, 1:322). This statement is in error as both Parley Pratt and Thomas Marsh were ordained to the office of Elder by Oliver Cowdery due to Joseph's absence.

77. *Autobiography of Parley P. Pratt* (1874), 46-47; 1961 ed., 45. Pratt's description of the log home agrees with that of Pomeroy Tucker who stated, "This house was divided into two rooms," adding that a bedroom wing was added later (*Origin, Rise, and Progress of Mormonism*, 13). Pratt wrote elsewhere: "Then, after finishing my visit to Columbia Co., I returned to the brethren in Ontario Co., where for the first time, I saw Mr. Joseph Smith, Jr.,

who had just returned from Pennsylvania, to his father's house, in Manchester" (Pratt, *Mormonism Unveiled* [New-York: Published by O. Pratt & E. Fordham, Third Edition, 1838], 41). The "History of Parley P. Pratt" also mentions "I saw for the first time Joseph Smith, the Prophet, at his father's house, in Manchester" (*Deseret News* 8 [19 May 1858]: 53).

78. *True Latter Day Saints' Herald* 3 (Oct. 1862): 79-83. When Thayer asked what was the price of the Book of Mormon, "Fourteen shillings" [$1.75] was the reply. He bought a copy (80). See Book of Commandments 35:14; LDS D&C 33:15; RLDS D&C 32:3c, where it is clear that Thayer and Northrop Sweet had already been ordained elders in the church because they could lay hands on individuals for the gift of the Holy Ghost. The "History of Parley P. Pratt" states that Pratt preached and at the close of the meeting there were "baptized seven persons" (*Deseret News* 8 [19 May 1858]: 53). Those baptized included Ezra Thayer, Northrop Sweet and Oliver Cowdery's step mother Keziah Cowdery.

79. 1830 U.S. Census, Manchester, Ontario County, New York, 170, Family #124, microfilm #017161, LDS Family History Library.

80. Nathan Pierce Docket Book, Manchester Town Office; microfilm of docket book, film 900, reel #62, Harold B. Lee Library, Brigham Young University. The fact that this summons was brought before Justice Nathan Pierce of Manchester, Ontario County, is further evidence that in June 1830 Hyrum Smith resided in Manchester rather than in Palmyra, Wayne County. See *Laws of the State of New York* (Albany: Printed by Leake & Croswell, 1824), 280. In the 1830 assessment records Hyrum Smith is taxed for fifteen acres on Lot 1. See 1830 Assessment Records of Manchester, New York, 5 July 1830, 23, Ontario County Historical Society, Canandaigua, New York; copy in our possession. Don Enders brought this document to our attention.

81. Printed Execution found unbound in Nathan Pierce Docket Book, Manchester Town Office, copy in our possession. The use of italics indicates where handwriting was filled in on the printed form.

The reverse side of the Execution records that $9.94 was received for "Levi Daggett by A K Daggett." This is probably Augustus K. Daggett, son of Levi Daggett, Sr. (see microfilm #017177, LDS Family History Library, Salt Lake City). See also Samuel Bradlee Daggett, *A History of the Doggett-Daggett Family* (Baltimore: Gateway Press, Inc., 1973), 149-50, 199.

82. The final item written in the docket book for this case was "Paid by Justice 4th April 1831," and the amount of $21.07 plus $1.60 for a total of $22.67. The reverse side of the execution contains the amount of $24.75, probably including the $12.81 already paid.

83. Richard L. Bushman, *Joseph Smith and the Beginnings of Mormonism* (Urbana: University of Illinois Press, 1984), 172.

84. Lucy Mack Smith, Preliminary MS, 124, 126; *Biographical Sketches* (1853), 158-62; *History of Joseph Smith* (1958), 178-82.

85. Lucy Mack Smith, Preliminary MS, 124-25; *Biographical Sketches* (1853), 162, 164-65; *History of Joseph Smith* (1958), 182, 185-86.

86. Diary of Eli Bruce, 5 Nov. 1830, in Rob Morris, *The Masonic Martyr: The Biography of Eli Bruce, Sheriff of Niagara County, New York* (Louisville, KY: Morris & Monsarrat, 1861), 266-67.

87. Dean C. Jessee, ed., *The Personal Writings of Joseph Smith* (Salt Lake City: Deseret Book, 1984), 231-32; see *Improvement Era* 9 (Dec. 1905): 168-69. See earlier letter of Joseph Smith to Martin Harris, 22 Feb. 1831, "see that Father Smiths family are taken care of and sent on. You will send to Colesville and have either Hiram [Smith] or Newel [Knight] to come immediately or both if they can be spared. You will not sell the books for less than 10 Shillings [$1.25]" (LDS archives, not in Jessee, *Personal Writings of Joseph Smith*). See also Pearson H. Corbett, *Hyrum Smith: Patriarch* (Salt Lake City: Deseret Book, 1963), 80.

In a "List of Articles belonging to Martin Harris & left in the hands of Thomas Lakely for safe keeping not to be delivered to any person except by the written order of the said Harris Dated May 3. 1831" is listed "300 Books of Mormon to be sold for $1.25 & account to the said Harris $1.00 for each copy, or deliver the said books to any person presenting the written order of the said Harris." The list was signed by Harris and is located in the Palmyra Library Vertical files, Thomas Lakey's "Record of Court Proceedings 1827-1830," in the King's Daughters Library, Palmyra, New York. Another Harris signature is located in the Inventory to the Estate of Seth Harris, Probate Record, 13 Jan. 1822, original in Ontario County Historical Society, Canandaigua, New York.

In a letter to Reverend Ancil Beach dated January 1832, six leading citizens of Canandaigua wrote: "Martin Harris lately testified on a trial which related to the work of printing and publishing the Book that he had sent 2300 copies of it to the west" (copy of letter in the Hubbell Papers, Princeton University Library, Princeton, New Jersey). Hyrum Smith's diary entries for 1832 as printed in *Hyrum Smith: Patriarch* mention that he sold the Book of Mormon in Ohio for $1.25 a copy (104, 111). The Book of Mormon was also used as an object of barter (103-104, 111).

88. "Newel Knight's Journal," in *Scraps of Biography* (Salt Lake City: Juvenile Instructor Office, 1883), 65. A journal of Newel Knight is located in LDS archives. Knight died on 11 January 1847.

89. Ibid., 65-67.

90. William G. Hartley, *"They Are My Friends": A History of the Joseph Knight Family, 1825-1850* (Provo, UT: Grandin Book Co., 1986), 60. The letter termed Pratt "another servant and apostle" and called the Colesville area "the seat of Satan." Cf. 1836 letter regarding the south part of Bainbridge, New York, in *History of Chenango and Madison Counties, New York* (Syracuse, NY: D. Mason & Co., 1880), 147. See also Elden J. Watson, comp., *The Orson Pratt Journals* (Salt Lake City: comp., 1975), 10.

91. BC 39:4; LDS D&C 37:3; RLDS D&C 37:2a.

92. Lucy Mack Smith, Preliminary MS, 135; *Biographical Sketches* (1853), 176; *History of Joseph Smith* (1958), 199. Lucy reported that she had learned "that Mr. Smith [her husband] and Hyrum had gone through to Kirtland by land, in order to be there by the first of April." At a conference held on 25 October 1831 at Orange, Ohio, "Br. Hyrum Smith said that he thought best that the information of the coming forth of the Book of Mormon be related by Joseph himself to the Elders present that all might know for themselves. Br. Joseph Smith jr. said that it was not intended to tell the world all the particulars of the coming forth of the book of Mormon, & also said that it was not expedient for him to relate these things &c" (Donald Q. Cannon and Lyndon W. Cook, eds., *Far West Record: Minutes of The Church of Jesus Christ of Latter-day Saints, 1830-1844* [Salt Lake City: Deseret Book Co., 1983], 23).

CHAPTER SEVEN

RESTORING THE
CHURCH OF CHRIST

B y 26 March 1830 5,000 copies of the Book of Mormon had been printed. Baptisms had been performed in May and June 1829, but no formal ecclesiastical organization had yet occurred.[1] In late March Joseph Knight drove Joseph Smith from Harmony, Pennsylvania, to the home of his father and brother Hyrum in Manchester. Knight later recalled that on the way Smith talked about anticipated success in selling the books and about organizing a church:

> Now in the Spring of 1830 I went with my Team and took Joseph out to Manchester to his Father. When we was on our way he told me that there must be a Church formed But did not tell when. Now when we got near to his fathers we saw a man some Eighty Rods Before us run acros[s] the street with a Bundle in his hand. "There," says Joseph, "there is Martin going a Cros[s] the road with some thing in his hand." Says I, "how Could you know him so far?" Says he, "I Believe it is him," and when we Came up it was Martin with a Bunch of morman Books. He Came to us and after Compliments he says, "The Books will not sell for no Body wants them." Joseph says, "I think they will sell well." Says he [Martin], "I want a Commandment." "Why," says Joseph, "fulfill what you have got." "But," says he, "I must have a Commandment." Joseph put him off. But he insisted three or four times he must have a Commandment. . . . In the morning he got up and said he must have a Commandment to Joseph and went home. And along in the after part of the Day Joseph and Oliver Received a Commandment.[2]

The title of the revelation as printed stated: "A commandment of God and not of man to you, Martin, given (Manchester, New-York, March, 1830,) by him who is eternal."[3] Knight stayed at the Smiths' residence a few days waiting for more copies of the Book of Mormon to be bound.

As Joseph Smith had predicted to Knight, the "Church of Christ" was organized very soon thereafter—on 6 April 1830. Traditional accounts locate this meeting at the home of Peter Whitmer in Fayette, New York. No minutes of the meeting have survived, but the earliest accounts and supporting evidence suggest the event occurred not at Fayette but in the Smiths' log home in Manchester.

The Book of Commandments, published in 1833, contained a collection of six revelations dated 6 April 1830, given to six people who attended the organizational meeting: Oliver Cowdery, Hyrum Smith, Samuel H. Smith, Joseph Smith, Sr., Joseph Knight, and Joseph Smith himself. These revelations were received, according to their headings, at Manchester. A round trip between Manchester and Fayette being fifty miles, it is unlikely the same six men could have attended an organizational meeting in Fayette on the same day. The revelations were first arranged and copied by Joseph Smith with the assistance of John Whitmer in July 1830 at Harmony, Pennsylvania, and later became chapters 2-27 of the Book of Commandments. On 20 July 1833 the press printing the revelations in book form was destroyed, but several of the yet-to-be-completed Book of Commandments were put together and used by early ministers of the church.[4]

In addition, all references in *The Evening and the Morning Star* before 1834 refer to the township of Manchester as the location of the church's organization.[5] For example, the following account of church origins appeared in April 1833:

> Soon after the book of Mormon came forth, containing the fulness of the gospel of Jesus Christ, the church was organized on the sixth of April, in Manchester; soon after, a branch was established in Fayette, and the June following, another in Colesville, New York. We shall not give, at this time, the particulars attending the organization of these branches of the church. . . . Twenty more [people] were added to the church in Manchester and Fayette, in the month of April; and on the 28th of June, thirteen were baptized in Coles-

ville. . . . In October, (1830) the number of disciples had increased to between seventy and eighty.[6]

As we have seen in previous chapters, the Smith house had become the center for many of the events associated with Joseph Smith's emerging religious vocation until the Smiths moved to Waterloo, New York, in the fall of 1830. William Smith remembered the organizational meeting being in Manchester.[7] Joseph Knight was staying with the Smiths when the church was organized. A neighbor and friend of the family, Benjamin Saunders, who recorded that the "<Smiths> held meetings at their house," was present at the baptisms and probably would not have gone out of his way to travel to Fayette for the occasion.[8]

Early references refer to six founding members.[9] As to the identity of the six members present at the foundational meeting, two early lists made in 1842-43 exist. It is possible there may have been no actual roll call made at the time and the names on the lists have slight variations. Brigham Young writing in 1843 identifies "The names of thouse [sic] present at the organization" on 6 April 1830 as Joseph Smith, Sr., Orrin Rockwell, Joseph Smith, Hyrum Smith, Samuel H. Smith, and Oliver Cowdery.[10] Jonathan Turner's *Mormonism in All Ages*, published in 1842, list is essentially the same as Young's except that Joseph Knight is mentioned rather than Orrin Rockwell.[11] By Knight's account, we know he was there, but he did not receive baptism on this day. The names mentioned in Joseph Smith's manuscript history of the church included Joseph Smith, Oliver Cowdery, Joseph Smith, Sr., Lucy Smith, Martin Harris, and a member of the Rockwell family, Sarah Rockwell. It is unlikely that Lucy Smith or Sarah Rockwell would be counted as one of the original six though they were present. More likely, the six original members were Joseph Smith, Oliver Cowdery, Hyrum Smith, Samuel H. Smith, Joseph Smith, Sr., and Martin Harris.[12] Years later, around 1858, several other lists were compiled reporting those baptized in May-June 1829 or having been present at the 6 April meeting.[13]

The revelation received by Joseph Smith during the founding organizational meeting itself (printed as chap. 22) was headed "A Revelation to Joseph, given in Manchester, New-York, April 6,

1830."[14] The location was changed in later editions to Fayette. Hyrum Smith was told:

> A Revelation to Hyrum, given in Manchester, New-York, April 6, 1830. Behold I speak unto you, Hyrum, a few words: For thou also art under no condemnation, and thy heart is opened, and thy tongue loosed; And thy calling is to exhortation, and to strengthen the church continually. Wherefore thy duty is unto the church forever; and this because of thy family. Amen.[15]

Circumstantial evidence places Hyrum Smith in the Palmyra-Manchester vicinity. He signed a note to Levi Daggett of Palmyra on 7 April.[16] Others receiving revelations in Manchester the same day included Oliver Cowdery, Samuel Harrison Smith, and Joseph Smith, Sr. Unlike the others', Joseph Knight's revelation exhorted him to "unite with the true church." He later wrote, "But I should a felt Better if I had a gone forward. But I went home and was Babtised in June with my wife and familey."[17]

Knight later recalled details regarding the exhortations and instructions which were part of the activities: "On the sixth Day of April 1830 he Begun the Church with six members and received the following Revelation, Book of Covenants [1835 ed.] Page 177. They all kneeld down and prayed and Joseph gave them instructions how to B[u]ild up the Church and ex[h]orted them to Be faithful in all things for this is the work of God."[18] The revelation to Smith instructed him to proceed with the first ordinations.[19] He ordained Oliver Cowdery an elder, and Cowdery ordained Smith a seer, translator, prophet, apostle, and first elder in the Church of Christ. Cowdery became known as the second elder. Joseph Smith's ordination as prophet and seer was the highlight ordinance on the day of the church's organization. William E. McLellin, who visited Oliver Cowdery in July 1847, wrote: "While I was on a visit with O. Cowdery, during the past summer, I asked him, to what did you ordain Joseph on the 6th of April, 1830? He answered, I ordained him to be a Prophet, Seer, &c., just as the revelation says."[20]

It was within this context that the 6 April revelation gave directions to members of the new church regarding its preeminent leader: "Wherefore, meaning the church, thou shalt give heed unto all his

[Joseph's] words, and commandments, which he shall give unto you, as he receiveth them, walking in all holiness before me: For his word ye shall receive, as if from mine own mouth, in all patience and faith."[21] Members were promised that if they obeyed, the gates of hell would not prevail against them, God would disperse the powers of darkness before them, and he would shake the heavens for their good.

At least four people seem to have been baptized as part of the activities surrounding the organization. Knight describes two of the four baptisms, the baptisms of Joseph Smith, Sr., and Martin Harris:

I had Be[e]n there several Days. Old Mr. Smith and Martin Harris Come forrod [forward] to Be Babtise[d] for the first. They found a place in a lot a small Stream ran thro and they ware Baptized in the Evening Because of persecution. They went forward and was Babtized Being the first I saw Babtized in the new and ever-lasting Covenant. . . . There was one thing I will mention that evening that old Brother Smith and Martin Harris was Babtised. Joseph was fil[le]d with the Spirrit to a grate Degree to see his Father and Mr. Harris that he had Bin [been] with so much he Bast [burst] out with greaf and Joy and seamed as tho the world Could not hold him. He went out into the Lot and appear[e]d to want to git out of site of every Body and would sob and Crie and seamed to Be so full that he could not live. Oliver and I went after him and Came to him and after a while he Came in. But he was the most wrot upon that I ever saw any man. But his joy seemed to Be full.[22]

Lucy Smith's narrative is similar:

In the spring Joseph came up <and preached to us> after <Oliver got throu[g]h> with the Book. <[My] Husband and> Martin H[a]rris was ba[p]tized. Joseph stood on the shore when his father came out of the water and as he took him by the hand, he cried out, Oh! my God I have lived to see my father baptized into the true church of Jesus Christ and <he> covered his face <in his father's bosom and wept aloud for joy as did> Joseph of old when he beheld his father coming up into the land of Egypt, this took pla<ace> on the sixth of April 1830, the d[a]y on which the church was organized.[23]

Lucy does not mention her own baptism. But a neighbor, Cornelius R. Stafford, recalled that as a young man he "saw old Jo Smith, his wife and Mrs. [Sarah W.] Rockwell baptized by prophet Jo Smith."[24]

Benjamin Saunders also remembered that the "<Smiths> held meetings at their house. I was there when they first baptized. Oliver Cowdery did the baptizing. Old brother <Smith> was baptized at that time and I think old Mrs. Rockwell."[25] Martin Harris years later recalled that he was not baptized "untill the church Was organised by Joseph Smith the Prophet then I Was Babtised by the Hands of Oliver Cowdery."[26]

The place of these baptisms was no doubt Crooked Brook (now Hathaway Creek), a stream in the northwest corner of the township of Manchester. Crooked Brook ran north past the Smith residence toward Palmyra. Joseph Knight described it as a "small Stream," which it still is.[27] According to a later newspaper account, the stream,

> not more than si[x]ty feet from the highway, is the first Mormon Jordan, a little creek which the Smith boys dammed at Joe's request and made a pool in which the first converts to Mormonism were baptized. It is a sing[i]n[g] meandering little brooklet about ten or fifte[e]n feet wide, with two or three feet of water standing in pools in the bends of the stream, but ordinarily the water is but a few inches deep.[28]

A history of Ontario County describes the stream in terms congruent with the accounts of those who claimed to be present at the church's organization: "Crooked brook, of Mormon fame, runs through the northwest part of the town[ship of Manchester], and it was in the waters of this stream that the Mormons baptized their early saints. Dr. [John] Stafford, an old resident of the village of Manchester, was present at the first baptism."[29] John Stafford, oldest son of William, "knew the Smith family well, and was present at the first baptism, when old Granny Smith and Sally Rockwell" were baptized.[30] The Stafford and Rockwell families were residents of the township of Manchester and lived within a mile of the Smith home.[31]

In 1839, when Joseph Smith, with the help of scribe James Mulholland, compiled the opening portion of his history, he was more vague about chronology but seemed to confirm the other accounts: "Several persons who had attended the above meeting [6 April 1830] and got convinced of the truth, came forward shortly after, and were received into the church, among the rest, my own father and mother were baptized to my great joy and consolation, and about the same time Martin Harris and A. [sic] Rockwell."[32] James Mulholland wrote at the bottom of what would be pages nine and ten of the 1839 draft: "Father Smith, Martin Harris baptized this evening 6th April. Mother Smith & Sister Rockwell 2 or 3 days afterward."[33] On the next page was recorded: "Several persons who attended this meeting, but who had <not> as yet been baptized, came forward shortly after. . . . Among the rest Father Smith, Martin Harris, Mother Smith."[34] The manuscript version behind the *Times and Seasons* edition added to the last phrase, "among the rest My own Father and Mother were baptized to my great joy and consolation, and about the same time, Martin Harris and a [blank] Rockwell."[35] Later the name "Orrin Porter" was mistakenly added in the blank space by someone other than James Mulholland.

Joseph Smith's 1839 history was not the first account to change the place of the church organization to Fayette, twenty-five miles away. The May 1834 edition of *The Evening and the Morning Star* contains probably the earliest error in the heading of the "MINUTES of a Conference of the Elders of the church of Christ, which church was organized in the township of Fayette, Seneca county, New-York, on the 6th of April, A.D. 1830." This conference of elders was held on 3 May 1834. Also, in the 1835 Doctrine and Covenants the texts of five of the six revelations received on 6 April 1830 and originally published in the 1833 Book of Commandments were amalgamated into a single revelation and the references to the location were deleted.[36]

Not all official accounts after 1834 reflected the error in location. In 1840 Orson Pratt prepared the pamphlet *Remarkable Visions* in which he stated that the church was organized in Manchester. In 1842 Smith used Pratt's pamphlet for wording in a letter to John Wentworth. As published in the *Times and Seasons*, Smith's letter read: "On the 6th of April, 1830, the 'Church of Jesus Christ of Latter-Day Saints,' was first organized in the town of Manchester, Ontario co., state of New York."[37] In 1844 this letter was used as a source for a history published by Daniel Rupp.[38] However, in 1848 the Manchester reference in Pratt's pamphlet *Remarkable Visions* was changed to Fayette to agree with Smith's history.[39] Nearly thirty years later, in 1876, the LDS Doctrine and Covenants included Fayette as the site of the church's founding, thereby canonizing the error.[40]

It is difficult to support the argument that the early references to Manchester may have been mistaken and that on 6 April the church was in fact organized at Fayette. The question becomes, then, why the confusion and contradictions about the location. Joseph Smith's history betrays other anachronisms and conflations. After gathering "at the house of the above mentioned Mr [Peter] Whitmer," Sr., Smith recalls: "I then laid my hands upon Oliver Cowdery and ordained him an Elder of the 'Church of Jesus Christ of Latter Day Saints.'" In fact the official name of the church in 1830 was the Church of Christ. The name was changed to the Church of the Latter Day Saints in 1834 and finally to the Church of Jesus Christ of Latter Day Saints in 1838.[41]

Memory often conflates events which were once separate and distinct. Events which occurred within days of the 6 April meeting at Manchester, events which demonstrably occurred at the Whitmer house in Fayette, might have assumed greater importance in Smith's mind over time. In Fayette there was an increase in the number of baptisms, the Articles and Covenants of the new church were written and accepted, licenses for lay ministers to preach were issued, and the first three churchwide conferences were convened.

One of the revelations given on 6 April 1830, a Tuesday, designated Oliver Cowdery to be "the first preacher of this church."[42] On 11 April, the first Sunday after the organization of the church, Cowdery delivered "the first public discourse," the Fayette branch of the church was organized, and Cowdery performed six baptisms. A week later, on 18 April, another baptismal service was held at Fayette, where Cowdery performed seven baptisms in Seneca Lake.[43] The manuscript history lists no one baptized at Fayette who lived in the Manchester/Palmyra area.

The next meeting was the first conference of the church, which convened on 9 June. For the first time the Manchester and Fayette branches came together. A copy of the minutes reads: "Minutes of the first Conference held in the Township of Fayette, Seneca County, State of New York."[44] Smith read "The Articles and Covenants of the church of Christ." They were "received by unanimous voice of the whole congregation."[45] The Articles and Covenants were then submitted as a confession of faith, members agreeing that the statement reflected their beliefs, including the callings of Joseph Smith and Oliver Cowdery, the Book of Mormon, and what were to be the teachings and practices of the infant church.

At the Fayette conference prospective members from Manchester township were baptized. They were Jerusha Smith (Hyrum Smith's wife), Katherine Smith, William Smith, Don Carlos Smith, Porter Rockwell, Caroline Rockwell, and Electa Rockwell (children of Sarah W. Rockwell).[46] These are the first baptisms of Manchester residents which can be documented as occurring in Fayette.

At the end of June, Smith and Cowdery were at Colesville, New York, to set up the church there. In the midst of opposition, Cowdery performed thirteen or fourteen baptisms and established the Colesville branch on Monday, 28 June 1830. Among those baptized were Joseph's wife Emma and Joseph and Polly Knight.[47]

Some historians have looked to David Whitmer, one of the three witnesses to the Book of Mormon, to substantiate the claim that the church was founded in Fayette, since he claimed to have been present at the meeting held on 6 April.[48] However, a closer look makes clear that the events Whitmer describes in Fayette parallel most closely events associated with meetings after the organization of the church. In 1887 Whitmer wrote:

> Now, when April 6, 1830, had come, we had then established three branches of the "Church of Christ," in which three branches were about seventy members: One branch was at Fayette, N.Y.; one at Manchester, N.Y., and one at Colesville, Pa. [New York] It is all a mistake about the church being *organized* on April 6, 1830, as I will show. We were as fully *organized*—spiritually—before April 6th as we were on that day. The reason why we met on that day was this; the world had been telling us that we were not a regularly organized church, and we had no right to officiate in the ordinance of marriage, hold church property, etc., and that we should organize according to the laws of the land. On this account we met at my

father's house in Fayette, N.Y., on April 6, 1830, to attend to this
matter of organizing according to the laws of the land. . . . Now
brethren, how can it be that the church was any more organized—
spiritually—on April 6th, than it was before that time? There were
six elders and about seventy members before April 6th, and the
same number of elders and members after that day.[49]

Whitmer's statement contains errors. He claims there were seventy
members in three branches of the church by 6 April 1830. However,
the "Far West Record" has the number at the time of the first
conference two months later, 9 June 1830, as only twenty-seven.[50]
Whitmer says there were three branches by 6 April, but the Fayette
branch was not founded until 11 April and the Colesville branch not
until the latter part of June.

Whitmer states that there were six elders. The only time there
were six elders was after the founding of the Fayette branch. Two of
these were Smith and Cowdery, who ordained each other at Manchester on 6 April, and the other four—Peter Whitmer, David Whitmer,
John Whitmer, and Ziba Peterson—all from Fayette, were evidently
ordained in April and received their licenses at the June conference,
where Samuel H. Smith became the seventh elder of the church.[51]

Edward Stevenson recorded an interview with Whitmer in January 1887 in which Whitmer told him, "on the 6th of April 1830, 6
Elders were at Peter Whitmers, David's Fathers. 2 Rooms were filled
with members about 20 from Colesville, 15 from Manchester Church
and about 20 from aro[u]nd about Father Whitmers. About 50 members & the 6 elders were presant."[52] The earliest possible date when
the Colesville church could have been represented at Fayette would
have been the second conference in September.

Another indication that Whitmer was recalling a latter meeting
is that J. W. Chatburn, who visited the Whitmers in the early 1880s,
recorded that Whitmer "said that he baptized fourteen in Seneca
Lake, a few days before the Church was organized. I asked his wife
[Julia Anne Jolly Whitmer] if she was present when the Church was
organized on April 6th, 1830. She replied, Yes; and was a baptized
member at that time."[53] The history of the church lists eleven people
baptized on 9 June by Whitmer, including his future wife Julia Jolly.[54]

Whitmer also declares that the organizational meeting was for legal purposes so the church could hold property and officiate in marriages. The cover of the Book of Commandments agrees that the Church of Christ was "Organized According to Law, on the 6th of April, 1830." However well-intentioned this event was, no records of incorporation have been found in the Fayette or Manchester/Palmyra area for 6 April 1830 or any other date.[55] Ultimately, the meeting was more spiritual than legalistic.

A state law at the time specified how a church was to incorporate. The minister of a group was to post public notice of time and date for a meeting of the male members to elect trustees. The congregation had to be notified "at least fifteen days before the day of election," and the notification was to be given for "two successive sabbaths or days on which such church, congregation or society, shall statedly meet for public worship" before the day of election.[56]

The Presbyterian congregation of West Bloomfield in Ontario County followed these specifications precisely: "Whereas at a meeting of the male members of the Presbyterian Congregation of West Bloomfield in the town of Bloomfield county of Ontario and state of New York convened agreeable to publick notice as directed by the statute in such cases made and provided at the Meeting House of said Congregation on the 31st day of May 1830."[57] Similar incorporations can be found in the Miscellaneous Records books of Wayne and Seneca counties.[58]

Joseph Smith was at neither Manchester nor Fayette long enough to give legal notice to incorporate. When he and Joseph Knight were on their way to Manchester, Knight says Smith told him "there must be a Church formed But did not tell when." This was at the most twelve days before 6 April. Knight was still at Manchester when the baptisms occurred and Smith "Begun the Church with six members."[59] Smith and Knight were not in Fayette at the end of March. David Marks, a Free-will Baptist evangelist, on 29 March 1830 "attended a meeting in Fayette, and tarried at the house of Mr. Whitmer." He saw two or three of Whitmer's sons, but Smith was not there.[60]

One early document states that the church was "regularly organized & established agreeable to the laws of our Country by the will & commandments of God." There are other early church licenses with similar wording.[61] This language might mean that the church was organized according to the freedom of religion clause amended to the United States Constitution in 1791. People were free to organize as a voluntary unincorporated religious society or church with no trustees. This is evidently what occurred on 6 April 1830. There were no known marriages performed in New York by ministers of the new church, no property that belonged to the church, and thus no compelling reason to organize according to the laws of New York state.

Certainly inaccuracies in both individual and community memory might account for the shift of the place of the church's organization from Manchester to Fayette. However, another intriguing possibility exists. The change in location may not have been inadvertent but part of a larger strategy for coping with the economic strains which plagued the church through the early years of its existence. As we have seen, what is probably the earliest reference to Fayette as the location of the 6 April events appears in a heading in *The Evening and Morning Star* to the minutes of a conference held in Kirtland, Ohio, on 3 May 1834. This conference was attended by Joseph Smith, Oliver Cowdery, Frederick G. Williams, Sidney Rigdon, and Newel K. Whitney, all leading elders of the church and members of the Kirtland United Firm. The minutes of that meeting report that it was decided that the church should be known by the name "The Church of the Latter Day Saints."[62] Perhaps after this conference the "Church of Christ" founded in Manchester, New York, became "The Church of the Latter Day Saints" founded in Fayette.

In the Book of Mormon, the simple title "Church of Christ" identifies the church as Jesus Christ's.[63] In 1829 Oliver Cowdery produced a document stating that the "Church shall be called The Church of Christ," and although other Christian churches before 1829 were similarly named, this name was confirmed in a revelation given on the day of its organization.[64]

Before the change in name, church leaders were concerned about obtaining donations to pay off the debts of the United Firm, to commence work on the Kirtland temple, and to provide funds for the forthcoming march of Zion's Camp to Missouri. In a letter from Kirtland on 5 December 1833, Smith wrote, "our means are already exhausted, and we are deeply in debt, and know of no means whereby we shall be able to extricate ourselves."[65] On 11 January 1834 Smith and his associates prayed "That the Lord would provide, in the order of his Providence, the bishop of this Church with means sufficient to discharge every debt that the Firm owes, in due season, that the Church may not be braught into disrepute, and the saints be afflicted by the hands of their enemies."[66] Less than a month before the name and place changes, the United Firm was dissolved and separated into two firms, one in Missouri and one in Kirtland. Members of the firm in Kirtland were instructed to divide the properties among themselves.[67] Additionally on 5 May the land designated for the Kirtland temple was transferred to Smith and his successor in the office of the presidency of the church.[68] By 1835 the identities of United Firm members were obscured by pseudonyms.[69] In a revelation received by Smith on 23 April 1834, shortly before the name and location changes, he was instructed: "Therefore, write speedily unto New York, and write according to that which shall be dictated by my spirit, and I will soften the hearts of those to whom you are in debt, that it shall be taken away out of <their> minds to bring afflictions upon you."[70]

All of these actions may well have been part of a larger attempt to frustrate church creditors or to avoid lawsuits. Unfortunately, there are no known letters extant written by Smith between 23 April and 5 May 1834, when he left Kirtland for Missouri. The evidence is too sketchy to reach a decisive conclusion, but this is an area of research worth pursuing and suggests a plausible motive for changing the church's name and relocating its place of organization to Fayette.

The Fayette location was unheard of until 1834. However, Fayette was important as the site of the first three church conferences, and the log home and farm of Peter Whitmer, Sr., should retain a fundamental historical and sentimental position in Smith's Church of Christ.

Why should we be concerned about accuracy in these details? LDS church educator T. Edgar Lyon once remarked, "[W]hy should Latter-day Saints concern themselves with authentic history? What difference does it make to the tourist if he is told fact or fiction? Personally, I do not appreciate being victimized by someone who, while posing as an authority, disseminates error, however trivial it may seem."[71]

NOTES

1. BC 9:17; LDS D&C 10:67-68; RLDS D&C 3:16; see also BC 15:1.

2. Dean C. Jessee, ed., "Joseph Knight's Recollection of Early Mormon History," *Brigham Young University Studies* 17 (Autumn 1976): 36-37. Minimal punctuation and editing has been added to clarify the account.

3. BC 16; LDS D&C 19; RLDS D&C 18. Robert J. Woodford noted that this commandment "can be dated between March 26 and March 31, 1830" (*The Seventh Annual Sidney B. Sperry Symposium*, 27 Jan. 1979, 34).

4. H. Michael Marquardt, "Early Texts of Joseph Smith's Revelations," *Restoration* 1 (July 1982): 8-11.

5. *The Evening and the Morning Star*, Independence, MO, 1 (Mar. 1833): 4 [p. 76] and 1 (Apr. 1833): 4 [p. 84].

6. Ibid., 1 (Apr. 1833): 4 [p. 84]; see also *Evening and Morning Star*, Kirtland, OH, reprint, Apr. 1833 (published June 1836), 167.

7. William Smith, *William Smith on Mormonism* (Lamoni, IA: Herald Steam Book and Job Office, 1883), 14. Although William seems to be incorrect in some of his recollections, he mentions that his family "went to my brother Hyrum's house" in 1829 and that "It was in this house that the first conference [sic] of the Church of Jesus Christ of Latter Day Saints [sic] was held, on the 6th day of April, 1830, at which I was present."

8. Interview of Benjamin Saunders, 1884, 27, Library-Archives, Reorganized Church of Jesus Christ of Latter Day Saints, Independence, Missouri (hereafter RLDS archives).

9. *The Evening and the Morning Star* 1 (Jan. 1833): 1 [p. 57]; and 1 (Mar. 1833): 4 [p. 76].

10. Brigham Young diary, page with date of 7 Oct. 1843, archives, historical department, Church of Jesus Christ of Latter-day Saints, Salt Lake City, Utah (hereafter LDS archives).

11. J[onathan]. B. Turner, *Mormonism in All Ages* (New York: Published by Platt & Peters, 1842), 22.

12. William E. McLellin, ed., *The Ensign of Liberty* 1 (Mar. 1847): 2. William E. McLellin includes Lucy Smith and Martin Harris in his list.

13. See Scott G. Kenney, ed., *Wilford Woodruff's Journal*, typescript, 1833-98, 9 vols. (Midvale, UT: Signature Books, 1983-85), 5:239-40, 18 Nov. 1858, original in LDS archives; copy of a statement dated 11 Aug. 1862 in Manuscript History of the Church, Book A-1, between pages 36 and 37, LDS archives; see also *History of the Church of Jesus Christ of Latter-day Saints* (Salt Lake City: Deseret Book Co., 1959), 1:76n, hereafter *History of the Church*; Diary of Edward Stevenson, 22 Dec. 1877 and 2 Jan. 1887, LDS archives;

Lyndon W. Cook, ed., *David Whitmer Interviews: A Restoration Witness* (Orem, UT: Grandin Book Co., 1991), 11, 214; *Ensign* 10 (June 1980): 44-45 and (Oct. 1980): 71.

14. BC 22; LDS D&C 21; RLDS D&C 19.

15. BC 18:1-4; LDS D&C 23:3; RLDS D&C 21:2.

16. Nathan Pierce Docket Book, 1827-30, 8 June 1830, facing page 77, located at Manchester Town Office; copy in our possession. See Richard L. Anderson, "Joseph Smith's New York Reputation Reappraised," *Brigham Young University Studies* 10 (Spring 1970): 292-93.

17. Jessee, "Joseph Knight's Recollection," 37.

18. Ibid. The revelation sec. 46 in the 1835 D&C; LDS D&C 21; RLDS D&C 19. When published in the 1835 D&C, this document did not indicate where it was received. In BC 22 the heading stated: "A Revelation to Joseph, given in Manchester, New-York, April 6, 1830" (45). The Manuscript History written in 1839 changes this for the first time to "Given at Fayette" (Jessee, *Papers of Joseph Smith*, 1:303).

19. BC 22:1, 13-14; LDS D&C 21:1, 10-11; RLDS D&C 19:1a, 3b.

20. William E. McLellin, ed., *The Ensign of Liberty* 1 (Dec. 1847): 42.

21. BC 22:2-5; LDS D&C 21:2-4; RLDS D&C 19: 1b-2b.

22. Jessee, "Joseph Knight's Recollection," 37.

23. Lucy Mack Smith, Preliminary Manuscript (MS), "History of Lucy Smith," 122, LDS archives (page numbering corresponds with a typed transcript in LDS archives and with the page numbers in the photocopy of the manuscript); Lucy Mack Smith, *Biographical Sketches of Joseph Smith the Prophet, and His Progenitors for Many Generations* (Liverpool: Published for Orson Pratt by S.W. Richards, 1853), 151; Lucy Mack Smith, *History of Joseph Smith By His Mother, Lucy Mack Smith* (Salt Lake City: Bookcraft, 1958), 168). The 1853 edition of Lucy's book, but not the Preliminary MS, reads: "On the morning of the sixth day of the same month, my husband and Martin Harris were baptized." Richard L. Bushman commented, "Lucy Smith said the baptism occurred in the morning, but Joseph Knight and Joseph Smith, Jr., placed it after the organizational meeting" (*Joseph Smith and the Beginnings of Mormonism* [Urbana: University of Illinois Press, 1984], 237n4).

24. Statement by C. R. Stafford in *Naked Truths About Mormonism* 1 (Jan. 1888): 3, original publication in the Yale University Library. Mrs. Rockwell was forty-four years old. Her daughter Caroline (b. 1 May 1812 and baptized 9 June 1830) said, "My mother was one of the first Mormon converts" (*Naked Truths About Mormonism* 1 [Apr. 1888]: 1).

25. Interview of Benjamin Saunders, 1884, RLDS archives.

26. Interview of Martin Harris by Edward Stevenson, 4 Sept. 1870, LDS archives.

27. Jessee, "Joseph Knight's Recollection," 37.

28. *New York Herald*, 25 June 1893. A photograph of Crooked Brook was taken by George Edward Anderson in 1907, see *Birth of Mormonism in Picture* (Salt Lake City: Deseret Sunday School Union, [ca. 1909]), 61; *Ensign* 8 (Nov. 1978): 53; and Richard Neitzel Holzapfel and T. Jeffery Cottle, *Old Mormon Palmyra and New England: Historic Photographs and Guide* (Santa Ana, CA: Fieldbrook Publications, 1991), 112.

29. John H. Pratt, in Charles F. Milliken's *A History of Ontario County, New York and Its People* (New York: Lewis Historical Publishing Co., 1911), 1:418.

30. *Shortsville Enterprise*, 18 Mar. 1904.

31. 1830 U.S. Census, Manchester, Ontario County, New York, 169-70.

32. *Times and Seasons* 4 (15 Nov. 1842): 12. This and subsequent publications make Mrs. Sarah Rockwell's first initial an "A."

33. Dean C. Jessee, ed., *The Papers of Joseph Smith* (Salt Lake City: Deseret Book Co., 1989), 1:243n1.

34. Ibid., 1:244.

35. Manuscript History A-1: 38; Jessee, *Papers of Joseph Smith*, 1:303-304.

36. See Preliminary Draft to History, 1839, and Manuscript History A-1: 37, in Jessee, *Papers of Joseph Smith*, 1:241-42, 302-303. See also BC 17-22; 1835 D&C 45-46; LDS D&C 21, 23; RLDS D&C 19, 21. For early references to the church being organized at Fayette, see Stanley R. Gunn, *Oliver Cowdery Second Elder and Scribe* (Salt Lake City: Bookcraft, 1962), 267, deed made on 5 May 1834; Nancy Clement Williams, *After One Hundred Years* (Independence, MO: Zion's Printing and Publishing Co., 1951), 228-30, deed of 5 May 1834; Deeds in Geauga Deed Records, Book 24:100, Geauga County, Ohio, microfilm #0020240, LDS Family History Library, Salt Lake City; see also Book 18:477-81, microfilm #0020237. For various writings that follow the decision of May 1834, that the Whitmer residence was the location of the church organization, see Richard L. Anderson, "The House Where the Church was Organized," *Improvement Era* 73 (Apr. 1970): 16-25; Doyle L. Green, "April 6, 1830: The Day the Church was Organized," *Ensign* 1 (Jan. 1971): 39-56; *Doctrine and Covenants Student Manual* (Salt Lake City: Church of Jesus Christ of Latter-day Saints, 1981), 43; John K. Carmack, "Fayette: The Place the Church was Organized," *Ensign* 19 (Feb. 1989): 15-19; Vivian Paulsen, "A Day Chosen by the Lord," *The Friend* 19 (Aug. 1989): 40-41; *Church History in the Fulness of Times* [Religion 341-43], (Salt Lake City: Church of Jesus Christ of Latter-day Saints, 1989), 67; Howard W. Hunter, "The Sixth Day of April, 1830," *Ensign* 21 (May 1991): 63-65; John K. Carmack, "Organization of the Church, 1830,"

Daniel H. Ludlow, ed., *Encyclopedia of Mormonism: The History, Scripture, Doctrine, and Procedure of the Church of Jesus Christ of Latter-day Saints* (New York: Macmillan Publishing Co., 1992), 1,049-50, see also 262, 505, 593, 603, 1,219, 1,335, 1,652); and Larry C. Porter, "Organizational Origins of the Church of Jesus Christ, 6 April 1830," in Larry C. Porter, Milton V. Backman, Jr., Susan Easton Black, eds., *Regional Studies in Latter-day Saint Church History: New York* (Provo, UT: Department of Church History and Doctrine, Brigham Young University, 1992), 149-64. G. Homer Durham explained, "Even Church records are not infallible" ("Why Study History?" *Ensign* 8 [Sept. 1978]: 59).

37. *Times and Seasons* 3 (1 Mar. 1842): 708. This was later changed to Fayette. See *History of the Church*, 4:538.

38. I Daniel Rupp, *He Pasa Ekklesia. An Original History of the Religious Denominations at Present Existing in the United States* (Philadelphia: Published by J. Y. Humphreys, 1844), 407. See *History of the Church*, 6:428.

39. O[rson]. Pratt, *Interesting Account of Several Remarkable Visions, and of the Late Discovery of Ancient American Records* (Edinburgh: Printed by Ballantyne and Hughes, 1840), 24. The change was made in one of the 1848 printings. The First Presidency of the LDS church has followed this tradition. Two examples are: (1) "On the sixth day of April, one hundred years ago today, Joseph Smith, with five others who had accepted the message of the restored Gospel, met at the home of Peter Whitmer, Sr., at Fayette, Seneca County, New York. The sacrament of bread and wine was administered and the Church of Jesus Christ of Latter-day Saints organized" (Centennial Message of the First Presidency, 6 Apr. 1930, in James R. Clark, ed., *Messages of the First Presidency* [Salt Lake City: Bookcraft, 1971], 5:283; also in David M. and Vonda S. Reay, *Selected Manifestations* [Oakland, CA: Comps., 1985], 227). (2) "On April 6, 1830, a small group assembled in the farmhouse of Peter Whitmer, in Fayette Township, in the state of New York. Six men participated in the formal organization procedures, with Joseph Smith as their leader" (Sesquicentennial Proclamation by the First Presidency and the Quorum of the Twelve Apostles of The Church of Jesus Christ of Latter-day Saints, 6 Apr. 1980, in *Selected Manifestations*, 310).

40. See 1876 LDS D&C 21. The designation "at Fayette" first appeared in RLDS D&C 19 in 1952, probably based on the LDS D&C.

41. Manuscript History A-1: 37; Jessee, *Papers of Joseph Smith*, 1: 302-303.

42. BC 22:15; LDS D&C 21:12; RLDS D&C 19:3c.

43. Manuscript History A-1: 39; Jessee, *Papers of Joseph Smith*, 1:304.

44. Donald Q. Cannon and Lyndon W. Cook, eds., *Far West Record: Minutes of The Church of Jesus Christ of Latter-day Saints, 1830-1844* (Salt Lake

City: Deseret Book, 1983), 1-2. Manuscript History A-1: 41, has the date of the conference as 1 June; see *Times and Seasons* 4 (1 Dec. 1842): 22; "Newel Knight's Journal," in *Scraps of Biography* (Salt Lake City: Juvenile Instructor Office, 1883), 52; and *History of the Church*, 1:84 and note.

45. Cannon and Cook, *Far West Record*, 1.

46. Manuscript History A-1: 42; *Times and Seasons* 4 (1 Dec. 1842): 23, spelling of Jerusha as "Jerushee" as in the manuscript. The name Porter Rockwell was written in the 1839 draft history. See Jessee, *Papers of Joseph Smith*, 1:246, 250. The manuscript history has the reading "Peter" Rockwell. This is a scribal error made by James Mulholland when copying from his draft history and should read Porter. See Jessee, *Papers of Joseph Smith*, 1: 309. William Smith correctly list Porter Rockwell as being baptized on 9 June 1830. See *William Smith on Mormonism*, 16.

Orrin Porter Rockwell was sixteen years old at the time of his baptism. In the 1820 Farmington and 1830 Manchester census records there is only one member of the Orin and Sarah Rockwell family in the age bracket of their son Porter. Consequently there is no "Peter" Rockwell who could have been baptized.

47. *The Evening and the Morning Star* 1 (Apr. 1833): 4 [p. 84]; Manuscript History A-1: 43; Jessee, *Papers of Joseph Smith*, 1:311. "H. P. [Hezekiah Peck] and wife have been baptized, & are very strong in the faith" (Letter to the Editor, *Brattleboro' Messenger* 9 [20 Nov. 1830]).

48. Carmack, "Fayette: The Place the Church was Organized," 19; Jessee, *Papers of Joseph Smith*, 1:242n2.

49. David Whitmer, *An Address to All Believers in Christ* (Richmond, MO: author, 1887), 33; emphasis in original.

50. Cannon and Cook, *Far West Record*, 3. The minutes state: "No. of the several members uniting to this Church since the last Conference, thirty-five, making in whole now belonging to this Church sixty-two." These minutes were copied from the original in 1838.

51. Ibid., 1.

52. Diary of Edward Stevenson, 2 Jan. 1887, LDS archives, in Cook, *David Whitmer Interviews*, 214.

53. *Saints' Herald* 29 (15 June 1882): 189.

54. Manuscript History A-1:42; *Papers of Joseph Smith*, 1: 309. The names of Julia Anne Jolly and Harriet Jolly were omitted when the history was published in 1842. See *Times and Seasons* 4 (1 Dec. 1842): 23. The history mentions that Whitmer performed a baptism in May 1830.

55. We have searched the records in the counties of Seneca, Ontario, and Wayne and have found no record of incorporation of the Church of

Christ on 6 April 1830 or any other date. Correspondence from the Department of State, State of New York, Albany, 6 Oct. 1986 and 23 Feb. 1987 to H. Michael Marquardt; research trip to New York in October 1986.

Further research indicates that there are no state records regarding incorporation of the Church of Christ, the Church of the Latter Day Saints, or the Church of Jesus Christ of Latter-day Saints in the state of New York. See Larry C. Porter, "A Study of the Origins of the Church of Jesus Christ of Latter-day Saints in the States of New York and Pennsylvania, 1816-1831," Ph.D. diss., Aug. 1971, Brigham Young University, 374-86; *Ensign* 8 (Dec. 1978): 26-27, also published in *A Sure Foundation: Answers to Difficult Gospel Questions* (Salt Lake City: Deseret Book, 1988), 196-99; and John K. Carmack in *Ensign* 19 (Feb. 1989): 16-17.

56. *Laws of the State of New-York, Revised and Passed at the Thirty-Sixth Session of the Legislature* (Albany: H. C. Southwick & Co., 1813), 2:214. For acts to amend "an act to provide for the incorporation of religious societies," passed 5 April 1813, see *Laws of the State of New-York* . . . (Albany: J. Buel, 1819), 34, and *Laws of the State of New-York* . . . (Albany: E. Croswell, 1826), 34-35.

57. Recorded 1 June 1830, Miscellaneous Records, Book D:23-24, Ontario County Clerk's Office, Canandaigua, New York.

58. See the incorporation of the First Baptist Church of Lodi, recorded 24 Nov. 1830, Miscellaneous Records Seneca County Book B:426-27, Seneca County Clerk's Office, Waterloo, New York; and of the First Congregational Society in Marion, signed 16 Mar. 1829; filed 28 Mar. 1829, Miscellaneous Docket 1:45, Lyons, Wayne County, New York.

59. Jessee, "Joseph Knight's Recollection," 36-37.

60. *The Life of David Marks* (Limerick, ME: Printed at the Office of the Morning Star, 1831), 340-41. Marks wrote concerning selling the Book of Mormon, "Five thousand copies were published - and they said the angel told Smith to sell the book at a price which was one dollar and eight cents per copy more than the cost, that they *'might have the temporal profit*, as well as the spiritual'" (341, emphasis in original). In an 1830 account, published shortly after his visit in March, he stated, "we went to Fayette & held one meeting" (*Morning Star*, Limerick, ME, 4 (28 Apr. 1830): 1).

61. MS Articles & Covenants, Zebedee Coltrin journal, LDS archives; cf. BC 24:2; LDS D&C 20:2; RLDS D&C 17:19. Some of the early preaching licenses had wording such as the following: "this Church of Christ established & regularly organized" (license of John Whitmer, given 9 June 1830, original in the Coe Collection, Yale University Library; and the priest license for

Joseph Smith, Sr., also given 9 June 1830, in the Joseph Smith Collection, LDS archives).

62. *The Evening and the Morning Star* 2 (May 1834): 160. See *History of the Church*, 2:62-63.

63. See LDS Mos. 18:17/RLDS 9:49; LDS 3 Ne. 26:21/RLDS 12:13; LDS 3 Ne. 28:23/RLDS 13:36; LDS 4 Ne. 1:1, 26, 29/RLDS 1:1, 28, 31; LDS//RLDS Moro. 6:4.

64. "A commandment from God unto Oliver," LDS archives; BC 22:14; LDS D&C 21:11; RLDS D&C 19:3b. For various arguments favoring the name change, see Oliver Cowdery, *The Evening and the Morning Star* 2 (May 1834): 158-59; 2 (June 1834): 164-65; Letter of John Smith to Elias Smith, 19 Oct. 1834, George Albert Smith Family Papers, Special Collections, Marriott Library, University of Utah, Salt Lake City; Thomas B. Marsh to Wilford Woodruff, *Elders' Journal* 1 (July 1838): 37.

65. In *History of the Church*, 1:450. A copy of the letter is in Joseph Smith Letterbook 1:68, LDS archives.

66. Joseph Smith's diary, 11 Jan. 1834, 45-46, LDS archives. Also in Jessee, *Papers of Joseph Smith*, 2:19.

67. "Kirtland Revelations" Book, 102-105, LDS archives; LDS D&C 104:19-59; RLDS D&C 101:3-10. See also "Kirtland Revelations" Book, 111, revelation dated Kirtland, 28 Apr. 1834; Joseph Smith's diary, 10 Apr. 1834, 71-72; also in Jessee, *Papers of Joseph Smith*, 2:29.

68. See, for example, the deed recorded in Geauga Deed Records, Book 18:478-79, Geauga County, Ohio; microfilm #0020237, LDS Family History Library. For some additional information on the Kirtland temple property, see *Restoration Studies IV* (Independence, MO: Herald Publishing House, 1988), 122n52.

69. See 1835 D&C 75, 86, 93, 96, 98.

70. "Kirtland Revelations" Book, 107; LDS D&C 104:81; RLDS D&C 101:13d.

71. T. Edgar Lyon, "How Authentic Are Mormon Historic Sites in Vermont and New York?," *Brigham Young University Studies* 9 (Spring 1969): 349, punctuation added.

CHAPTER EIGHT

EXPRESSIONS OF FAITH

In June 1830 baptisms into the Church of Christ were performed in Colesville, New York, in a branch established there by Smith and Oliver Cowdery. The coming of the new church to the Colesville area occasioned a series of confrontations—between the state of New York and Joseph Smith, between the Presbyterian church and the Church of Christ, and between the Coburn and Knight families.[1]

The family of Joseph Knight became the nucleus of the new church in Colesville just as the Smiths had been the nucleus in Manchester and the Whitmers in Fayette. And the Knights were at the center of difficulties erupting during the church's first summer in the area. The Knight family home and mill were located just across the Susquehanna River from the little village of Nineveh in Colesville Township. Joseph Smith had worked with Knight and others in the Colesville area while conducting his treasure-digging activities, and the Knights had helped Smith while he was working on the Book of Mormon.[2] It was in the latter part of March 1830, while Joseph Knight was transporting Smith to Manchester, that Smith first spoke to Knight about the need to establish a church. After witnessing the baptisms of Smith's father and Martin Harris, Knight obtained copies of the Book of Mormon and returned home to Colesville to sell them.

After the first church conference in Fayette, Smith and Oliver Cowdery made their way to Colesville.[3] Cowdery preached at the Knight home on Sunday, 27 June. Baptisms were to be performed that Sunday, but antagonists destroyed the dam erected for the purpose. On Monday, 28 June 1830, members of the Knight family and others were baptized near the Knight home, and the Colesville church began to take shape.[4]

Among those baptized was Newel Knight's wife Sarah Coburn (known as Sally).[5] Newel had been a Universalist and Sally a Presbyterian. Sally's father Amasa Coburn was an accomplished musician and earned part of his living by giving music and vocal lessons in the town of Guilford, Chenango County, where the Coburn family had established their residence sometime before 1820. Sally had grown up surrounded by music and had joined the local church choir.[6] The Presbyterian church of Harpursville in 1827 was nearest to her home but was eventually absorbed into the church at Nineveh, just across the river from where they lived.[7]

A few days after Sally Knight's baptism, a young medical doctor, Abram W. Benton, a Presbyterian, swore out a warrant for Smith's arrest.[8] Smith's history records that "a young man named Benton, of the same religious [Presbyterian] faith, swore out the first warrant against me."[9] Constable Ebenezer Hatch was dispatched south to Colesville to arrest Joseph and return him to Bainbridge for trial.

Joseph Knight provided lawyers for Smith's defense and later recalled:

> they made a Catspaw of a young fellow By the name of Docter Benton in Chenengo County to sware out a warrent against Joseph for, as they said, pretending to see under ground. A little Clause they found in the [New] york Laws against such things. The of[f]icer Came to my house near knite [night] and took him. I harnesed my horses and we all went up to the village. But it was so late they Could not try him that nite and it was put of[f] till morning. I asked Joseph if [he] wanted Counsell he said he tho[ugh]t he should. I went that nite and saw Mr. James Davi[d]son a man I was acquainted with. The next morning ther[e] gather[e]d a multitude of peopel [sic] that ware against him [Smith]. Mr. Davi[d]son said it looked like a squaley [squally] Day; he thot we had Better have John Read [Reed] a pretty good speaker near by. I told him we would, so I imployed them Both. So after a trial all Day jest at nite he was Dismissed.[10]

Smith's history describes how he was "visited by a constable" at Knight's home and "arrested by him on a warrant, on the charge of being a disorderly person." "On the day following," the history continues, "a court was convened for the purpose of investigating those charges," where there were "many witnesses called up against me."[11]

One of Smith's defense lawyers, John Reed, recalled that they "had him arraigned before Joseph Chamberlain, a justice of the peace, a man that was always ready to deal justice to all, and a man of great discernment of mind." The case started "about 10 o'clock, A.M.," and "closed about 12 o'clock at night."[12]

The bills submitted to the county by the constable and the justice at Smith's examination confirm the account in Smith's history. The bill submitted by Constable Ebenezer Hatch "Dated at South Bainbridge July 4th 1830" reads:

```
To Serving warrant on Joseph Smith & keeping
him twenty four hours          $2=00
3 meals Victuel & 1 Lodging      =50
Suppoenying 5 witness          62 1/2
                              $3=13 1/2
                                 75
                              $2.37 1/2
```

It is not evident why the costs were reduced by seventy five cents, but the $2.37 1/2 total, rounded off to $2.38, was recorded next to Hatch's name in the "Supervisor's Journal," confirming that Smith was in fact arrested one day, held over night, and tried the next day. It further shows that Hatch delivered five subpoenas to witnesses to take part in the hearing.

A second bill submitted by Justice Chamberlain for cases tried between 1 June and August 1830 includes the state of New York "vs Joseph Smith Jr a Disorderly person July 1st 1830," supplying the exact date of the trial, 1 July 1830, a Thursday.[13] That the examination in this case was lengthy is reflected in the itemized listing of Chamberlain's costs:

```
oath on Complaint          6 [cents]
filing Complaint           3
warrant                    19
Examination 1 Day          1[.]00
10 Subpoenis               60
Swearing 12 witnesses      72
```

This bill shows there were actually twelve witnesses, indicating that another constable served seven additional subpoenas. Chamberlain's expenses for six cases totaled $11.74 for a three-month period. This amount was entered on the back of the bill and is recorded beside his name in the "Supervisor's Journal" under the Town of Bainbridge for the year 1830.[14]

The earliest printed account of this hearing appeared less than a year later in the 9 April 1831 issue of the *Evangelical Magazine and Gospel Advocate*. It was dated at South Bainbridge, March 1831, and signed A. W. B., identified by Dale L. Morgan, who uncovered this account, as Abram W. Benton who brought the complaint against Smith. Benton related the Bainbridge trial as follows:

> During the trial it was shown that the Book of Mormon was brought to light by the same magic power by which he pretended to tell fortunes, discover hidden treasures, &c. Oliver Cowd[e]ry, one of the three witnesses to the book [of Mormon], testified under oath, that said Smith found with the plates, from which he translated his book, two transparent stones, resembling glass, set in silver bows. That by looking through these, he was able to read in English, the reformed Egyptian characters, which were engraved on the plates.

Benton recalled an attempt to have Josiah Stowell admit that Smith had lied to him about his ability to locate buried treasure. Benton described the questioning of Stowell and his responses:

> Josiah Stowell, a Mormonite, being sworn, testified that he positively knew that said Smith never had lied to, or deceived him, and did not believe he ever tried to deceive any body else. The following questions were then asked him, to which he made the replies annexed.
> [Q] Did Smith ever tell you there was money hid in a certain place which he mentioned?
> [A] Yes.
> [Q] Did he tell you, you could find it by digging?
> [A] Yes.
> [Q] Did you dig?
> [A] Yes.
> [Q] Did you find any money?

[A] No.

[Q] Did he not lie to you then, and deceive you?

[A] No! the money was there, but we did not get quite to it!

[Q] How do you know it was there?

[A] Smith said it was![15]

Joseph Smith's history adds the following testimony:

Among many witnesses called up against me [Joseph Smith], was Mr. Josiah Stoal [Stowell] (of whom I have made mention, as having worked for him some time) and examined to the following effect. -

Q. Did not the prisoner Joseph Smith have a horse of you?

Ansr. Yes.

Q. Did not he go to you and tell you, that an angel had appeared unto him, and authorised him to get the horse from you?

Ansr. No, he told me no such story.

Q. Well; How had he the horse of you?

Ansr. He bought him of me, as another man would do.

Q. Have you had your pay?

Ansr. That is not your business.

The question being again put, the witness replied, "I hold his note for the price of the horse, which I consider as good as the pay - for I am well acquainted with Joseph Smith Jr, and know him to be an honest man; and if he wishes I am ready to let him have another horse on the same terms".

Mr. Jonathan Thompson was next called up, and examined.

Q. Has not the prisoner, Joseph Smith Jr had a yoke of oxen of you?

Ansr. Yes.

Q. Did he not obtain them of you by telling you that he had a revelation to the effect that he was to have them?

Ansr. No, He did not mention a word of the kind concerning the oxen; he purchased them, the same as another man would.[16]

Smith's account also adds Stowell's two daughters, probably Rhoda and Miriam, to the list of witnesses, and Benton adds Joseph Knight and his son Newel.[17] Benton related that Newel "testified, under oath, that he positively had a devil cast out of himself by the instrumentality of Joseph Smith, jr., and that he saw the devil after it was out, but could not tell how it looked!"[18]

Smith's history indicated that he was "acquitted by this court."[19] According to John Reed, one of Smith's attorneys, "the court pronounced the words 'not guilty,' and the prisoner was di[s]charged."[20]

According to Joel K. Noble of Colesville, before whom Smith was brought on a similar charge the next day, 2 July, Smith won his dismissal by appealing to the statute of limitations. Noble wrote, "Jo. was arrested examination had Jo. plead in bar Statute of Limitations."[21] Since New York law limited misdemeanor charges to three years, and four years had elapsed since Smith was originally charged in Bainbridge, the case was dismissed.

However, the opposition did not give up that easily. No sooner had Smith stepped out of Justice Chamberlain's court in South Bainbridge, Chenango County, than he was served another warrant and taken a few miles south across the county line into Colesville, Broome County, where he was arraigned before Justice Noble.

Joseph Knight recalled: "Then there was a nother of[f]icer was Ridy [ready] and took him on the same Case Down to Broom[e] County Below forth with. I hired Boath these Lawyers and took them Down home with me that nite. The next Day it Continued all Day till midnite. But they Could find no thing against him therefore he was Dismist [dismissed]."[22]

Justice Noble expressed his disgust with the proceedings:

> Jo was no Sooner Set on terifirma than arrested again, brought before me in a adjoining County only 6 miles Distant, trial protracted 23 hours the pros[e]cuti[on] was Cond[ucted] by a Gent[leman] well Skil[l]ed in [the] Science of Law, proof manifested by I think 43 Witnesses. . . . Jo. was asked by witness if he could see or tel[l] more than others Jo. said he could not and says any thing for a living. I now and then Get a Sh[i]lling.[23]

The well-skilled attorney who conducted the prosecution was probably William Seymour, another Presbyterian, the "Lawyer Seymour" mentioned in Smith's history. He pursued Smith's money-digging past.[24]

Newel Knight was called as a witness and described his testimony during this trial:

> As soon as I had been sworn, Mr. Seymour proceeded to interrogate

me as follows:

Question. - "Did the prisoner, Joseph Smith, Jun., cast the devil out of you?"

Answer. - "No, sir."

Q. - "Why, have you not had the devil cast out of you?"

A. - "Yes, sir."

Q. - "And had not Joseph Smith some hand in it being done?"

A. - "Yes, sir."

Q. - "And did he not cast him out of you?"

A. - "No, sir, it was done by the power of God, and Joseph Smith was the instrument in the hands of God on this occasion. He commanded him to come out of me in the name of Jesus Christ."

Q. - "And are you sure it was the devil?"

A. - "Yes, sir."

Q. - "Did you see him after he was cast out of you?"

A. - "Yes, sir, I saw him."

Q. - "Pray, what did he look like?"

(Here one of the lawyers on the part of the defense told me I need not answer that question.) I replied:

"I believe, I need not answer you that question, but I will do it if I am allowed to ask you one, and you can answer it. Do you, Mr. Seymour, understand the things of the Spirit?"

"No," answered Mr. Seymour, "I do not pretend to such big things."

"Well, then," I replied, "it will be of no use for me to tell you what the devil looked like, for it was a spiritual sight and spiritually discerned, and, of course, you would not understand it were I to tell you of it."

The lawyer dropped his head, while the loud laugh of the audience proclaimed his discomfiture.[25]

Noble wrote, "a Mormon Swore in open court Jo. Smith cast a Devil out of him (M[ormo]n) and said how D[evi]l Looked. Said Devil was a body of Light."[26] According to Smith's history, "The Court finding the charges against me, not sustained, I was accordingly acquitted."[27] Newel Knight also remembered that "he was discharged."[28]

"[T]hrough the instrumentality of my new friend, the Constable," continued Smith's history, "I was enabled to escape them, and make my way in safety to my wifes sister's house, where I found my wife awaiting with much anxiety the issue of those ungodly proceedings: And with her in company next day arrived in safety at my house."[29]

Against this backdrop of dramatic public conflict, the Knight family played out parallel tensions within the more private arena of their extended family. When news reached Emily Coburn in Sandford that her sister Sally was interested in joining the Mormon church, she doubted the report, "believing her to be of an unshaken mind and principle." Emily visited her sister "to try if possible to convince her of the error into which she had innocently been decoyed and deceived."[30]

Emily, who had recently joined the Presbyterian church in Sandford, had a special concern about her sister. On Emily's several previous visits to her older sister's home in Colesville, she had become acquainted with young Smith and his treasure-seeking activities which centered on Sally's father-in-law's farm. She recalled:

> I had seen him two or three times, while visiting at my sister's, but did not think it worth my while to take any notice of him. I never spoke to him, for he was a total stranger to me. However, I thought him odd looking and queer. He also told his friends that he could see money in pots, under the ground. He pretended to foretell people's future destiny, and, according to his prognostication, his friends agreed to suspend their avocations and dig for the treasures, which were hidden in the earth; a great share of which, he said, was on Joseph Knight's farm.

According to Emily's recollections, Sally's father-in-law, Joseph Knight, shared in the money-digging excursions on his own land:

> Old Uncle Joe, as we called him, was a wool carder, and a farmer; yet he abandoned all business, and joined with a number of others, to dig for money on his premises. While I was visiting my sister, we have walked out to see the places where they dug for money, and laughed to think of the absurdity of any people having common intellect to indulge in such a thought or action.

One story about the treasure-seekers' adventures stood out in Emily's mind:

> in the time of their digging for money and not finding it attainable,

Joe Smith told them there was a charm on the pots of money, and if some animal was killed and the blood sprinkled around the place, then they could get it. So they killed a dog, and tried this method of obtaining the precious metal; but again money was scarce in those diggings. Still, they dug and dug, but never came to the precious treasure. Alas! how vivid was the expectation when the blood of poor Tray was used to take off the charm, and after all to find their mistake.[31]

In the years after these early encounters with Colesville folklife Emily lived with her brother Esick Lyon Coburn. He had married a milliner from Philadelphia and subsequently moved to Sandford. There he pursued his trade as a tanner, and his wife opened a millinery establishment. About 1828 Emily began a two-year apprenticeship with her sister-in-law. As Emily began her third year of residence she was caught up in a neighborhood religious excitement and joined the newly organized Presbyterian church in Sandford.

Sandford and Colesville had both been created in 1821 from the township of Windsor, which originally covered the entire eastern end of Broome County.[32] The Presbyterian church had been in the Windsor area since 1800, but the separate Sandford church was organized in the winter of 1829-30.[33] On 1 February 1830, Reverend John Sherer was commissioned by the American Home Missionary Society to serve the Colesville and Sandford churches for a twelve-month period, with three months' salary in hand and the next three months pledged.[34] Sherer, then thirty-nine, was a graduate of Andover and had been ordained in 1825. He had served a pastorate in Litchfield, New Hampshire, and was a member of the Oneida Conference before being assigned to Broome County. He arrived on the field in February, and after completing six months of labor, he reported to the New York office on the status of his work. At its organization the Sandford church consisted of five members and "As many more were examined and propounded for admission." By this he meant that five more were examined regarding their personal experience of conversion and their understanding of the gospel message of repentance and faith in Jesus Christ. "These," he added, "have been received since. At another communion Three have been added, at another one <by letter>; and there now stand propounded, three others. A few more it is hoped will unite themselves." He adds, "Thus a vine has been planted, where a dreary moral waste has long <existed>. This little Flock of Christ appear to be 'steadfast, unmovable, always abounding in the work of the Lord,' though opposed on every side."

Concerning Colesville he wrote: "In Colesville every good object seems to be opposed by some. Yet even here, hope seems to be lighting up. There have been a few cases of conversion, since I came here, and now there is an appearance of seriousness on the minds of several. In a distant part of the society where for a few sabbaths past I have appointed meetings at 5 o'Clock, there begins to be some favorable appearances."[35]

Emily Coburn had been a new Presbyterian convert. She found her sister's religious enthusiasm more than a match for her own. "She was as firm as the everlasting hills in the belief of Mormonism," Emily wrote, "and seemed to have the whole Bible at her tongue's end. She was of the belief that God had again visited His People, and again set His hand, the second time, to recover the house of Israel." Sally warned Emily against condemning what she did not understand.

Emily had determined it was useless to try to change her sister's mind and she decided to return to her brother's in Sandford. Emily and the Knight family attended services at her sister's home on Sunday, 27 June. Emily recalled, "The discourse was delivered by Oliver Cowd[e]ry, an elder of the Mormon church, and a witness to the gold plates."[36] A message came to Emily that her brother Esick wished to see her in a grove some distance from the house:

> I felt reluctant in granting his request, but through the advice of my sister I ventured to go. I at this time attempted to make plain to him the reason of my tarrying at my sister's, and I then believed he understood me perfectly. While in the midst of our conversation, who should come but the Rev. Mr. Sherer, pastor of our church in Sandford. He came and took my hand and holding it so long and firmly I thought it odd.[37]

Holding her hand tightly, the pastor tried to move her down the lane to a spot where her uncle was waiting with a horse and buggy to take her back to Sandford. For some reason Sherer failed to mention this detail, and it was only gradually that she learned what their real intent was. At the time Emily felt Sherer's behavior inexplicable, holding so tenaciously to her hand. She asked her brother to help her, but he refused, saying she should listen to Sherer's advice.

At that point her sister, accompanied by other Mormons, arrived at the grove. Sally rushed up to Emily and wrenched Sherer's hand from hers, yelling, "What are you doing with my sister? What are you doing with my sister?" Emily remembered Sally's white face as she repeated these words. The confrontation proved too much for Sherer and her brother, and Emily slipped into the house while the others argued for about half an hour.

Finally Sally and her companions returned to the house and once more were seated and quietly talking and singing when, Emily remembered, her uncle Henry

> rode up to the door on a white, stately, beautiful horse, and as he drew up he exclaimed, "You are happy now you have accomplished your purpose, and I hope you enjoy it; but this will not be of long endurance, let me tell you." "O, yes," said one of the [Mormon] elders, "you are an attorney, probably you will take steps in this matter, but not to-day." "Sir," said another Mormon elder, "you are mad; you look as white as the horse you are riding; to-day is the holy Sabbath, and you are a deacon; don't indulge in such a passion." Many hard words were used on both sides; and here the subject ended, by putting spurs to the white steed, under a two hundred and twenty [pound] burden, which seemed light and easy for the noble animal.[38]

The matter did not end there. That evening, although it was dark and rainy, her brother-in-law spurred his horse on "through darkness, mud and rain, and dead of night" to her father's house in Guilford, some thirty miles away, where he obtained their permission to consult an attorney and seize Emily in her parents' name. Returning in the morning, he came to Emily and informed her that he now had authority to take her away. Emily replied that she would willingly have gone without protest if they had asked her and provided some means of getting back. In fact, she had on her own concluded to return to her brother's, but Newel Knight had not yet found time or a team to take her. She returned to Sandford, where she was met with "sober faces and cold hands." Still she remembered that she managed to "choke down" her feelings.

This incident appears in condensed form in Joseph Smith's history. Smith's history states:

> Amongst the many present at this meeting was one Emily Coburn sister to the wife of Newel Knight. The Revd. Mr. Shearer, a divine of the presbyterian faith, who had considered himself her pastor, came to understand that She was likely to believe our doctrine, and had a short <time> previous to this, our meeting, came to labor with her, but having spent some time with her without being able to persuade her against us, he endeavored to have her leave her sisters house, and go with him to her father's, who lived at a distance of at least some [blank] miles off: For this purpose he had recourse to stratagem, He told her that one of her brothers was waiting at a certain place, wishful to have her go home with him. He succeeded thus to get her a little distance from the house when, seeing that her brother was not in waiting for her, She refused to go any further with him; upon which he got hold of her by the arm to force her along; but her sister, was soon with them; the two women were too many for him and he was forced to sneak off without his errand, after all his labor and ingenuity. Nothing daunted however he went to her Father, represented to him something or other, which induced the Old Gentleman to give him a power of Attorney, which, as soon as our meeting was over, on the above named Sunday evening, he immediately served upon her and carried her off to her father's residence, by open violence, against her will. All his labor was in vain, however, for the said Emily Coburn, in a short time afterwards, was baptized and confirmed a member of "the Church of Jesus Christ of Latter Day Saints."[39]

After Emily returned home from Colesville, a rumor came to the attention of her family that she too was planning to join the Mormon church. "I received daily visits from the pastor of our church, who gave me a prayer book and wished me to learn some of the prayers," she reported, "but I returned the book, saying I wished to be led and taught by one who said, 'Take my yoke upon you, and learn of me.'"[40] Those words betray the pain and stubbornness of a strong-willed young woman.

In keeping with the Presbyterian procedures of church discipline, a course of gospel labor was commenced. Patterned on Matthew 18, the first step was for an individual privately to approach the offending party and seek to restore that person. If this failed one or two others were taken along for a second visit to assist in the settlement and to serve as witnesses in the event the matter had to be brought before the entire church.

The final stage in the process was lodging a formal complaint with the church and holding a public hearing. In Emily's case the complaint was lodged by officers of the church, including her own brother Esick Lyon Coburn.[41] It read:

> To the Church of Christ, in Sandford:
> WHEREAS, E[mily]. M. [Coburn], a member of said church, embraces a most wicked and dangerous heresy; and whereas, we have taken with her the first and second steps of gospel labor, without obtaining satisfaction, we therefore make complaint to the church of which said E. M. [Emily Coburn] is a member, praying that the brethren of said church would bring her to an account for her unchristian conduct; and, as in duty bound, your servants will ever pray.
>
>

H. M.
> E. L.
> B. S.[42]

Looking back, Emily acknowledged that her attitude could have been "more pleasing, cheerful, delightful." Yet each of the three separate times they visited her to labor with her, she assured them that

> I had no thought of joining them (the Mormons). This they did not seem to hear; and, to sum up the matter, their uncharitable actions drove me farther and still farther from believing in anything good. I was not yet eighteen years of age. My heart was stricken, and I could see no love manifested. In the advancement of time I perceived they still believed I intended joining that church, without listening to what I told them or trying to ascertain the truth in regard to it. They did not come to me in love and ask me to go with them to my brother's or my father's.[43]

The pastor continued to make his customary visits and eventually raised the matter of settling the complaint against her with the church. He informed her that there would be a meeting at church the following day, and since the matter concerned her, he wished her to be present. "I did not intend to be obstinate," she recalled, "but my feelings revolted against it." Nevertheless she went and "as the meeting was expressly to the purpose of bringing me to an account," she stood before the church in her own defense. "I arose and told them the charges brought against me were incorrect," she reports, "and I was very sorry that so much hard labor had been done under false colors; but this I would say, for the satisfaction of the church, that inasmuch as I had been the means of so much dissatisfaction, I felt heartily sorry, and hoped that God and the church would pardon that mistake. This seemed to be all that was necessary, and they gave me the hand of fellowship, and here the trouble ended."[44]

Peace was short-lived. Sometime in late September or early October Emily returned to her father's home in Guilford. There she and her sister Jane braided straw bonnets and enjoyed the fall sunsets and the autumn trees. The painful events of the summer still lingered in her mind. "Why did not my father come or send after me when he heard of my intention to join the Mormon church? Why did they give a power of attorney to disgrace and ignominiously drag away this poor child." Such unanswered questions flooded her mind.

Still her religious views remained the same, and she continued to pray that her life would be spent serving God and that her example would lead many to Christ. Then one day in autumn, when "the outward world seemed in slumber," the thought came to her that her sister Sally, whom she had not heard from for "several months," would arrive within two hours. Her mother refused to accept such a premonition. Yet within a short time Sally and her husband Newel arrived. Even more startling was the willingness of her parents to let Emily return to the Knight farm in Colesville. Even "more strange" was "when, as if by some unknown power, I was baptized and confirmed in the Mormon church the next Sabbath after!" Such an intention had not entered her mind when she left her father's house, she confessed. All she could say in later reflection was that she was following her religious duty. Was it the utter confidence she had in her older sister's integrity? she wondered. Whatever the motivation that led her to unite with the Mormon church, it profoundly altered the course of her life.

The consternation and sorrow resulting from Emily Coburn's baptism in the Mormon church can be seen in the letter of Reverend John Sherer written in November describing events of the summer:

> I will relate a circumstance that has given me pain. A member of the church in Sandford, a young female, has renounced her connexion with the church, and joined <another> in Colesville founded by Joseph Smith. This man has been known, in these parts, for some time, as a kind of Juggler, who has pretended, through a glass, to see money under ground &c, &c. The book, on which he founds his new religion, is called the "Book of Mormon". It contains not much, and is rather calculated to suit the marvelous, and unthinking. No man in his right mind can think the Book or the doctrines it contains, worthy of the least notice; yet there are a number who profess to believe in it. Since the church was formed, which was some time in July, about twenty have gathered around their stand- ard, and have subscribed themselves to be the followers [of] Christ; for they call themselves a church of Christ, and the only church of Christ. All professing christians who do not adhere to their system, they consider as formalists; "having the form of Godliness, but denying the power." They have pretended to work miracles, such as casting out devils, and many other things, too blasphemous to mention. — It is believed, however, they have [atta]ined to about the zenith of their glory in this place. Their books remain unsold; <except> here and there an individual, none will buy them. It is thought the greatest speculation, which they probably anticipated, will prove a losing business. May the Lord speedily turn their counsels head long, and deliver those, whose feet have been taken in their snare.[45]

Meanwhile, at Fayette in October 1830, the month after the second church conference, a minister named Peter Bauder spent a full day at the Peter Whitmer home. He spoke with Joseph Smith personally and published his recollection in 1834:

> I called at P[eter]. Whitmer's house, for the purpose of seeing [Joseph] Smith, and searching into the mystery of his system of religion, and had the privilege of conversing with him alone, several

hours, and of investigating his writings, church records, &c. I improved near four and twenty hours in close application with Smith and his followers: he could give me no christian experience, but told me that an angel told him he must go to a certain place in the town of Manchester, Ontario County, where was a secret treasure concealed, which he must reveal to the human family.[46]

While staying in Fayette in November, Joseph Smith met nineteen-year-old convert Orson Pratt. Pratt wrote, "By my request, on the 4th of Nov., the Prophet Joseph inquired of the Lord for me, and received the revelation published in the Doctrine and Covenants."[47] Pratt later added: "I went into that chamber [in the second story of the Peter Whitmer Sr.'s home] with the Prophet Joseph Smith, to inquire of the Lord; and he received a revelation for my benefit, which was written from the mouth of the Prophet by John Whitmer, one of the witnesses of the Book of Mormon."[48]

When Pratt and his traveling companion, Joseph F. Smith, visited David Whitmer in 1878, Pratt provided further insight into the way Smith obtained this revelation. In a letter written three weeks after the event, James R. B. Vancleave reports asking Pratt about "his belief in the seer stone":

at Peter Whitmer Sr's residence he [Orson Pratt] asked Joseph whether he could not ascertain what his mission was, and Joseph answered him that he would see, & asked Pratt and John Whitmer to go upstairs with him, and on arriving there Joseph produced a small stone called a seer stone, and putting it into a Hat soon commenced speaking and asked Elder P[ratt]. to write as he would speak, but being too young and timid and feeling his unworthiness he asked whether Bro. John W[hitmer]. could not write it, and the Prophet said that he could: Then came the revelation to the Three named given Nov. 4th 1830.[49]

David Whitmer stated that many of Smith's early revelations were received through the seer stone. He wrote, "The revelations in the Book of Commnadments [sic] up to June, 1829, were given through the 'stone,' through which the Book of Mormon was translated."[50] Smith received many of his revelations from July 1828 to June 1829 (when he was dictating the text of the Book of Mormon) by a stone placed in his hat—the same method he used in hunting for lost treasure.[51]

Sidney Rigdon, a new convert from Ohio, met Smith the following month in December. He had first heard about Mormonism early in November and received baptism on 8 November 1830.[52] He was ordained an Elder by Oliver Cowdery in Ohio. Rigdon, with Smith, visited the branch of the church in Colesville.[53] While there Rigdon evidently checked the docket books of both Joseph Chamberlain and Joel K. Noble. Reportedly when he returned to Ohio about 1 February 1831, he "with a great show of good nature, commenced a long detail of his researches after the character of Joseph Smith; he declared that even his enemies had nothing to say against his character; he had brought a transcript from the docket of two magistrates, where Smith had been tried as a disturber of the peace, which testified that he was honorably acquitted."[54]

During the early months of 1831 the Smith, Whitmer, and Knight families together with many converts would join Rigdon and others into Kirtland, Ohio, now the gathering place of the Saints at their new church headquarters.

NOTES

1. These events were recorded by members of the Mormon church, by the minister of the Presbyterian church, by one of the sisters involved, Emily Coburn, and by a judge at one of Joseph Smith's trials. The Mormon account is recorded in Manuscript History Book A-1: 43, archives, historical department, Church of Jesus Christ of Latter-day Saints, Salt Lake City, Utah (hereafter LDS archives); Dean C. Jessee, ed., *The Papers of Joseph Smith* (Salt Lake City: Deseret Book Co., 1989), 1:310-11. The account in Book A-1 may have been based in part on Newel Knight's recollections. Joseph Smith's 1839 diary records for the dates 4-5 July: "Thursday & Friday (assisted by Br Newel Knight) dictating History" (Joseph Smith diary, kept by James Mulholland, LDS archives; Jessee, *Papers of Joseph Smith*, 2:326). Newel Knight's published account is found in *Scraps of Biography* (Salt Lake City: Juvenile Instructor Office, 1883), 54. For the experience of Joseph Knight, see Dean C. Jessee, ed., "Joseph Knight's Recollection of Early Mormon History," *Brigham Young University Studies* 17 (Autumn 1976): 38; minimal punctuation and editing has been added to clarify account.

2. Albert L. Zobell, Jr., "Writing Paper for the Book of Mormon Manuscript," *Improvement Era* 72 (Feb. 1969): 54-55.

3. For problems in the Fayette area, see the letter of Rev. Diedrich Willers, 18 June 1830, trans. and ed. by D. Michael Quinn in *New York History* 54 (July 1973): 317-33.

4. Knight, *Scraps of Biography*, 53-55.

5. *Latter Day Saints' Messenger and Advocate* 1 (Oct. 1834): 12, Kirtland, Ohio, has the date of Sally Knight's baptism as 29 June 1830. Since the day of baptisms was a Monday, the correct date is probably 28 June. See *Utah Genealogical Magazine* 26 (Oct. 1935): 147-48.

6. Newel Knight, *Scraps of Biography*, 47.

7. From 1824 to 1830 the work at Nineveh declined, being without a pastor. In 1830 it emerged as the Bainbridge and Ninevah Presbyterian church (J. S. Pattengill, *History of the Presbytery of Binghamton*, 16). None of the early records appear to have survived.

8. According to records in the family Bible, Abram Willard Benton was "born July 16, 1805." He died on 9 March 1867 at Fulton, Illinois. His brief comments about Smith's 1830 Bainbridge trial appeared in "Mormonites," *Evangelical Magazine and Gospel Advocate*, New Series, 2 (9 Apr. 1831): 120, original periodical in Meadville Theological Seminary, Chicago, Illinois.

9. Manuscript History Book A-1: 48; Jessee, *Papers of Joseph Smith*, 1:318.

10. Jessee, "Joseph Knight's Recollection," 38. The New York law Knight cited was part of the vagrancy law which regarded as a misdemeanor "pretending . . . to discover where lost goods may be found" (*Laws of the State of New York, Revised and Passed in the Thirty-Sixth Session of the Legislature* [1813], 1:114).

11. Manuscript History A-1: 44; Jessee, *Papers of Joseph Smith*, 1:312-13.

12. John Reed's speech was given on 17 May 1844 and appeared in *Times and Seasons* 5 (1 June 1844): 549-50; this quote is on page 550. See also footnote in Joseph Smith et al., *History of the Church of Jesus Christ of Latter-day Saints* (Salt Lake City: Deseret Book, 1959), 1:94-96; 6:392-97. Our spelling of the name "Reed" comes from the 1839 draft of the Manuscript History (see Jessee, *Papers of Joseph Smith*, 1:253, 257); *Times and Seasons*; and bills from Bainbridge, New York, for the years 1826 and 1830.

13. These bills were discovered in 1971 in the dead storage in the basement of the Norwich jail, with the 1826 bills, as described in chap. 4. Chamberlain's bill is now in the Office of the Clerk of the Board of Supervisors, Chenango County Office Building, Norwich, New York.

14. If we could locate Justice Chamberlain's docket book, we might have a more complete record of the testimony of the witnesses, but the book's

location, if it is still extant, is unknown to members of his family. We could trace only three descendants, none of whom knew of any docket book that belonged to their great-grandfather.

15. A. W. Benton, "Mormonites," *Evangelical Magazine* 2 (9 Apr. 1831): 120. Josiah Jones wrote that in the fall of 1830, "He [Oliver Cowdery] stated that Smith looked onto or through the transparent stones to translate what was on the plates" (in Milton V. Backman, Jr., "A Non-Mormon View of the Birth of Mormonism in Ohio," *Brigham Young University Studies* 12 [Spring 1972]: 309). See LDS Mosiah 28:13; RLDS Mosiah 12:18.

According to Benton, Addison Austin testified "that at the very same time that Stowell was digging for money, he, Austin was in company with said Smith alone, and asked him to tell him honestly whether he could see this money or not. Smith hesitated some time, but finally replied, 'to be candid, between you and me, I cannot, any more than you or any body else; but any way to get a living'" (A. W. Benton, "Mormonites," *Evangelical Magazine* 2 (9 Apr. 1831): 120).

16. Manuscript History Book A-1: 44-45; Jessee, *Papers of Joseph Smith*, 1:313-14. Smith wrote to Oliver Cowdery in 1829, "I have bought a horse of Mr. Stowell and want some one to come after it as soon as convenient" (Smith to Cowdery, 22 Oct. 1829, Joseph Smith Letterbook 1:9, LDS archives). See Dean C. Jessee, comp., *The Personal Writings of Joseph Smith* (Salt Lake City: Deseret Book Co., 1984), 228.

17. On Josiah Stowell's family, see William H. H. Stowell, *Stowell Genealogy* (Rutland, VT: The Tuttle Co., 1922), 230.

18. Benton, "Mormonites," 120.

19. Manuscript History Book A-1: 45; Jessee, *Papers of Joseph Smith*, 1:314.

20. *Times and Seasons* 5 (1 June 1844): 550; *History of the Church* 1:95n and 6:394.

21. Joel K. Noble to Jonathan B. Turner, 8 Mar. 1842, Jonathan B. Turner Collection, Illinois State Historical Library, Springfield. The limitation on a misdemeanor was set forth in *Laws of the State of New York, Revised and Passed* (1813), 1:187, which read:

all suits, informations and indictments which shall hereafter be brought or exhibited for any crime or misdemeanor, murder excepted, shall be brought or exhibited within three years next after the offence shall have been committed, and not after, and if brought or exhibited after the time hereby limited the same shall be void: *Provided however,* That if the person, against whom such suit, information or indictment shall be brought or exhibited, shall not have been an inhabitant or usually resident within this state during the said three years, then the same shall or may be brought or exhibited against such a person at anytime within three years, during which he shall be an inhabitant or usually resident within this state, after the offence committed.

Smith's opponents may have felt that, due to Smith's absence from New York while in Pennsylvania, the statue of limitations had not been exceeded.

22. Jessee, "Joseph Knight's Recollection," 38.

23. Noble to Jonathan B. Turner, 8 Mar. 1842. John Reed mentioned, "The prisoner was to be tried by three justices of the peace" (*Times and Seasons* 5 [1 June 1844]: 551). Since no bills for this trial in Colesville have yet been found we cannot verify this statement.

24. Manuscript History Book A-1: 46; Jessee, *Papers of Joseph Smith*, 1:315. William Seymour had been a pioneer settler in Binghamton and after studying law moved to Windsor Township, next to Colesville. There he became an elder and clerk of session in the Presbyterian church as well as a justice of the peace and town clerk. Returning to Binghamton, he became a county judge, a member of the U.S. Congress, and finally judge of the Court of Common Pleas. He died on 28 December 1848, highly commended by the Bar Association (*Binghamton Democrat*, 2 Jan. 1849, 3).

25. Knight, *Scraps of Biography*, 59-60, cf. Manuscript History, Book A-1: 46; Jessee, *Papers of Joseph Smith*, 1:316.

26. Noble to Turner, 8 Mar. 1842. A newspaper printed a portion of a letter written in 1830 which said, "we have seen none of their miracles here, except N.N. [Newel Knight] I heard say in meeting, that he had the devil cast out" (letter dated 8 Oct. 1830, in *Brattleboro' Messenger*, 20 Nov. 1830, as cited in John Phillip Walker, ed., *Dale Morgan on Early Mormonism: Correspondence and a New History* [Salt Lake City: Signature Books, 1986], 344).

27. Manuscript History Book A-1: 47; Jessee, *Papers of Joseph Smith*, 1:317.

28. Knight, *Scraps of Biography*, 61. W. R. Hine also reported that "Jo was discharged" (*Naked Truths About Mormonism* 1 [Jan. 1888]: 2, original publication in the Yale University Library). George A. Smith, in a discourse given on 18 March 1855, repeated what he had heard from Emer Harris, an older brother of Martin Harris:

> Forty-seven times he [Joseph Smith] was arraigned before the tribunals of law, and had to sustain all the expense of defending himself in those vexatious suits, and was every time acquitted. He was never found guilty but once. I have been told, by Patriarch Emer Harris, that on a certain occasion he was brought before a magistrate in the

State of New York, and charged with having cast out devils; the magistrate, after hearing the witnesses, decided that he was guilty, but as the statutes of New York did not provide a punishment for casting out devils, he was acquitted (*Journal of Discourses*, 26 vols. [Liverpool, Eng.: Latter-day Saints' Book Depot, 1854-86], 2:213).

29. Manuscript History Book A-1: 47; Jessee, *Papers of Joseph Smith*, 1:317.

30. Emily Coburn's account is in her book under the name Emily M. Austin, *Mormonism; or, Life Among the Mormons* (Madison, WI: M. J. Cantwell, Book and Job Printers, 1882), 35-36.

31. Ibid., 32-33. William G. Hartley wrote, "It is possible, although evidence is lacking, that the Knights had interest in money digging ventures, such as friend Stowell sponsored, and that their interest in Joseph's story about gold plates might have had a profit motive at first. But their devotion to Joseph Smith for the next two decades was religious, not commercial" (*"They Are My Friends": A History of the Joseph Knight Family, 1825-1850* [Provo, UT: Grandin Book Co., 1986], 22).

32. Thomas F. Gordon, *Gazetteer of the State of New York* (Philadelphia: T. K. and P. G. Collins, 1836), 362.

33. The church was first organized as the North Branch of the Presbyterian Church of Windsor, and in 1812 it became a separate church known as the Colesville Presbyterian church. It had its central meeting place on Cole's Hill, where Nathaniel Cole had built the tavern that gave the area its name. By 1820 there was a house of worship there. J. S. Pattengill, *History of the Presbytery of Binghamton* (Binghamton, NY: Carl, Stoppard & Co., 1877), 18-20. The General Assembly of the Presbyterian church (U.S.A.) first listed the Sandford church in its May 1830 *Minutes*. The last time it appeared was in the May 1833 *Minutes*, after which it dissolved or was merged with another church.

34. American Home Missionary Society (AHMS) archives, "Fourth Report," 34, #321. All papers and correspondence are housed in the Amistad Research Center, Tilton Hall, Tulane University, New Orleans, Louisiana.

35. John Sherer to Reverend Absalom Peters, 20 Aug. 1830, AHMS archives. Part of this letter was edited for publication and printed in *The Home Missionary, and American Pastor's Journal* 3 (1 Nov. 1830): 143.

36. Austin, *Mormonism*, 36. Joseph Smith's history records, "The Sabbath arrived and we held our meeting, Oliver Cowdery preached" (Manuscript History A-1: 42; Jessee, *Papers of Joseph Smith*, 1:309). This appears to be the Sabbath service that both Emily and Joseph Smith's history refer to when Oliver Cowdery preached. Cowdery and Smith returned to Colesville in July

1830 to confirm those who had been baptized but they were prevented and had to leave because of persecution (Jessee, *Papers of Joseph Smith*, 1:317-18).

37. Austin, *Mormonism*, 40.

38. Ibid., 41-42.

39. Manuscript History Book A-1: 43; Jessee, *Papers of Joseph Smith*, 1:310-11, cf. 251. The name of the church at this time was the Church of Christ but by the time Smith's history was written it was called the Church of Jesus Christ of Latter Day Saints, which is what appears in the text. See Knight, *Scraps of Biography*, 54.

40. Austin, *Mormonism*, 44.

41. Ibid., 251. The initials E. L. on the complaint refer to her brother Esick Lyon [Coburn]. It is likely also that the initials H. M. represent the uncle she elsewhere (25) refers to as H. M. C.: Hanry Cobourn listed in the 1830 census of Sandford as living just a few houses from Esek Cobourn (63). This is also probably the "Henry" Coburn recorded in the 1825 Sandford census.

42. Ibid., 43, emphasis in original.

43. Ibid., 39.

44. Ibid., 47-48.

45. Sherer to Peters, 18 Nov. 1830. Smith's history reported Newel Knight's experience with the devil as occurring in April or May 1830: "he saw the devil leave him and vanish from his sight" (Manuscript History A-1: 40; Jessee, *Papers of Joseph Smith*, 1:306). Emily soon moved west with the Colesville church to Ohio, then on to Missouri. She eventually settled in Nauvoo, Illinois, only to leave the church she had joined some ten years before.

46. Peter Bauder, *The Kingdom and Gospel of Jesus Christ: Contrasted with that of Anti-Christ* (Canajohrie, NY: Printed by A. H. Calhoun, 1834), 36. One of the focuses of Bauder's pamphlet was his understanding that Christian churches had throughout history lost the spirit of personal forgiveness and instead turned to domineering priestcraft. Therefore, he found it important that he could find no such experience of personal salvation in his conference with Smith.

47. "History of Orson Pratt," Deseret News 8 (2 June 1858): 62; also in Eldon J. Watson, comp., *The Orson Pratt Journals* (Salt Lake City: comp., 1975), 9. BC 36; 1835 D&C 56; LDS D&C 34; RLDS D&C 33.

48. *Journal of Discourses* 7: 311 (18 Sept. 1859); see also 12:88 (11 Aug. 1867) and 17:290 (7 Feb. 1875).

49. James R. B. Vancleave to Joseph Smith III, 29 Sept. 1878, "Miscellaneous Letters and Papers," Library-Archives, Reorganized Church of Jesus Christ of Latter Day Saints, Independence, Missouri (hereafter RLDS archives). See also Lyndon W. Cook, ed., *David Whitmer Interviews: A Restoration*

Witness (Orem, UT: Grandin Book Co., 1991), 239-40. Orson Pratt and Joseph F. Smith visited David Whitmer on Sunday, 8 September 1878.

Shortly after the visit Pratt and Smith reported to President John Taylor and Council of Twelve Apostles that when Pratt spoke to a small group meeting at Plano, Illinois, on 12 September 1878, he "explained the circumstances under which several revelations were received by Joseph the Prophet, and the manner in which he received them, he being present on several occasions of the kind. Declared that sometimes Joseph used a seer stone when enquiring of the Lord, and receiving revelation . . . he oftener received them without any instrument" ("Report of Elders Orson Pratt and Joseph F. Smith," *Deseret Evening News*, [23 Nov. 1878], 1; *Latter-day Saints' Millennial Star* 40 [16 Dec. 1878]: 787).

50. David Whitmer, *An Address to All Believers in Christ* (Richmond, MO: Author, 1887), 53.

51. Joseph Smith's history records that eight revelations were received through the "Urim and Thummim" (seer stone in a hat) between July 1828 and June 1829. It is probable that all the revelations during this period were received through the stone as David Whitmer states.

In a letter from John Logan Traughber to "Dear Friend," dated 10 October 1881, he wrote: "John C. Whitmer, a son of Jacob, told me that when O. Pratt and J. F. Smith were at Richmond to see 'D.C.,' [David Whitmer] in 1878, he asked Orson how he first understood the B[ook]. of M[ormon]. was translated, and Orson said 'twas by means of the Seer-stone. He said he asked Orson if he ever knew of the stone's being used after the translation, and he answered that he did; and that Joe took him upstairs at Whitmers, in Fayette, N. Y., after meeting, one Sunday, and sat down and put the stone in his hat, and the hat over his face, and read off to him a revelation, as John Whitmer wrote it down. This was in November, 1830" (in A. T. Schroeder Collection, State Historical Society of Wisconsin, Madison). The reference to Sunday may be in error.

52. Copy of Oliver Cowdery letter, dated 12 Nov. 1830, in a Newel Knight journal currently in private possession.

53. John Whitmer's History, as cited in F. Mark McKiernan and Rodger D. Launius, eds., *An Early Latter Day Saint History: The Book of John Whitmer Kept by Commandment* (Independence, MO: Herald Publishing House, 1980), 31-32, 35-36, original in RLDS archives. Emily Coburn mentions a visit of Sidney Rigdon but places it at an earlier time frame in her account (Austin, *Mormonism*, 37).

54. "Mormonism," *The Telegraph* 2 (15 Feb. 1831), Painesville, Ohio; reprinted in the *Evangelical Inquirer* 1 (7 Mar. 1831): 226, Dayton, Ohio, ed.

David S. Burnet; also published in E. D. Howe, *Mormonism Unvailed* (Paines-ville [OH]: by the Author, 1834), 113. Richard L. Anderson identified the article's author "M. S. C." as probably Matthew S. Clapp ("The Impact of the First Preaching in Ohio," *Brigham Young University Studies* 11 [Summer 1971]: 480).

CONCLUSION

This study might be called the search for the historical Joseph. Although it has become fashionable in some quarters to quote Martin Heidegger's axiom that "there are no facts, only interpretation," we believe that facts exist and that an array of different interpretations is possible. We trust most readers will agree.

One feels considerable empathy for Joseph Smith as his life unfolds from court records and other scraps of history. When the Smiths default on their mortgage, when a young women dies and friends grapple with the meaning of death, when money diggers demand their share of the treasure, when Joseph is jeered at in open court for crystal-gazing, when a potential convert is abducted by her Presbyterian minister—these are not stories of public relations invention. What we encounter is an understanding of the complexity of the times and that these issues were an important part of everyday life.

As the documents reveal, some events differed from what has been traditionally taught. Was Smith less than forthcoming in later years about his evolution from Manchester farmboy to a new prophet? Did he or others alter the record intentionally? Having been involved in our own quest for the past thirty years searching archives for clues to this and other mysteries, we have long since abandoned the simple prophet-fraud dichotomy that others still find so compelling. Our intent is to understand, not to debunk.

The question of volition is open-ended. Smith believed that he spoke with supernatural beings, and he produced impressive tran-

197

scripts of interviews with them. Whether he actually did is ultimately a matter of faith.

Those interested in the origin of Mormonism will soon discover that to have only Joseph Smith's recollections of his early years misses the richness of the times. When Smith told his life's history, his understanding at that later time shaped the story of his extraordinary visions. Magical incantations, guardian spirits, treasures in hills, use of a special stone for secular and religious purposes—these were all de-emphasized while the story became conflated and simplified. Supernatural encounters were amplified and polished to accommodate more orthodox views. To us, the original accounts ring more authentic.

Whether readers peruse our book in search of their own spiritual moorings or out of historical inquisitiveness, it should assist them in clarifying some of the issues surrounding the beginnings of this new religious movement. Predominantly a summary of primary documents and recollections, our book allows room for people of all perspectives to expand rather than confine their perceptions.

Joseph Smith is an important figure in western religious development, and he deserves a preeminent place among other millennialists of his time. Much of the subsequent history and world view of the United States was influenced by such reformers whose social experiments, redaction of religious tradition, and consideration of alternative futures brought us to where we are today.

Names of Possessors.	Remarks by Assessors.	Description of Real Estate.	Amount of Real Estate. Dollars.	Cents.	Amount of Personal Estate. Dollars.	Cents.	Total, Real and Personal Estate. Dollars.	Cents.	Tax to be paid thereon. Dollars.	Cents.
Sawyer Luke	Lot no 32, pt Lot 187, incr No 2 Pt 200		1.800	"	45	"	1.845		4	16
Chichester Samuel	Pct 108	(3) Do	1	350	"	"	350			79
Moraigne? Persons	Pct 20	(2) Do	3/4	450	"	"	450		1	01
Simons John	Pct 22	(2) Do	1 1/2	360	"	"	360			65
Smith Robert	Pct 108	(3) Do	1	200	"	"	200			45
Sprague William	Pct 102	(2) Do	2	400	"	"	400			90
Francis George	Lot 24	(2) Do	160	1920	242	"	2.162		4	89
Smith James F	Pct 15	(2) Do	3/4	657	"	"	657			25
Sheffield John	Pct 113	(2) Do	1	150	"	"	151			43
Olsorne? Craftes	Pct 110	(2) Do	50	325	"	"	325			74
Smith & Bowers	Lot 20 & 94	(2) Do	125	1492	"	"	1.492		3	36
Morse Alpheus	Lots 7 in Sharon title	(2) Do	2	510	510	"	1.000		2	26
Smith Isaac	31.128.129.135.137	Do	24	561	"	"	560		1	26
Smith Joseph	Pt Lot no 1	Do	100	700	"	"	700		1	58
			$9397		787		10.184		22	98

One hundred acres of Lot 1 taxed to Joseph Smith, Sr., for the first time in Farmington (Manchester), New York. (From Assessment Roll, Farmington [Manchester], New York, 7 July 1821; courtesy Ontario County Records Center and Archives, Canandaigua, New York.)

J. A. Steere, Printer

Samuel Wagstaff	Asa Lilly
Alex McIntyre	Moses Hotchkiss
James Lewis	Daniel Hendee
Joel McCollum	Joseph Smith
James White	Alvin Smith
Thos. J. Stimpson	William White
Calvin Perkins	James Shaw
Eber Barnes	Dennis Davenport
George Ford	Ashley VanDuzer
Enoch Lilly	Samuel Allen
Solomon Tice	Azel Howe
Wm. Hayward	David Richardson
Levi Hall	Zebulon Reeves
Silas Shirtliff	Dorastus Cole
David S. Jackway	David P. Daggett
Gain Robinson	Cleason Hall
Jonathan Eggleston	Josiah [Joseph] D. Hayward
Orrin Warner	James Culver
Patrick Boyle	John Woodward
Wm. Jackway	Platt Williams
Wm. Hutchinson	Fitch Averill
William Hunt	Thomas Bukit
Michael Eggleston	Isaac C. Bills
Jedediah Bennett	Stephen Cook
Zebulon Williams	Daniel Lane
Jeremiah Hurlbut	Luther Wilder
Levi Daggett	Robert Talford

Palmyra Highway Tax Record for 1822, District 26. (From typed copy by Doris Nesbitt, preserved on microfilm in copies of old village records, Palmyra, New York, 1793-1867).

April the 16 day the year 1827. S. Harrison Smith Son of Joseph Smith began to Work for me by the month. is to Work 7 Months for the use of the place Where said Joseph Smith Lives

Lemuel Durfee, Sr., Account Book, 16 April 1827.

Transcription:

April the 16 day the year 1827 S. Harrison Smith Son of
Joseph Smith began to Work for me by the month. is to
Work 7 Months for the use of the place Where said Joseph Smith Lives

(Courtesy Ontario County Historical Society, Canandaigua, New York.)

1826 Bill of Justice Albert Neely. (Courtesy Clerk of the Board of Supervisors, Chenango County Office Building, Norwich, New York.)

Chenango County to Albert Neely   Dr

People)
vs)   Assault & Battery
Tunis Brazee)   trial at G. A. Leadbetters
                             Justices

same)   James Humphry)
vs)   Zechariah Tarbel)
Peter Brazee)   Albert Neely)

same)
vs)
John Sherman)   To my fees in trial)
                   of above cause)   3.68

People)
vs)
Samuel May)   Assault & Battery
March 22. 1826)   To my fees in this cause $1.99

same)
vs)   Misdemeanor
Joseph Smith)
The Glass looker)   To my fees in examination)
March 20. 1826)   of the above cause)   2.68

same)
vs)   Champerty
Newel Evans)   To examination of above cause   2.18
Sept. 2. 1826)

same)   Assault & Battery
vs)
Josiah Evans)   To my fees in above cause   1.46

same)
vs)
Robert Darnell)   Petit Larceny
Oct 3. 1826)   To fees in above cause   1.85

same)   Assault and Battery
vs)
Ira Church)   To fees in above cause   2.53
Nov 9. 1826)

              Albert Neely, Jus of Peace $16.37

16.37
  93
15.44

Transcription of 1826 Bill of Justice Albert Neely.

Hill Cumorah, Manchester, New York. (Photograph by George E.
Anderson, 1907).

THE

BOOK OF MORMON:

AN ACCOUNT WRITTEN BY THE HAND OF MOR-MON, UPON PLATES TAKEN FROM THE PLATES OF NEPHI.

Wherefore it is an abridgment of the Record of the People of Nephi; and also of the Lamanites; written to the Lamanites, which are a remnant of the House of Israel; and also to Jew and Gentile; written by way of commandment, and also by the spirit of Prophesy and of Revelation. Written, and sealed up, and hid up unto the LORD, that they might not be destroyed; to come forth by the gift and power of GOD unto the interpretation thereof; sealed by the hand of Moroni, and hid up unto the LORD, to come forth in due time by the way of Gentile; the interpretation thereof by the gift of GOD; an abridgment taken from the Book of Ether.

Also, which is a Record of the People of Jared, which were scattered at the time the LORD confounded the language of the people when they were building a tower to get to Heaven: which is to shew unto the remnant of the House of Israel how great things the LORD hath done for their fathers; and that they may know the covenants of the LORD, that they are not cast off forever; and also to the convincing of the Jew and Gentile that JESUS is the CHRIST, the ETERNAL GOD, manifesting Himself unto all nations. And now if there be fault, it be the mistake of men: wherefore condemn not the things of GOD, that ye may be found spotless at the judgment seat of CHRIST.

BY JOSEPH SMITH, JUNIOR,

AUTHOR AND PROPRIETOR,

PALMYRA:

PRINTED BY E. B. GRANDIN, FOR THE AUTHOR.

1830.

Title page of 1830 Book of Mormon.

January 1830 Joseph Smith, Sr., and Martin Harris Agreement. In Simon Gratz Autograph Collection, Case 8, Box 17 (American Miscellaneous), under Smith, Joseph, Sr., Historical Society of Pennsylvania, Philadelphia, Pennsylvania. (Courtesy Historical Society of Pennsylvania; used by permission.)

I hereby agree that Martin Harris shall have an equal privilege with me & my friends of selling the Book of Mormon of the Edition now printing by Egbert bB Grandin until enough of them shall be sold to pay for the printing of the same or until such times as the said Grandin shall be paid for the printing the aforesaid Books or copies

Manchester   January the 16th 1830   Joseph Smith Sr

Witness Oliver H P Cowdery

Transcription of Joseph Smith, Sr., and Martin Harris Agreement: [opposite page]

CHAPTER XVII.

1 *A Revelation to Oliver, given in Manchester, New-York, April 6, 1830.*

BEHOLD I speak unto you, Oliver, a few words. 2 Behold thou art blessed, and art under no condemnation.

3 But beware of pride, lest thou shouldst enter into temptation.

4 Make known thy calling unto the church, and also before the world; and thy heart shall be opened to preach the truth from henceforth and forever. Amen.

———————

CHAPTER XVIII.

1 *A Revelation to Hyrum, given in Manchester, New-York, April 6, 1830.*

BEHOLD I speak unto you, Hyrum, a few words:

2 For thou also art under no condemnation, and thy heart is opened, and thy tongue loosed;

3 And thy calling is to exhortation, and to strengthen the church continually.

4 Wherefore thy duty is unto the church forever, and this because of thy family. Amen.

Revelations of 6 April 1830, given in Manchester, New York. A Book of Commandments, for the Government of the Church of Christ (in press 1833).

44

CHAPTER XIX.

1 *A Revelation to Samuel, given in Manchester, New-York, April 6, 1830.*
BEHOLD I speak a few words unto you, Samuel:

2 For thou also art under no condemnation, and thy calling is to exhortation, and to strengthen the church.

3 And thou art not as yet called to preach before the world. Amen.

CHAPTER XX.

1 *A Revelation to Joseph, the father of Joseph, given in Manchester, New-York, April 6, 1830.*
BEHOLD I speak a few words unto you, Joseph:

2 For thou also art under no condemnation, and thy calling also is to exhortation, and to strengthen the church.

3 And this is thy duty from henceforth and forever. Amen.

CHAPTER XXI.

1 *A Revelation to Joseph (K.,) given in Manchester, New-York, April 6, 1830.*
BEHOLD I manifest unto you by these words, that you must take up your cross, in the which you must pray vocally before the world, as well as

Revelations of 6 April 1830, given in Manchester, New York. A Book of Commandments, for the Government of the Church of Christ (in press 1833).

in secret, and in your family, and among your friends, and in all places.

2 And behold it is your duty to unite with the true church, and give your language to exhortation continually, that you may receive the reward of the laborer. Amen.

CHAPTER XXII.

1 *A Revelation to Joseph, given in Manchester, New-York, April* 6, 1830.

BEHOLD there shall be a record kept among you, and in it thou shalt be called a seer, a translator, a prophet, an apostle of Jesus Christ, an elder of the church through the will of God the Father, and the grace of our Lord Jesus Christ;

2 Being inspired of the Holy Ghost to lay the foundation thereof, and to build it up unto the most holy faith;

3 Which church was organized and established, in the year of our Lord eighteen hundred and thirty, in the fourth month, and on the sixth day of the month, which is called April.

4 Wherefore, meaning the church, thou shalt give heed unto all his words, and commandments, which he shall give unto you, as he receiveth them, walking in all holiness before me:

5 For his word ye shall receive, as if from mine own mouth, in all patience and faith;

6 For by doing these things, the gates of hell shall not prevail against you:

7 Yea, and the Lord God will disperse the powers of darkness from before you; and cause the

B7

Revelations of 6 April 1830, given in Manchester, New York. A Book of Commandments, for the Government of the Church of Christ (in press 1833).

Crooked Brook on Smith Farm, Manchester, New York. (Photograph by George E. Anderson, 1907. Published in *Birth of Mormonism in Picture* [Salt Lake City: Deseret Sunday School, ca. 1909].)

Nathan Pierce Docket Book, 1827-30, case of Hyrum Smith, 28 June 1830.
(Courtesy Manchester Town Office, Manchester, New York). Transcription
on facing page.

[Side of Document]	[body of document]

Levi Daggett   8th June 1830 Sum pleas trespass on the Case

vs   Ret 18th June my house 3 oclock after noon

Hyram Smith   and returned served by copy S. Southworth

14th August 1830   18th June 1830 another Summons issued Ret 28th

Execution issued   day of June 1830 at one oclock after noon to

to Erastus Cole [?]   S. Southworth and returned served by Copy 21st of

13th September 1830   June 1830   Smith

this Execution returned   28th June 1830 Joseph ^ father of the Defendant appeared

in ____ by N. Harrington   and the Case was called and the plaintif declared

that he had collected   for a note and account Note dated 7th

$12.81 and paid plaintif   April 1830 for $20.07 on Interest and on account

9.94 by receipt on   for Shoeing horses of ballance due on account of $0.69

Execution and   Joseph Smith sworn and saith that his Son the Defendant

I received of said   engaged him to Come down at the return of the sum

constable $1.79 court   mons and direct the Justice to enter Judgment against

costs   the defendant for the amount of the note & account

The above Execution   Judgment for the plaintif for twenty one dollars seven cents $21.07

received and _____

Costs S. Southworth Court fees $0.80		Paid by Justice	
Witness fees	.12½	4th April 1831	1.60
Lamar Pick [?] served sub	.12½		22.67
Justice costs	.55		
	1.60		

Side column continues:

to plaintif this

27th Sept 1830

for to collect these [?]

amount due—

26th October 1830

Execution returned

no property nor body

to be found by

N. Harrington Constable

Transcription of Nathan Pierce Docket Book, case of Hyrum Smith, 28 June 1830.

~~~~~~~~~~~~~~~ EXECUTION ~~~~~~~~~~~~~~~

COUNTY, ss.—The People of the State of New York, by the Grace of God Free and Independent:

To any Constable of the said County, Greeting:

WHEREAS Judgment was rendered before me *Nathan Pierce* Esq. one of the Justices of the Peace of the said county, on the *28th* day of *June 1830* against *Hyrum Smith*

in favor of *Levi Daggett* for

twenty one Dollars *Seven* Cents, the damages, and *one*

Dollars *twenty nine* Cents, the costs:—THESE are therefore to command you to levy on the goods and chattels of the said defendant (except such as are by law exempted from execution) the amount of the said judgment, and bring the money before me, on the *13th* day of *September 1830* at my office in the town of *Manchester* in the said county, to render to the said plaintiff— And if no goods or chattels can be found, or not sufficient to satisfy this execution, then you are hereby commanded to take the body of the said defendant and convey *him* to the common Jail of the county aforesaid, there to remain until this execution shall be satisfied and paid. Hereof fail not at your peril. Given under my hand, at *Manchester* this *14th* day of *August* in the year of our Lord, 1830

Damages $ 21.07
Costs   1.79
Interest   .18
            $23.04

This Execution received from to Collect this amount this 27th September 1830

for Payment Nathaus Pierce Justice of the Peace.

~~~~ Sold by Bemis & Ward, Canandaigua. ~~~~

Execution against Hyrum Smith (front), 14 August 1830, in Nathan Pierce Docket Book, 1827-30. (Courtesy Manchester Town Office, Manchester, New York.)

Execution against Hyrum Smith (back), 14 August 1830, in Nathan Pierce Docket Book, 1827-30. (Courtesy Manchester Town Office, Manchester, New York.)

this Execution renewed for to collect this
amount due there on this 27th September 1830
fees 19 cents

Execution [printed]—handwritten on it:

[back side of Execution]:

Rec__ed of Nathan Harrington $9.94 Cents for
Levi dgget [Daggett] Septtember the 13th 1830

Received on this execution   Levi Daggett
$12.81 this 13th day of September   By
1830   Nathan Harrington   A K Daggett
              Constable

No property to be found Nor Boddy and I return
this Execution   October the 26 1830
                   N Harrington
                              Constable

[amounts on side]: $23 04
                               1 59
                            _____
                            $24.63
                                12
                            _____
                            $24 75

Transcription of back and front of Execution against Hyrum Smith, in Nathan Pierce Docket Book, 1827-30.

APPENDICES

APPENDICES

1. Joseph Smith's 1832 Account of His Early Life

In November 1832, after the birth of Joseph Smith III, Joseph Smith, Jr., commenced to dictate an account of his early life to his scribe Frederick G. Williams in Kirtland, Ohio. John Whitmer, official church historian, was residing in the Independence, Missouri, area. This account was written in Smith's ledger book now known as "Joseph Smith Letterbook 1," the first of two letterbooks. At some unknown time, these pages (3 leaves, 6 pages) were cut out but are located in archives, historical department, Church of Jesus Christ of Latter-day Saints, Salt Lake City, Utah. This short history of six pages was rediscovered in the 1960s, and a typescript appeared in Paul R. Chessman, "An Analysis of the Accounts Relating Joseph Smith's Early Visions," M.A. thesis, Brigham Young University, May 1965, 127-32. Another transcription of the early portion of the manuscript was done by Dean C. Jessee and published in *Brigham Young University Studies* 9 (Spring 1969): 278-80. The account has been subsequently published by Jessee in *The Personal Writings of Joseph Smith* (Salt Lake City: Deseret Book, 1984), 4-8, and *The Papers of Joseph Smith* (Salt Lake City: Deseret Book, 1989) 1:3, 5-10.

The account that follows is from the opening four pages and part of page five. The handwriting starts with that of Frederick G. Williams. Bold type indicates words in the handwriting of Joseph Smith. Williams's writing ends the portion we have extracted. The transcript has been divided into shorter paragraphs for easier reading.

A History of the life of Joseph Smith Jr. an account of his marvilous experience and of all the mighty acts which he doeth in the name of Jesus Ch[r]ist the son of the living God of whom he beareth record and also an account of the rise of the church of Christ in the eve of time according as the Lord brough<t> forth and

established by his hand <firstly> he receiving the testamony from on
high seccondly the ministering of Angels thirdly the reception of the
holy Priesthood by the minist[e]ring of Aangels to admin[i]ster the
letter of the Gospel—<the Law and commandments as they were
given unto him> and the ordinencs fo[u]rthly a confirmation and
reception of the high Priesthood after the holy order of the son of
the living God power and ordinence from on high to preach the
Gospel in the administration and demonstration of the spirit **the
Kees of the Kingdom of God confered upon him and the continu-
ation of the blessings of God to him &c —**

**I was born in the town of Charon [Sharon] in the <State> of
Vermont North America on the twenty third day of December AD
1805 of goodly Parents who spared no pains to instructing me in
<the> christian religion at the age of about ten years my Father
Joseph Smith Siegnior moved to Palmyra Ontario County in the
State of New York and being in indigent circumstances were
obliged to labour hard for the support of a large Family having
nine chilldren and as it required the exertions of all that were able
to render any assistance for the support of the Family therefore
we were deprived of the bennifit of an education suffice it to say
I was mearly instructid in reading writing and the ground <rules>
of Arithmatic which const[it]uted my whole literary acquirements.**

**At about the age of twelve years my mind become seriously
imprest with regard to the all importent concerns for the wellfare
of my immortal Soul which led me to searching the scriptures
believeing as I was taught, that they contained the word of God
thus applying myself to them and my intimate acquaintance with
those different denominations led me to marvel exce[e]dingly for
I discovered that <they did not> of adorn their profession by a holy
walk and Godly conversation agreeable to what I found contained
in that sacred depository this was a grief to my Soul**

**thus from the age of twelve years to fifteen I pondered many
things in my heart concerning the sittuation of the world of
mankind the contentions and divi[si]ons the wicke[d]ness and
abominations and the darkness which pervaded the minds of
mankind my mind become exce[e]dingly distressed for I become
convicted of my sins and by searching the scriptures I found that
<mankind> did not come unto the Lord but that they had aposta-
tised from the true and liveing faith and there was no society or
denomination that built upon the gospel of Jesus Christ as re-**

corded in the new testament and I felt to mourn for my own sins and for the sins of the world

for I learned in the scriptures that God was the same yesterday to day and forever that he was no respector to persons for he was God for I looked upon the sun the glorious luminary of the earth and also the moon rolling in their magesty through the heavens and also the stars shining in their courses and the earth also upon which I stood and the beast of the field and the fowls of heaven and the fish of the waters and also man walking forth upon the face of the earth in magesty and in the strength of beauty whose power and intiligence in governing the things which are so exceding great and marvilous even in the likeness of him who created <them> and when I considered upon these things my heart exclaimed well hath the wise man said <it is a> fool <that> saith in his heart there is no God

my heart exclaimed all all these bear testimony and bespeak an omnipotant and omnipreasant power a being who makith Laws and decreeth and bindeth all things in their bounds who filleth Eternity who was and is and will be from all Eternity to Eternity and when I considered all these things and that <that> being seeketh such to worship him as worship him in spirit and in truth

therefore I cried unto the Lord for mercy for there was none else to whom I could go and obtain mercy and the Lord heard my cry in the wilderness and while in <the> attitude of calling upon the Lord <in the 16th year of my age> a piller of light above the brightness of the sun at noon day come down from above and rested upon me and I was filled with the spirit of god and the <Lord> opened the heavens upon me and I saw the Lord and he spake unto me saying Joseph <my son> thy sins are forgiven thee. go thy <way> walk in my statutes and keep my commandments behold I am the Lord of glory I was crucifyed for the world that all those who believe on my name may have Eternal life <behold> the world lieth in sin at this time and none doeth good no not one they have turned asside from the gospel and keep not <my> commandments they draw near to me with their lips while their hearts are far from me and mine anger is kindling against the inhabitants of the earth to visit them ac[c]ording to th[e]ir ungodliness and to bring to pass that which <hath> been spoken by the mouth of the prophets and Ap[o]stles behold and lo I come quickly as it [is] **written of me in the cloud ‹clothed› in the glory of my Father**

and my soul was filled with love and for many days I could rejoice with great Joy and the Lord was with me but [I] could find none that would believe the he[a]v[e]nly vision nevertheless I pondered these things in my heart

but after many days I fell into transgressions and sinned in many things which brought a wound upon my soul and there were many things which transpired that cannot be writ[t]en and my Fathers family have suffered many persicutions and afflictions

and it came to pass when I was seventeen years of age I called again upon the Lord and he shewed unto me a heavenly vision for behold an angel of the Lord came and stood before me and it was by night and he called me by name and he said the Lord had forgiven me my sins and he revealed unto me that in the Town of Manchester Ontario County N.Y. there was plates of gold upon which there was engravings which was engraven by Maroni [Moroni] & his fathers the servants of the living God in ancient days and deposited by the commandments of God and kept by the power thereof and that I should go and get them and he revealed unto me many things concerning the inhabitants of the earth which since have been revealed in commandments & revelations

and it was on the 22d day of Sept. AD 1822 and thus he appeared unto me three times in one night and once on the next day and then I immediately went to the place and found where the plates was deposited as the angel of the Lord had commanded me and straight-way made three attempts to get them and then being exce[e]dingly frightened I supposed it had been a dreem of Vision but when I consid[e]red I knew it was not

therefore I cried unto the Lord in the agony of my soul why can I not obtain them behold the angel appeared unto me again and said unto me you have not kept the commandments of the Lord which I gave unto you therefore you cannot now obtain them for the time is not yet fulfilled therefore thou wast left unto temptation that thou mightest be made acquainted with the power of the advisary therefore repent and call on the Lord thou shalt be forgiven and in his own due time thou shalt obtain them

for now I had been tempted of the advisary and saught the Plates to obtain riches and kept not the commandment that I should have an eye single to the glory of God therefore I was chastened and

saught diligently to obtain the plates and obtained them not untill
I was twenty one years of age and in this year I was married to Emma
Hale Daughter of Isaach [Isaac] Hale who lived in Harmony Susque-
han[n]a County Pen[n]sylvania on the 18th January AD. 1827, on
the 22d day of Sept of this same year I obtained the plates

2. Interview of Martin Harris

In late January 1859, Martin Harris, who resided at Kirtland,
Ohio, was interviewed by Joel Tiffany. This interview was later published in New York City in *Tiffany's Monthly* 5 (Aug. 1859): 163-70.
The article was titled, "Mormonism—No. II." An original copy is
located at the American Antiquarian Society, Worcester, Massachusetts. The quotation marks have been deleted and some paragraphs
shortened for easier reading.

The following narration we took down from the lips of Martin
Harris, and read the same to him after it was written, that we might
be certain of giving his statement to the world. We made a journey
to Ohio for the purpose of obtaining it, in the latter part of January,
1859. We did this that the world might have a connected account of
the origin of Mormonism from the lips of one of the original
witnesses, upon whose testimony it was first received. For it will be
remembered that Martin Harris is one of the three witnesses selected to certify to the facts connected with the origin of that
revelation.

Mr. Harris says: Joseph Smith, jr., found at Palmyra [Manches-
ter], N.Y., on the 22d day of September, 1827, the plates of gold
upon which was recorded in Arabic, Chaldaic, Syriac, and Egyptian,
the Book of Life, or the Book of Mormon. I was not with him at the
time, but I had a revelation the summer before, that God had a work
for me to do. These plates were found at the north point of a hill
two miles north of Manchester village. Joseph had a stone which was
dug from the well of Mason Chase, twenty-four feet from the
surface. In this stone he could see many things to my certain
knowledge. It was by means of this stone he first discovered these
plates.

In the first place, he told me of this stone, and proposed to bind it on his eyes, and run a race with me in the woods. A few days after this, I was at the house of his father in Manchester, two miles south of Palmyra village, and was picking my teeth with a pin while sitting on the bars. The pin caught in my teeth, and dropped from my fingers into shavings and straw. I jumped from the bars and looked for it. Joseph and Northrop Sweet also did the same. We could not find it. I then took Joseph on surprise, and said to him—I said, "Take your stone," I had never seen it, and did not know that he had it with him. He had it in his pocket. He took it [out] and placed it in his hat—the old white hat—and placed his face in his hat. I watched him closely to see that he did not look [to] one side; he reached out his hand beyond me on the right, and moved a little stick, and there I saw the pin, which he picked up and gave to me. I know he did not look out of the hat until after he had picked up the pin.

Joseph had had this stone for some time. There was a company there in that neighborhood, who were digging for money supposed to have been hidden by the ancients. Of this company were old Mr. Stowel[l]—I think his name was Josiah—also old Mr. Beman, also Samuel Lawrence, George Proper, Joseph Smith, jr., and his father, and his brother Hiram Smith. They dug for money in Palmyra, Manchester, also in Pennsylvania, and other places. When Joseph found this stone, there was a company digging in Harmony, Pa., and they took Joseph to look in the stone for them, and he did so for a while, and then he told them the enchantment was so strong that he could not see, and they gave it up. There he became acquainted with his future wife, the daughter of old Mr. Isaac Hale, where he boarded. He afterwards returned to Pennsylvania again, and married his wife, taking her off to old Mr. Stowel[l]'s, because her people would not consent to the marriage. She was of age, Joseph was not.

After this, on the 22nd of September, 1827, before day, Joseph took the horse and wagon of old Mr. Stowel[l], and taking his wife, he went to the place where the plates were concealed, and while he was obtaining them, she kneeled down and prayed. He then took the plates and hid them in an old black oak tree top which was hollow. Mr. Stowel[l] was at this time at old Mr. Smith's, digging for money.

It was reported by these money-diggers, that they had found boxes, but before they could secure them, they would sink into the earth. A candid old Presbyterian told me, that on the Susquehannah flats he dug down to an iron chest, that he scraped the dirt off with his shovel, but had nothing with him to open the chest; that he went away to get help, and when they came to it, it moved away two or three rods into the earth, and they could not get it.

There were a great many strange sights. One time the old log school-house south of Palmyra, was suddenly lighted up, and frightened them away. Samuel Lawrence told me that while they were digging, a large man who appeared to be eight or nine feet high, came and sat on the ridge of the barn, and motioned to them that they must leave. They motioned back that they would not; but that they afterwards became frightened and did leave. At another time while they were digging, a company of horsemen came and frightened them away. These things were real to them, I believe, because they were told to me in confidence, and told by different ones, and their stories agreed, and they seemed to be in earnest—I knew they were in earnest.

Joseph did not dig for these plates. They were placed in this way: four stones were set up and covered with a flat stone, oval on the upper side and flat on the bottom. Beneath this was a little platform upon which the plates were laid; and the two stones set in a bow of silver by means of which the plates were translated, were found underneath the plates.

These plates were seven inches wide by eight inches in length, and were of the thickness of plates of tin; and when piled one above the other, they were altogether about four inches thick; and they were put together on the back by three silver rings, so that they would open like a book.

The two stones set in a bow of silver were about two inches in diameter, perfectly round, and about five-eighths of an inch thick at the centre; but not so thick at the edges where they came into the bow. They were joined by a round bar of silver, about three-eighths of an inch in diameter, and about four inches long, which, with the two stones, would make eight inches.

The stones were white, like polished marble, with a few gray streaks. I never dared to look into them by placing them in the hat, because Moses said that "no man could see God and live," and we could see anything we wished by looking into them; and I could not keep the desire to see God out of my mind. And beside, we had a command to let no man look into them, except by the command of God, lest he should "look aught and perish."

These plates were usually kept in a cherry box made for that purpose, in the possession of Joseph and myself. The plates were kept from the sight of the world, and no one, save Oliver Cowdery, myself, Joseph Smith, jr., and David Whitmer, ever saw them. Before the Lord showed the plates to me, Joseph wished me to see them. But I refused, unless the Lord should do it.

At one time, before the Lord showed them to me, Joseph said I should see them. I asked him, why he would break the commands of the Lord? He said, you have done so much I am afraid you will not believe unless you see them. I replied, "Joseph, I know all about it. The Lord has showed to me ten times more about it than you know."—Here we inquired of Mr. Harris—How did the Lord show you these things? He replied, I am forbidden to say anything how the Lord showed them to me, except that by the power of God I have seen them.

Mr. Harris continues: I hefted the plates many times, and should think they weighed forty or fifty pounds.

When Joseph had obtained the plates, he communicated the fact to his father and mother. The plates remained concealed in the tree top until he got the chest made. He then went after them and brought them home. While on his way home with the plates, he was met by what appeared to be a man, who demanded the plates, and struck him with a club on his side, which was all black and blue. Joseph knocked the man down, and then ran for home, and was much out of breath. When he arrived at home, he handed the plates in at the window, and they were received from him by his mother. They were then hidden under the hearth in his father's house. But the wall being partly down, it was feared that certain ones, who were trying to get possession of the plates, would get under the house and dig them out.

Joseph then took them out, and hid them under the old cooper's shop, by taking up a board and digging in the ground and burying them. When they were taken from there, they were put into an old Ontario glass-box. Old Mr. Beman sawed off the ends, making the box the right length to put them in, and when they went in he said he heard them jink [clink], but he was not permitted to see them. He told me so.

The money-diggers claimed that they had as much right to the plates as Joseph had, as they were in company together. They claimed that Joseph had been [a] traitor, and had appropriated to himself that which belonged to them. For this reason Joseph was afraid of them, and continued concealing the plates. After they had been concealed under the floor of the cooper's shop for a short time, Joseph was warned to remove them. He said he was warned by an angel. He took them out and hid them up in the chamber of the cooper's shop among the flags [flax]. That night some one came, took up the floor, and dug up the earth, and would have found the plates had they not been removed.

These things had all occurred before I talked with Joseph respecting the plates. But I had the account of it from Joseph, his wife, brothers, sisters, his father and mother. I talked with them separately, that I might get the truth of the matter.

The first time I heard of the matter, my brother Presarved [Preserved] Harris, who had been in the village of Palmyra, asked me if [I] had heard about Joseph Smith, jr., having a golden bible. My thoughts were that the money-diggers had probably dug up an old brass kettle, or something of the kind. I thought no more of it. This was about the first of October, 1827.

The next day after the talk with my brother, I went to the village, and there I was asked what I thought of the Gold Bible? I replied, The Scripture says, He that answereth a matter before he heareth it, it is foolishness unto him. I do not wish to make myself a fool. I don't know anything about it. Then said I, what is it about Joe's Gold Bible? They then went on to say, that they put whiskey into the old man's cider and got him half drunk, and he told them all about it. They then repeated his account, which I found afterwards to agree substantially with the account given by Joseph. Then said I to them, how do you know that he has not got such gold plates? They replied, "Damn him! angels appear to men in this enlightened age! Damn him, he ought to be tarred and feathered for telling such a damned lie!" Then I said, suppose he has told a lie, as old Tom Jefferson said, it did [not] matter to him whether a man believed in one god or twenty. It did not rob his pocket, nor break his shins. What is it to us if he has told a lie? He has it to answer for [it] if he has lied. If you should tar and feather all the liars, you would soon be out of funds to purchase the material.

I then thought of the words of Christ, The kingdom divided against itself cannot stand. I knew they were of the devil's kingdom, and if that is of the devil, his kingdom is divided against itself. I said in my heart, this is something besides smoke. There is some fire at the bottom of it. I then determined to go and see Joseph as soon as I could find time.

A day or so before I was ready to visit Joseph, his mother came over to our house and wished to talk with me. I told her I had no time to spare, she might talk with my wife, and, in the evening when I had finished my work I would talk with her. When she commenced talking with me, she told me respecting his bringing home the plates, and many other things, and said that Joseph had sent her over and wished me to come and see him. I told her that I had a time appointed when I would go, and that when the time came I should then go, but I did not tell her when it was. I sent my boy to harness my horse and take her home. She wished my wife and daughter to go with her; and they went and spent most of the day. When they came home, I questioned them about them. My daughter said, they were about as much as she could lift. They were now in the glass-box, and my wife said they were very heavy. They both lifted them. I waited a day or two, when I got up in the morning, took my breakfast, and told my folks I was going to the village, but went directly to old Mr. Smith's.

I found that Joseph had gone away to work for Peter Ingersol[l] to get some flour. I was glad he was absent, for that gave me an opportunity of talking with his wife and the family about the plates. I talked with them separately, to see if their stories agreed, and I found they did agree. When Joseph came home I did not wish him to know that I had been talking with them, so I took him by the arm and led him away from the rest, and requested him to tell me the story, which he did as follows. He said: "An angel had appeared to him, and told him it was God's work." Here Mr. Harris seemed to wander from the subject, when we requested him to continue and tell what Joseph then said. He replied, Joseph had before this described the manner of his finding the plates. He found them by looking in the stone found in the well of Mason Chase. The family had likewise told me the same thing.

Joseph said the angel told him he must quit the company of the money-diggers. That there were wicked men among them. He must have no more to do with them. He must not lie, nor swear, nor steal. He told him to go and look in the spectacles, and he would show him the man that would assist him. That he did so, and he saw myself, Martin Harris, standing before him. That struck me with surprise. I told him I wished him to be very careful about these things. "Well," said he, "I saw you standing before me as plainly as I do now." I said, if it is the devil's work I will have nothing to do with it; but if it is the Lord's, you can have all the money necessary to bring it before the world. He said the angel told him, that the plates must be translated, printed and sent before the world. I said, Joseph, you know my doctrine, that cursed is every one that putteth his trust in man, and maketh flesh his arm; and we know that the devil is to have great power in the latter days to deceive if possible the very elect; and I don't know that you are one of the elect. Now you must not blame me for not taking your word. If the Lord will show me that it is his work, you can have all the money you want.

While at Mr. Smith's I hefted the plates, and I knew from the heft that they were lead or gold, and I knew that Joseph had not credit enough to buy so much lead. I left Mr. Smith's about eleven o'clock and went home. I retired to my bedroom and prayed God to show me concerning these things, and I covenanted that if it was his work and he would show me so, I would put forth my best ability to bring it before the world. He then showed me that it was his work, and that it was designed to bring in the fullness of his gospel to the gentiles to fulfill his word, that the first shall be last and the last first. He showed this to me by the still small voice spoken in the soul. Then I was satisfied that it was the Lord's work, and I was under a covenant to bring it forth.

The excitement in the village upon the subject had become such that some had threatened to mob Joseph, and also to tar and feather him. They said he should never leave until he had shown the plates. It was unsafe for him to remain, so I determined that he must go to his father-in-law's in Pennsylvania.

He wrote to his brother-in-law Alvah Hale, requesting him to come for him. I advised Joseph that he must pay all his debts before starting. I paid them for him, and furnished him money for his journey. I advised him to take time enough to get ready, so that he might start a day or two in advance: for he would be mobbed if it was known when he started. We put the box of plates into a barrel about one-third full of beans and headed it up. I informed Mr. Hale of the matter, and advised them to cut each a good cudgel and put into the wagon with them, which they did. It was understood that they were to start on Monday; but they started on Saturday night and got through safe. This was the last of October, 1827. It might have been the first of November.

3. Memorandum of John H. Gilbert

John H. Gilbert, who set up the majority of the type for the Book of Mormon, prepared a statement in preparation for the World's Fair held in Chicago, Illinois, in 1892. The following transcript was published by Wilford C. Wood in *Joseph Smith Begins His Work*, Vol. 1 (Salt Lake City: Deseret News Press, 1958): Introductory pages.

Memorandum, made by John H. Gilbert, Esq.,
Sept. 8th, 1892, Palmyra, N.Y.

I am a practical printer by trade. I have been a resident of Palmyra, N.Y., since about the year 1824, and during all that time have done some type-setting each year. I was aged ninety years on the 13th day of April 1892, and on that day I went to the office of the Palmyra Courier and set a stick-ful of type.

My recollection of past events, and especially of the matter connected with the printing of the "Mormon Bible," is very accurate and faithful, and I have made the following memorandum at request, to accompany the photographs of "Mormon Hill," which have been made for the purpose of exhibits at the World's Fair in 1893.

In the forepart of June 1829, Mr. E. B. Grandin, the printer of the "Wayne Sentinel," came to me and said he wanted I should assist him in estimating the cost of printing 5000 copies of a book that Martin Harris wanted to get printed, which he called the "Mormon Bible."

It was the second application of Harris to Grandin to do the job,—Harris assuring Grandin that the book would be printed in Rochester if he declined the job again.

Harris proposed to have Grandin do the job, if he would, as it would be quite expensive to keep a man in Rochester during the printing of the book, who would have to visit Palmyra two or three times a week for manuscript, &c. Mr. Grandin consented to do the job if his terms were accepted.

A few pages of the manuscript were submitted as a specimen of the whole, and it was said there would be about 500 pages.

The size of the page was agreed upon, and an estimate of the number of ems in a page, which would be 1000, and that a page of manuscript would make more than a page of printed matter, which proved to be correct.

The contract was to print and bind with leather, 5000 copies for $3,000. Mr. Grandin got a new font of Small Pica, on which the body of the work was printed. When the printer was ready to commence work, Harris was notified, and Hyrum Smith brought the first installment of manuscript, of 24 pages, closely written on common foolscap paper—he had it under his vest, and vest and coat closely buttoned over it. At night Smith came and got the manuscript, and with the same precaution carried it away. The next morning with the same watchfulness, he brought it again, and at night took it away. This was kept up for several days. The title page was first set up, and after proof was read and corrected, several copies were printed for Harris and his friends. On the second day—Harris and Smith being in the office—I called their attention to a grammatical error, and asked whether I should correct it? Harris consulted with Smith a short time, and turned to me and said: "The Old Testament is ungrammatical, set it as it is written."

After working a few days, I said to Smith on his handing me the manuscript in the morning; "Mr. Smith, if you would leave this manuscript with me, I would take it home with me at night and read and punctuate it." His reply was, "We are commanded not to leave it." A few mornings after this, when Smith handed me the manuscript, he said to me:—"If you will give your word that this manuscript shall be returned to us when you get through with it, I will leave it with you." I assured Smith that it should be returned all right when I got through with it. For two or three nights I took it home with me and read it, and punctuated it with a lead pencil. This will account for the punctuation marks in pencil, which is referred to in the Mormon Report, an extract from which will be found below.

Martin Harris, Hyrum Smith and Oliver Cowdery were very frequent visitors to the office during the printing of the Mormon Bible. The manuscript was supposed to be in the handwriting of Cowdery. Every Chapter, if I remember correctly, was one solid paragraph, without a punctuation mark, from beginning to end.

Names of persons and places were generally capitalized, but sentences had no end. The character or short &, was used almost invariably where the word and, occurred, except at the end of a chapter. I punctuated it to make it read as I supposed the Author intended, and but very little punctuation was altered in proof-reading. The Bible was printed 16 pages at a time, so that one sheet of paper made two copies of 16 pages each, requiring 2500 sheets of paper for each form of 16 pages. There were 37 forms of 16 pages each,—570 pages in all.

The work was commenced in August 1829, and finished in March 1830,—seven months. Mr. J. H. Bortles and myself done the press work until December taking nearly three days to each form.

In December Mr. Grandin hired a journeyman pressman, Thomas McAuley, or "Whistling Tom," as he was called in the office, and he and Bortles did the balance of the press-work. The Bible was printed on a "Smith" Press, single pull, and old fashioned "Balls" or "Niggerheads" were used—composition rollers not having come into use in small printing offices.

The printing was done in the third story of the west end of "Exchange Row," and the binding by Mr. Howard, in the second story the lower story being used as a book store, by Mr. Grandin, and now—1892—by Mr. M. Story as a dry-goods store.

Cowdery held and looked over the manuscript when most of the proofs were read. Martin Harris once or twice, and Hyrum Smith once, Grandin supposing these men could read their own writing as well, if not better, than any one else; and if there are any discrepancies between the Palmyra edition and the manuscript these men should be held responsible.

Joseph Smith, Jr. had nothing to do whatever with the printing or furnishing copy for the printers, being but once in the office during the printing of the Bible, and then not over 15 or 20 minutes.

Hyrum Smith was a common laborer, and worked for any one as he was called on.

Cowdery taught school winters—so it was said—but what he done summers, I do not know.

Martin Harris was a farmer, owning a good farm, of about 150 acres, about a mile north of Palmyra village, and had money at interest. Martin,—as every body called him,—was considered by his neighbors a very honest man; but on the subject of Mormonism, he was said to be crazy. Martin was the main spoke in the wheel of Mormonism in its start in Palmyra, and I may say, the only spoke. In the fall of 1827, he told us what wonderful discoveries Jo Smith had made, and of his finding plates in a hill in the town of Manchester, (three miles south of Palmyra,)—also found with the plates a large pair of spectacles, by putting which on his nose and looking at the plates, the spectacles turned the hyroglyphics into good English. The question might be asked here whether Jo or the spectacles was the translator?

Sometime in 1828, Martin Harris, who had been furnished by someone with what he said was a fac-simile of the hyroglyphics of one of the plates, started for New York. On his way he stopped at Albany and called on Lt. Gov. Bradish,—with what success I do not know. He proceeded to New York, and called on Prof. C. Anthon, made known his business and presented his hyroglyphics.

This is what the Professor said in regard to them—1834—

"The paper in question was, in fact, a singular scroll. It consisted of all kinds of singular characters, disposed in columns, and had evidently been prepared by some person who had before him at the time a book containing various alphabets; Greek and Hebrew letters, crosses and flourishes, Roman letters inverted or placed sidewise [sideways], arranged and placed in perpendicular columns, and the whole ended in a rude delineation of a circle, divided into various compartments, arched with various strange marks, and evidently copied after the Mexican Calendar, given by Humboldt, but copied in such a way as not to betray the source whence it was derived. I am thus particular as to the contents of the paper, inasmuch as I have frequently conversed with my friends on the subject since the Mormon excitement began, and well remembered that the paper contained anything else but 'Egyptian Hyroglyphics.'["]

Martin returned from his trip east satisfied that "Joseph" was a "little smarter than Prof. Anthon."

Martin was something of a prophet:—He frequently said that "Jackson would be the last president that we would have; and that all persons who did not embrace Mormonism in two years would be stricken off the face of the earth." He said that Palmyra was to be the New Jerusalem, and that her streets were to be paved with gold.

Martin was in the office when I finished setting up the testimony of the three witnesses,—(Harris—Cowdery and Whitmer) I said to him,—"Martin, did you see those plates with your naked eyes?" Martin looked down for an instant, raised his eyes up, and said, "No, I saw them with a spiritual eye."

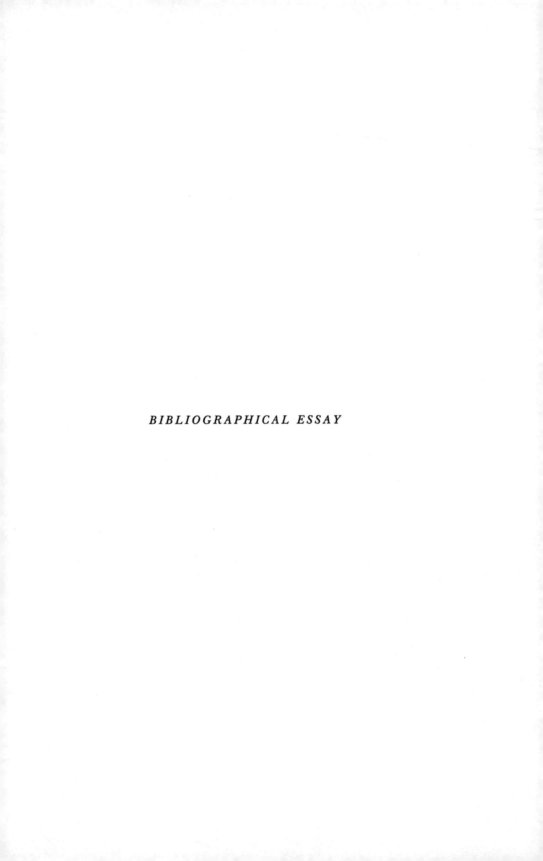

BIBLIOGRAPHICAL ESSAY

BIBLIOGRAPHICAL ESSAY

1. Smith Family Recollections

JOSEPH SMITH

The Manuscript History of the Church was commenced in 1838 when Joseph Smith dictated the early portion from his birth in December 1805 to about September 1827. A rough draft was evidently made before the final copy. This 1838 draft was copied in 1839 into a bound book and is known as the 1838-39 manuscript history. The volume is labeled Book A-1 and is located in LDS archives. The history is a first person narrative of events. How much of the history was actually dictated by Smith is not known. Smith had dictated and written a short history in 1832 which covered events to April 1829.

For December 1805 to January 1831 the pages are in the following handwritings: pages 1-59 (Dec. 1805-Sept. 1830), James Mulholland; pages 60-75 (Sept.-Nov. 1830), Robert B. Thompson; and pages 75-92 (Nov. 1830-Jan. 1831), William W. Phelps. The text on pages 131-33 was written by Willard Richards after publication in the *Times and Seasons*.

There is a note in the front of the manuscript about Smith's oldest brother Alvin. The year of his death has been corrected to 1823. The note reads:

In Memory of Alvin Smith
Died the 19th Day of November
In the 25 year of his age year 1823
Joseph Smith Joseph
In Memory of Alvin S

The history covering December 1805 through January 1831 appeared in the following publications: *Times and Seasons* 3 (15 Mar. 1842): 726 through 4 (15 Oct. 1843): 354, Nauvoo, Illinois; *The Latter-Day Saints' Millennial Star* 3 (June 1842): 21 through 5 (Aug. 1844): 35, Liverpool, England. It also appeared in the *Millennial Star* 14 (Supplement, 1852): 1-56. Extracts covering December 1805 through May 1829 were published in the *Pearl of Great Price* in 1851. The *Pearl of Great Price* was revised and then canonized on 10 October 1880 by the Church of Jesus Christ of Latter-day Saints and is known as Joseph Smith-History (JS-H). In 1902 the "History of Joseph Smith" up to January 1831 was published by the LDS church as *The History of the Church of Jesus Christ of Latter-day Saints* 1:1-145. This publication contains editing by B. H. Roberts. It first appeared in a paperback edition in 1978. For a convenient publication of the Manuscript History, see Dean C. Jessee, ed., *The Papers of Joseph Smith: Autobiographical and Historical Writings* (Salt Lake City: Deseret Book, 1989), 1:267-346. An early 1839 draft covering May 1829 through September 1830 can be found on pages 231-64.

The Reorganized Church of Jesus Christ of Latter Day Saints, headquartered in Independence, Missouri, published *The History of the Reorganized Church of Jesus Christ of Latter Day Saints*, written and compiled by Joseph Smith III and Heman C. Smith in 1897; republished in Independence, Missouri, by Herald House in 1967, 1:6-168.

Joseph Smith only "corrected 42 pages" (p. 42 covers part of June 1830) after its publication in the *Times and Seasons*. See Heber C. Kimball's diary in *On the Potter's Wheel: The Diaries of Heber C. Kimball*, edited by Stanley B. Kimball (Salt Lake City: Signature Books in association with Smith Research Associates, 1987), 100; also *History of the Church* 7:389.

LUCY MACK SMITH

The Preliminary Manuscript to the "History of Lucy Smith" was dictated by her to Martha Jane Coray. Martha's husband, Howard, in his autobiography written in 1883, recalled that it was in the winter of 1844-45 that his wife was asked to serve as amanuensis for Lucy Smith (see Howard C. Searle, "Early Mormon Historiography: Writing the History of the Mormons, 1830-1858," Ph.D. diss., University of California, Los Angeles, 1979, 362). Lucy wrote to her son William: "I have by the council of the 12 undertaken a history of the family that is my father's family and my own" (ibid., 369, letter dated 23 Jan. 1845). The original of the Preliminary Manuscript is in LDS archives. There is also a small notebook housed in Special Collections, Harold B. Lee Library, Brigham Young University, Provo, Utah.

Orson Pratt used another manuscript that had been compiled and revised by Martha and Howard Coray from the earlier Preliminary Manuscript and other papers. Extracts from the "History of Joseph Smith" in the *Times and Seasons* were used in this revision. The title page of the revised manuscript is as follows: "The History of Lucy Smith Mother of the Prophet." The copyright of 18 July 1845 has: "The History of Lucy Smith . . . an account of the many persecutions, trials and afflictions which I and my family have endured in bringing forth the Book of Mormon, and establishing the church of Jesus Christ of Latter Day Saints" (Copyright Records, Illinois, Vol. 18 [1821-48], 18 July 1845, Library of Congress, Washington, D.C.).

The first publication of Lucy's history was *Biographical Sketches of Joseph Smith the Prophet, and His Progenitors for Many Generations* in Liverpool, England, for Orson Pratt by Samuel W. Richards in 1853. This work is as much an autobiography of Lucy as it is a biography of Joseph Smith.

Five years later, in 1859, Brigham Young remarked that he wanted the book revised and corrected (Wilford Woodruff journal, 13 Feb. 1859, LDS archives). Later in 1865 Young had *Biographical Sketches* recalled because of assumed inaccuracies. The 1853 publication was revised by George A. Smith and Elias Smith. This revision was published in 1902 with an introduction by Joseph F. Smith. It did not indicate where the text had been altered nor the reason. The 1902 edition was further edited with notes and comments by Preston Nibley in 1945 and published by Bookcraft of Salt Lake City under the title *History of Joseph Smith By His Mother, Lucy Mack Smith*.

An edition was published by the Reorganized Church of Jesus Christ of Latter Day Saints in 1880 and 1908 as *Biographical Sketches of Joseph Smith the Prophet, and His Progenitors for Many Generations*. It was republished in 1912 with notes by Heman C. Smith, and a paperback edition was printed by Herald Publishing House, Independence, Missouri, in 1969. A reproduction of the 1853 first edition was issued by Modern Microfilm Co., Salt Lake City, in 1965 with an introduction by Jerald and Sandra Tanner, and a printing by Arno Press and the *New York Times* was published in 1969.

For additional information, see Jan Shipps, *Mormonism: The Story of a New Religious Tradition* (Urbana: University of Illinois Press, 1985), 87-107.

WILLIAM SMITH

On 18 April 1841 William Smith was interviewed by Reverend James Murdock, who included excerpts from the interview in a letter dated 19 June 1841 written to *The Congregational Observer*, Hartford and New-Haven, Connecticut, 2 (3 July 1841): 1. About 1875 William wrote about his early life in New York. This is known as "Notes Written on 'Chamber's Life of Joseph Smith.' by William Smith," and was sent to the LDS church in 1925 by Charles Knecht of Yakima, Washington.

William Smith's published narrative was printed in 1883 when he was seventy-two years old as *William Smith on Mormonism* (Lamoni, IA: Printed at Herald Steam Book and Job Office). On 8 June 1884 he preached a sermon at Deloit, Iowa, that was published in *Saints' Herald* 31 (4 Oct. 1884): 643-44. In October 1893, a month before William died, he was interviewed by E. C. Briggs and J. W. Peterson. This interview was printed in the following publications: *Zion's Ensign* 5 (13 Jan. 1894): 6; *Deseret Evening News* 27 (20 Jan. 1894): 11; *Latter-day Saints' Millennial Star* 61 (26 Feb. 1894): 132-34; and excerpted in *Church News*, 16 Mar. 1968, 11, 13.

2. The 1826 Examination

ITEMIZED BILLS BY JUSTICE ALBERT NEELY
AND CONSTABLE PHILIP DE ZENG

The itemized bills of Justice Albert Neely and Constable Philip

De Zeng, officials who participated in the arrest and examination of Joseph Smith, were discovered on 28 July 1971 by Wesley Walters and Fred Poffarl among dead-storage documents in the basement of the county jail in Norwich, New York. These two bills were bound together in a bundle with other 1826 Bainbridge bills submitted to the County Board of Supervisors for approval and payment. They were tied with pink string, which had been placed around them when the treasurer packaged them for storage after they had been marked "passed" and the total due each claimant had been carefully entered into the "Supervisor's Journal" beside his name.

These and other bills relating to Joseph Smith's Bainbridge court hearings were removed by Walters and Poffarl from the water-soaked box in which they were found and hand-carried to Yale University's Beinecke Rare Book and Manuscript Library. They were received back by Chenango County in October 1971. Photographs are on file at the library of Westminster Theological Seminary in Philadelphia.

Neely's bill was first published by Jerald Tanner from a photocopy (see *Salt Lake City Messenger* 32 [Aug. 1971]: 2). It, along with the constable's bill, appeared shortly thereafter in *Joseph Smith's 1826 Trial* (Salt Lake City: Modern Microfilm Co., 1971), 6, 12-13. Both bills were also reproduced from photostats in Marvin S. Hill's "Joseph Smith and the 1826 Trial: New Evidence and New Difficulties," *Brigham Young University Studies* 12 (Winter 1972): 227, 233.

The 1826 bill which Neely submitted to the county for payment carries this entry:

same	[i.e. The People]	
vs		Misdemeanor
Joseph Smith		
The Glass looker		To my fees in
March 20. 1826		examination of
		the above cause 2.68

The phrase "Glass looker" on Neely's bill is Joseph Smith's preferred term to describe his occupation at the time, and is the same word Abram W. Benton used in his 1831 account to describe the peep-stone or glass placed in a hat to locate hidden treasures. Smith's father-in-law, Isaac Hale, in a sworn affidavit published in their county newspaper in 1834, mentions that "Smith stated to me, that he had given up what he called 'glass-looking,' and that he expected to work hard for a living, and was willing to do so" (*Susquehanna Register, and Northern Pennsylvanian*, 9 [1 May 1834]: 1; Howe, *Mormonism Unvailed*, 264).

The bill submitted by De Zeng gives further details concerning this court procedure by listing:

Serving Warrant on Joseph Smith & t[ravel]	1.25
Subpoening 12 Witnesses & travel	2.50 [3.50?]
attendance with Prisoner two days & 1 nigh[t]	1.75
notifying two Justices	1.__
10 Miles travel with Mittimus to take him	1.__

The dollar amounts are barely visible in the water-soaked area. It is not entirely certain if the costs for subpoenaing witnesses and travel read $2.50 or $3.50.

Neely's itemized bill of $16.37, which included a number of other cases besides the examination of Joseph Smith, was "passed" by the Chenango County supervisors for $15.44. De Zeng's bill of $41.15 was passed, together with another bill for $26 for a total of $67.15. The total amounts of the bills for each year were entered into the "Supervisor's Journal" beside the name of the official in each town. This journal was housed in a separate building from that in which the bills were kept.

Bainbridge had four justices of the peace and two constables. Each justice handled cases in which one or both of the constables served warrants and subpoenas, and sometimes two or three justices were called together to form a court of special sessions to try a particular case. Therefore the costs for some of the cases appear on the bills of several different officials. For example, the 1825 cases of Luke Crandall and Lewis Porter appear on the bills of Constable De Zeng, who made the arrest, and on the bills of Justices Levi Bigelow, James Humphrey, and Zechariah Tarble, who served as a court of special sessions to try the cases (see "Arrangement of Bills of Justices of the Peace and Constables for Bainbridge, Chenango County, New

York, 1820-30," comp. H. Michael Marquardt, July 1988). This inter-relatedness of bills substantiates the genuineness of any particular bill. In addition each bill is in the distinctive handwriting of that individual, which can be validated from bills submitted in other years.

THE WILLIAM D. PURPLE ACCOUNT

William D. Purple of Greene, New York, had moved to South Bainbridge to begin a medical practice in 1825. While in South Bainbridge he became a Mason and was soon secretary of the local lodge. As Warden of Friendship Lodge, he "was representative in Grand Lodge in June, 1827" (William D. Purple, *Historical Reminiscences of Eastern Light Lodge, No. 126, F. & A. M., of Greene, Chenango County, N.Y., From 5811 [1811] To 5897 [1897], with Biographical Sketches*, revised and published by the Lodge, 1897 [Greene, NY: Hall's Steam Print, 1897], 40). He also served as clerk of the village of Bainbridge when it was incorporated on 21 April 1829 (James H. Smith, *History of Chenango and Madison Counties, New York* [Syracuse, NY: D. Madson & Co., 1880], 167). Near the end of 1830 he removed to Coventry and then to Greene, New York, where he continued his practice. "He was Inspector of Common Schools in 1834, Postmaster eight years, and Greene's first Historian" (Mildred English Cochrane, *From Raft to Railroad: A History of the Town of Greene, Chenango County, New York 1792-1867* [Ithaca, NY: Cayuaga Press, 1967], 89, 99-101). He died on 18 May 1886.

When the examination of Joseph Smith was held early in 1826, Purple, then twenty-three years old, was invited by his friend Justice Neely to take notes. In all probability his notes provided the basis for the record of the examination in Neely's docket book. From time to time thereafter he told acquaintances about the legal difficulties encountered by young Smith in Bainbridge. In 1877 he committed his reminiscences to writing. They appeared in *The Chenango Union* 30 (3 May 1877): 3, Norwich, New York, under the heading "Joseph Smith, the Originator of Mormonism, Historical Reminiscences of the town of Afton," dated "Greene, April 28, 1877." A copy is located in the Guernsey Memorial Library, Norwich, New York. Another copy put in a scrapbook can be found in the A. T. Schroeder Collection, under "Mormonism: Pamphlets, Vol. 2, Item 5," State Historical Society of Wisconsin, Madison. A different printing can be found pasted in the "Dr. Purple Scrapbook," 60-[62], Moore Memorial Library in Greene, New York. The account also became the basis of an article in *The Democrat*, Montrose, Pennsylvania, 19 Sept. 1877. Purple's presence in Bainbridge in 1826 is attested to by a bill of Justice of the Peace Zechariah Tarble in issuing a search warrant on 16 and 26 May 1826, "on the application of William D. Purple," to search for his stolen coat. It is further evidenced in a bill of "Knapp & Purple" for medical services to persons in the township from 9 to 21 February 1827.

The official record and the bills correct Purple as to the exact date of the examination, 20 March 1826. However, Purple had dated the hearing the end of February, remarkably close considering his reminiscence was written some fifty years after the event. Purple's character and memory are praised in several obituaries in the "Dr. Purple Scrapbook," pp. 54-56; excerpts in Fawn Brodie's notes in the Utah State Historical Society preserved among the papers of Stanley Ivins.

THE OFFICIAL RECORD

Four years before Purple's account was published, the actual record taken from Neely's docket book was made public. It has been questioned whether there even was an Albert Neely, justice of the peace in Bainbridge in 1826. However, the papers commissioning him as such, dated 16 November 1825, were found in May 1971, as well as more information establishing that he was in Bainbridge at this time. The record of the examination was torn from Neely's docket book by his niece, Emily Pearsall, and taken to Utah when she went to serve as a missionary under Episcopalian bishop Daniel S. Tuttle.

Neely held this office in 1826, 1827, and January 1828. He was evidently a merchant in Bainbridge who had arrived there before February 1825 (Smith, *History of Chenango and Madison Counties*, 143, 168-69). Neely's name appears in the civil Docket Book of Zechariah Tarble as a plaintiff in cases from 26 February 1825 through 14

January 1826. His signature is contained under a judgment entered 19 September 1825 (Original Docket Book of Zechariah Tarble, Bainbridge Town Hall, Bainbridge, New York). He was a defendant in 1825 and 1828-30 (Docket of Judgements, Justice Court, 5 May 1818-4 July 1844, Chenango County Clerk's Office, Norwich, New York, microfilm #826053, LDS Family History Library).

Neely was a vestryman of the Protestant Episcopal church (Smith, *History of Chenango and Madison Counties,* 176, and Charlah Ireland Skinner, *History of St. Peter's Church: Bainbridge, New York 1825 to 1975* [Bainbridge, NY: Broadcaster Press, 1975], 1). He was elected a Commissioner of Schools on 7 March 1826 (see Neely's 1826 bills submitted to the Chenango County Board of Supervisors, Clerk of the Board of Supervisors, Chenango County Office Building, Norwich, New York). The value of his personal estate for 1826 was put at $1,500 (1826 Assessment Roll, 14, Bainbridge Town Hall, Bainbridge, New York). He married Phebe Pearsall (b. 11 July 1809), and they were living in the town of Manlius, Onandaga County, when the 1830 census was taken (Clarence E. Pearsall, ed., *History and Genealogy of the Pearsall Family in England and America* 2 [1928]: 1,144; U.S. Census for Manlius, Onandaga County, New York, 372, microfilm #017160, LDS Family History Library). Neely was a justice of the peace of the town of Manlius in 1838. (See *Laws of the State of New York . . .* [Albany: Printed by E. Croswell . . . , 1838], 17-18). He died in 1857.

On Pearsall, see Daniel Tuttle, *Reminiscences of a Missionary Bishop* (New York: T. Whittaker, 1906), 272, 397-98; and Clarence and Hettie May Pearsall and Harry L. Neal, *History and Genealogy of the Pearsall Family in England and America* (1928), 2:1,143-44, 1,151. Emily Pearsall was born on 25 January 1833 to Robert Pearsall and his wife Flavia. Robert was an older brother of Phebe Pearsall, wife of Albert Neely. Emily was baptized on 26 May 1844 when she was eleven years old at St. Peter's Episcopal Church in Bainbridge, New York (New York County Records, 113:16, Daughters of the American Revolution Library, Washington, D.C.). She was confirmed on 14 May 1850 (St. Peter's Parish Register, vol. 1, 1838-1907, Bainbridge, New York). Bishop Tuttle in his autobiography wrote that "Smith was up more than once, when a youth, before justices of the peace in Central New York for getting money under false pretenses, by looking with his *peep* stone" (*Reminiscences of a Missionary Bishop*, 327, emphasis in original).

Before Pearsall's death in 1872, Charles Marshall, a British journalist visiting Salt Lake City, was shown the pages from Neely's docket book, copied it, and upon returning to England published it as "The Original Prophet. By a Visitor to Salt Lake City," *Fraser's Magazine* 7 (Feb. 1873): 229-30; reprinted in *Eclectic Magazine* 17 (Apr. 1873): 483. It is clear from a comparison with the first printing of the official record that neither account borrowed from the other. See *Joseph Smith and Money Digging* (Salt Lake City: Modern Microfilm Co., 1970), 23-29, which errs in making Horace and Arad Stowell sons instead of cousins of Josiah.

Marshall described how he obtained his transcript: "During my stay in Salt Lake [City] permission was courteously accorded me to copy out a set of such judicial proceedings not hitherto published. I cannot doubt their genuineness. The original papers were lent me by a lady of well-known position, in whose family they had been preserved since the date of the transactions."

After Pearsall's death, Tuttle fell heir to the Neely court record, and, unaware of its previous publication by Marshall, announced he was publishing it for the first time in "Mormons," *New Schaff-Herzog Encyclopedia* 2 (1883): 1,576. LDS scholar Hugh Nibley wrote: "Now, Bishop Tuttle, *if* this court record is authentic it is the most damning evidence in existence against Joseph Smith" (*The Myth Makers* [Salt Lake City: Bookcraft, 1961], 142; also in *Tinkling Cymbals and Sounding Brass: The Art of Telling Tales about Joseph Smith and Brigham Young* [Salt Lake City: Deseret Book Co., and Provo, UT: Foundation for Ancient Research and Mormon Studies, 1991], 246), emphasis in original.

Tuttle omitted the court costs which appeared at the end of the record in the *Fraser's Magazine* printing, apparently feeling they were unimportant for his general article on Mormons. Before the bishop left Utah in September 1886, he gave the record to Methodists there who printed it, including court costs, in their *Utah Christian Advocate* along with a thirty-five word summary of Horace Stowell's testimony which was not included in *Fraser's Magazine*, probably due to a copying error. See "A Document Discovered," *Utah Christian Advocate*

3 (Jan. 1886): 1 [misnumbered vol. 2, no. 13], Salt Lake City (copies at Drew University and Utah State Historical Society). Tuttle after his service in Utah was appointed Bishop of Missouri on 9 August 1886 (*Reminiscences of a Missionary Bishop*, 303) and moved to St. Louis where he spent the remaining years of his service until his death there in 1923. The document apparently was not returned to the bishop since it is not on file at the Diocesan Office, or with his personal effects preserved by his grandson, Wallace Tuttle of St. Louis, or with his library at the St. Louis Public Library.

If the document had been returned to the Episcopal church in Salt Lake City, it would have perished in the fire that destroyed their records many years ago (Richard S. Watson, letter 10 Mar. 1970). The Methodist Rocky Mountain Conference does not have it in its holdings (Robert Runnells, letter 28 July 1970; telephone call to archivist Martin Rist, 1970). It is possible that the editor of the *Utah Christian Advocate*, Samuel J. Carroll, may have kept it. Since mission work in Utah had been placed under several different conferences, it is remotely possible that it may still be somewhere among their records.

Justice of the peace docket books are not required to be kept on file at the county court house, although the townships could require them to be filed with them. Most were handed down in the justice's family or eventually discarded.

In the letter Tuttle wrote: "The Ms. was given me by Miss Emily Pearsall who, some years since, was a woman helper in our mission and lived in my family, and died here. Her father or uncle was a Justice of the Peace in Bainbridge, Chenango Co., New York, in Jo. Smith's time, and before him Smith was tried. Miss Pearsall tore the leaves out of the record found in her father's house and brought them to me." Although Tuttle did not give the uncle's name, the *Pearsall Genealogy* makes it clear that her uncle was *the* Albert Neely.

COMPARISON OF DOCUMENTS

The pages torn from Justice Neely's docket book and the bill he submitted to the county agree on the charge, date, location, and total amount due Neely. As printed in *Fraser's Magazine*, the docket listed Neely's costs as:

Warrant, 19c. [cents] Complaint upon oath, 25 $\frac{1}{2}$c. Seven witnesses, 87 $\frac{1}{2}$c. Recognizances, 25c. Mittimus, 19c. Recognizances of witnesses, 75c. Subpoena, 18c. −$2.68.

These billed amounts are in keeping with standard established law at the time (see *A New Conductor Generalis: Being a Summary of the Law Relative to the Duty and Office of Justices of the Peace, Sheriffs, Coroners, Constables, Jurymen, Overseers of the Poor* (Albany, NY: E. R. Backus, 1819), 481-82).

In addition to the correlations between the Neely docket and his 1826 bill, further verification of the authenticity of the Neely record is found in the fact that the names of all those whom he lists as participants in the examination can be verified as people who were actually living in the South Bainbridge area in 1826. For example, Arad Stowell, listed as a witness, was a relative of Josiah's and also a school commissioner during that year, with his bill appearing among the 1826 school bills from Bainbridge. Arad Stowell was one of the first trustees of the South Bainbridge Presbyterian Church, organized in 1825 (Smith, *History of Chenango and Madison Counties*, 150). The following people mentioned in the court record are listed in the 1826 Assessment Roll of Bainbridge: Arad Stowell, Horace Stowell, Josiah Stowell, Jonathan Thompson, and more than one McMaster (Bainbridge Town Hall, Bainbridge, New York). For further information on the participants, see Stanley Ivins's notes in Utah State Historical Society; Tanner, *Joseph Smith and Money Digging*, 36-38; and John Phillip Walker, ed., *Dale Morgan on Early Mormonism: Correspondence and a New History* (Salt Lake City: Signature Books, 1986), 397-99. In Neely's court record Josiah Stowell says it was while he was at Simpson Stowell's home that Joseph Smith demonstrated his skill with a seer stone. A land purchase on 29 January 1827 was made by "Simpson Stowell of the town of Manchester" (see Deed Liber 45: 400-01, Ontario County Records Center and Archives, Canandaigua, New York). Simpson, sometimes spelled as Simeon, was Josiah Stowell's oldest son. See 1820 Census of Bainbridge, Chenango County, New York, microfilm #193721, p. 158, LDS Family History Library.

SELECTED BIBLIOGRAPHY

Allen, James B. "The Significance of Joseph Smith's First Vision in Mormon Thought," *Dialogue: A Journal of Mormon Thought* 1 (Autumn 1966): 28-45.

Anderson, Mary Audentia. *Ancestry and Posterity of Joseph Smith and Emma Hale.* Independence, MO: Herald Publishing House, 1929.

Anderson, Richard L. *Joseph Smith's New England Heritage: Influences of Grand-fathers Solomon Mack and Asael Smith.* Salt Lake City: Deseret Book, 1971.

Anderson, Rodger I. *Joseph Smith's New York Reputation Reexamined.* Salt Lake City: Signature Books, 1990.

Arrington, Leonard J. "Mormonism: From Its New York Beginnings," *New York History* 61 (Oct. 1980): 387-410.

Austin, Emily M. *Mormonism; or, Life Among the Mormons.* Madison, WI: M.J. Cantwell, 1882.

Backman, Milton V., Jr. *Joseph Smith's First Vision: The First Vision in its Historical Context.* 2d ed., Salt Lake City: Bookcraft, 1980.

_____. *Eyewitness Accounts of the Restoration.* Orem, UT: Grandin Book, 1983.

Brodie, Fawn M. *No Man Knows My History: The Life of Joseph Smith, the Mormon Prophet.* 2nd ed., New York: Alfred A. Knopf, 1971.

Bushman, Richard L. *Joseph Smith and the Beginnings of Mormonism.* Urbana: University of Illinois Press, 1984.

Cannon, Donald Q., and Lyndon W. Cook, eds. *Far West Record: Minutes of The Church of Jesus Christ of Latter-day Saints, 1830-1844.* Salt Lake City: Deseret Book, 1983. Ms titled "The Conference Minutes and Record Book of Christ's Church of Latter Day Saints."

Gilbert, John H. "Memorandum," 8 Sept. 1892. Typescript, King's Daughter's Free Library, Palmyra, New York. Printed in *Joseph Smith Begins His*

Work. Vol. 1:introductory pages. Salt Lake City: Deseret News Press for Wilford C. Wood, 1958.

Hill, Donna. *Joseph Smith: The First Mormon.* Garden City, NY: Doubleday, 1977.

Hill, Marvin S. "Secular or Sectarian History? A Critique of *No Man Knows My History,*" *Church History* 43 (Mar. 1974): 79-96.

_____. *Quest for Refuge: The Mormon Flight from American Pluralism.* Salt Lake City: Signature Books, 1989.

Howard, Richard P. *Restoration Scriptures: A Study of Their Textual Development.* Independence, MO: Herald Publishing House, 1969.

Jessee, Dean C. comp. and ed. *The Personal Writings of Joseph Smith.* Salt Lake City: Deseret Book, 1984.

_____. *The Papers of Joseph Smith: Autobiographical and Historical Writings.* Vol. 1. Salt Lake City: Deseret Book, 1989.

_____. ed., "Joseph Knight's Recollection of Early Mormon History," *Brigham Young University Studies* 17 (Autumn 1976): 29-39. Ms. LDS archives.

Knight, Newel. "Journal." Ms. LDS archives.

_____. "Newel Knight's Journal." *Scraps of Biography.* Salt Lake City: Juvenile Instructor Office, 1883.

Lambert, Neal E., and Richard H. Cracroft, "Literary Form and Historical Understanding: Joseph Smith's First Vision," *Journal of Mormon History* 7 (1980): 31-42.

Lyon, T. Edgar. "How Authentic Are Mormon Historic Sites in Vermont and New York?" *Brigham Young University Studies* 9 (Spring 1969): 341-50.

Newell, Linda K., and Valeen Tippetts Avery. *Mormon Enigma: Emma Hale Smith.* Garden City, NY: Doubleday, 1984.

Porter, Larry C. "A Study of the Origins of The Church of Jesus Christ of Latter-day Saints in the States of New York and Pennsylvania, 1816-1831." Ph.D. dissertation, Brigham Young University, 1971.

Pratt, Parley P. *Autobiography of Parley Parker Pratt.* Parley P. Pratt, Jr., ed. 1874; 5th ed. Salt Lake City: Deseret Book, 1961.

Quinn, D. Michael. *Early Mormonism and the Magic World View.* Salt Lake City: Signature Books, 1987.

Searle, Howard C. "Early Mormon Historiography: Writing the History of the Mormons, 1830-1858." Ph.D. dissertation, University of California at Los Angeles, 1979.

Smith, Joseph. Ms. materials, LDS archives. The Manuscript History, Kirtland Revelations Book and Joseph Smith Letterbooks are available on microfilm at LDS archives, Salt Lake City, Utah; RLDS archives, Independence, Missouri; and Harold B. Lee Library, Brigham Young University, Provo, Utah.

_____. *Book of Mormon.* Palmyra [NY]: E.B. Grandin, 1830. Current editions include Salt Lake City: Church of Jesus Christ of Latter-day Saints, 1981. Independence, MO: Reorganized Church of Jesus Christ of Latter Day Saints, 1908, 1966; Church of Christ (Temple Lot), 1990.

_____. *A Book of Commandments, for the Government of the Church of Christ* . . . Zion [Independence, MO]: W.W. Phelps & Co., 1833.

_____. Compiled by Joseph Smith, Junior, Oliver Cowdery, Sidney Rigdon, Frederick G. Williams. *Doctrine and Covenants of the Church of the Latter Day Saints: Carefully Selected from the Revelations of God.* Kirtland, OH: Frederick G. Williams & Co., 1835.

Smith, Joseph, et al. *History of the Church of Jesus Christ of Latter-day Saints.* 6 vols. Introduction and Notes by B.H. Roberts. Salt Lake City: Deseret Book, 1959. Behind this revised history are preliminary manuscripts and the bound books of the Manuscript History of Joseph Smith, also known as the Manuscript History of the Church, LDS archives.

Smith, Joseph III and Smith, Heman C. *The History of the Reorganized Church of Jesus Christ of Latter Day Saints.* 4 vols. Lamoni, IA: Herald House, 1896-1903. Reprinted 1967.

Smith, Lucy [Mack]. Preliminary Manuscript. Ms. 1844-45. LDS archives.

_____. "The History of Lucy Smith Mother of the Prophet." MS. LDS archives. Revised in 1845 from Preliminary Manuscript. A copy of this revision used for 1853 printed version.

_____. *Biographical Sketches of Joseph Smith the Prophet, and His Progenitors for Many Generations.* Liverpool, Eng.: Published for Orson Pratt by S.W. Richards, 1853.

Smith, William. "Notes Written on 'Chamber's Life of Joseph Smith,' by William Smith." About 1875. Typescript of Charles Knecht, 1925. LDS archives.

_____. *William Smith on Mormonism*. Lamoni, IA: Herald Steam Book and Job Office, 1883.

Stott, G. St. John. "Joseph Smith's 1823 Vision: Uncovering the Angel Message," *Religion* 18 (Oct. 1988): 347-62.

Walker, John Phillip, ed. *Dale Morgan on Early Mormonism: Correspondence and a New History*. Salt Lake City: Signature Books, 1986.

Walker, Ronald W. "Martin Harris: Mormonism's Early Convert," *Dialogue: A Journal of Mormon Thought* 19 (Winter 1986): 29-43.

Walters, Wesley P. "New Light on Mormon Origins from the Palmyra (N.Y.) Revival," *Bulletin of the Evangelical Theological Society* 10 (Fall 1967): 227-44, printed with Selected Bibliography. Revised and enlarged in *Dialogue: A Journal of Mormon Thought* 4 (Spring 1969): 60-81.

INDEX

ABOUT THE AUTHORS

H. Michael Marquardt is the author of *The Strange Marriages of Sarah Ann Whitney*, *The Book of Abraham Revisited*, and editor of *Joseph Smith's Diaries*. His essays have appeared in the *Journal of Pastoral Practice*, *Restoration*, and *Sunstone*. He and his wife Dorothy reside in Sandy, Utah, and are the parents of five children.

Wesley P. Walters was pastor of the Marissa Presbyterian church in Illinois until his death in 1990. He has been published in *Dialogue: A Journal of Mormon Thought*, *Journal of the Evangelical Theological Society*, *Journal of the Westminster Theological Society*, and the *Journal of Pastoral Practice*. He was married to Helen Rambo; they are the parents of five children.